Ethnicity and Resource Competition in Plural Societies

World Anthropology

General Editor

SOL TAX

Patrons

CLAUDE LÉVI-STRAUSS
MARGARET MEAD
LAILA SHUKRY EL HAMAMSY
M. N. SRINIVAS

MOUTON PUBLISHERS · THE HAGUE · PARIS
DISTRIBUTED IN THE USA AND CANADA BY ALDINE, CHICAGO

Ethnicity and Resource Competition in Plural Societies

Editor

LEO A. DESPRES

MOUTON PUBLISHERS · THE HAGUE · PARIS

DISTRIBUTED IN THE USA AND CANADA BY ALDINE, CHICAGO

Acknowledgements

The thought that a book of this nature might be of some value to anthropologists interested in the study of ethnic group relations originated in discussions with my friend and former colleague, Jacques Maquet. It materialized as a project when Sol Tax suggested it might make a worthy contribution to the IXth International Congress of Anthropological and Ethnological Sciences. I extend my gratitude to both of these gentlemen.

I also want to thank each of the contributors to this volume not only for their individual efforts but also for making my task as editor a pleasant one. In many respects, their ideas have been grist for my own intellectual mill. Hopefully, I have not detracted from the merit and independence of their individual contributions. In any event, they should understand that I deeply appreciate their assistance in bringing this project to fruition.

Finally, I should like to thank the Department of Anthropology of Case Western Reserve University for giving freely of its secretarial assistance. Anne Wade has been particularly helpful with the typing and distribution of manuscripts and to her I owe a special debt of gratitude.

January, 1975   LEO A. DESPRES

General Editor's Preface

No fact of human history is more important in the lives of nations than that their populations are heterogenous. When populations are conscious of different historical origins, their group interests become intertwined with ethnic identity and both are reinforced. This book analyzes the specific interplay of economic interests and ethnic sentiment, and does so in new ways by examining some of history's lesser known cases. The cases, coming from widely separated parts of developing areas in Asia, Africa, and Latin America, are analyzed in the context of social science theory emanating mainly from European and North American data. The result is the broad comparative perspective so characteristic of anthropology as it increasingly moves between modern and traditional societies, and as it recruits its scholars from Third World nations.

Like most contemporary sciences, anthropology is a product of the European tradition. Some argue that it is a product of colonialism, with one small and self-interested part of the species dominating the study of the whole. If we are to understand the species, our science needs substantial input from scholars who represent a variety of the world's cultures. It was a deliberate purpose of the IXth International Congress of Anthropological and Ethnological Sciences to provide impetus in this direction. The *World Anthrology* volumes, therefore, offer a first glimpse of a human science in which members from all societies have played an active role. Each of the books is designed to be self-contained; each is an attempt to update its particular sector of scientific knowledge and is written by specialists from all parts of the world. Each volume should be read and reviewed individually as a separate volume on its own given subject. The set as a whole will indicate what changes are in store for anthropology as scholars from the developing countries join in studying the species of which we are all a part.

The IXth Congress was planned from the beginning not only to include as many of the scholars from every part of the world as possible, but also with a view toward the eventual publication of the papers in high quality volumes. At previous Congresses scholars were invited to bring papers which were then read out loud. They were necessarily limited in length; many were only summarized; there was little time for discussion; and the sparse discussion could only be in one language. The IXth Congress was an experiment aimed at changing this. Papers were written with the intention of exchanging them before the Congress, particularly in extensive pre-Congress sessions; they were not intended to be read aloud at the Congress, that time being devoted to discussions — discussions which were simultaneously and professionally translated into five languages. The method for eliciting the papers was structured to make as representative a sample as was allowable when scholarly creativity — hence self-selection — was critically important. Scholars were asked both to propose papers of their own and to suggest topics for sessions of the Congress which they might edit into volumes. All were then informed of the suggestions and encouraged to re-think their own papers and the topics. The process, therefore, was a continuous one of feedback and exchange and it has continued to be so even after the Congress. The some two thousand papers comprising *World Anthropology* certainly then offer a substantial sample of world anthropology. It has been said that anthropology is at a turning point; if this is so, these volumes will be the historical direction-markers.

As might have been foreseen in the first post-colonial generation, the large majority of the Congress papers (82 percent) are the work of scholars identified with the industrialized world which fathered our traditional discipline and the institution of the Congress itself: Eastern Europe (15 percent); Western Europe (16 percent); North America (47 percent); Japan, South Africa, Australia, and New Zealand (4 percent). Only 18 percent of the papers are from developing areas: Africa (4 percent); Asia-Oceania (9 percent); Latin America (5 percent). Aside from the substantial representation from the U.S.S.R. and the nations of Eastern Europe, a significant difference between this corpus of written material and that of other Congresses is the addition of the large proportion of contributions from Africa, Asia, and Latin America. "Only 18 percent" is two to four times as great a proportion as that of other Congresses; moreover, 18 percent of 2,000 papers is 360 papers,

10 times the number of "Third World" papers presented at previous Congresses. In fact, these 360 papers are more than the total of ALL papers published after the last International Congress of Anthropological and Ethnological Sciences which was held in the United States (Philadelphia, 1956). Even in the beautifully organized Tokyo Congress in 1968 less than a third as many members from developing nations, including those of Asia, participated.

The significance of the increase is not simply quantitative. The input of scholars from areas which have until recently been no more than subject matter for anthropology represents both feedback and also long-awaited theoretical contributions from the perspectives of very different cultural, social, and historical traditions. Many who attended the IXth Congress were convinced that anthropology would not be the same in the future. The fact that the next Congress (India, 1978) will be our first in the "Third World" may be symbolic of the change. Meanwhile, sober consideration of the present set of books will show how much, and just where and how, our discipline is being revolutionized.

As the Editor points out in his concluding chapter, a sizable proportion of the entire Congress was devoted to discussion of ethnic studies and no less than twenty-six titles of the books which have resulted bear, in different ways, on the subject. To those directly on ethnicity, migration, and economic-political problems may be added books on urbanization, on the women's movement, on geographic areas where other cases of ethnic pluralism are recorded, and on the response of anthropological theory to social problems related to colonialism.

Chicago, Illinois   Sol Tax
September 6, 1974

Table of Contents

Acknowledgements   V

General Editor's Preface   VII

Introduction   I
by *Leo A. Despres*

Resource Competition, Monopoly, and Socioracial Diversity   9
by *Harmannus Hoetink*

Ethnic Boundary Maintenance, Readaptation, and Societal Evolution
in the San Blas Islands of Panama   27
by *Regina E. Holloman*

Jungle Quechua Ethnicity: An Ecuadorian Case Study   41
by *Norman E. Whitten, Jr.*

Ethnicity and Class in Highland Peru   71
by *Pierre L. van den Berghe*

Ethnicity and Resource Competition in Guyanese Society   87
by *Leo A. Despres*

Resource Competition and Inter-Ethnic Relations in Nigeria   119
by *Onigu Otite*

Competition Within Ethnic Systems in Africa   131
by *Elliott P. Skinner*

Ethnogenesis and Resource Competition Among Tibetan Refugees
in South India 159
by Melvyn C. Goldstein

Toward a Theory of Ethnic Phenomena 187
by Leo A. Despres

Biographical Notes 209

Index of Names 213

Index of Subjects 215

Introduction

LEO A. DESPRES

Without recapitulating the details of history (cf. Banton 1967, 1970; Harris 1968), it may be stated that the study of ethnic and racial phenomena is deeply rooted in the intellectual tradition of anthropology and related social science disciplines. The range and specificity of focus attending the investigation of these phenomena have varied considerably in terms of the theoretical currents of particular disciplines, and, clearly, these theoretical currents are as much the product of economic and political forces as they are the product of independent thought. Thus, the unsettled conditions accompanying the rather sweeping economic and political changes that followed World War II, the persistence of poly-ethnic systems in the tide of such changes, and the apparent relationship of these systems to existing patterns of intra- and inter-national exploitation have all contributed to a renewed interest among social scientists in ethnic and racial phenomena. This renewed interest has been marked in recent years by a rash of studies of group relations carried out in respect to the colonial and post-colonial societies of Africa, Asia, and America. Similar studies have also appeared in reference to the industrial and imperial societies of Europe and North America.[1]

Among anthropologists, the conventional focus of research in respect to ethnic phenomena has been the ethnic group, or some unit of population distinguished by characteristic cultural features (Narroll 1964). Friendly critics (cf. e.g. Barth 1969: 10–12; van den Berghe 1970: 12)

---

[1] For a review of these developments, see Shibutani and Kwan (1965), Banton (1967), Mason (1970), Schermerhorn (1970), van den Berghe (1967, 1970), and Zubaida (1970).

have suggested that this focus has deflected the attention of anthropologists from the analysis of problems relating to the nature and persistence of ethnic boundaries, the organization of ethnic groups, and the dynamics of inter-ethnic relations. There are, of course, notable exceptions to this criticism. More importantly, regarding anthropological studies of less recent vintage, it cannot be overlooked that many of the very best (e.g. Evans-Pritchard 1940; Fortes 1945; Leach 1954) are replete with data relating to the genesis and ethnic identity of particular populations.

Still, the context of anthropological research has changed significantly over the past fifteen to twenty years. Not only have the colonial blinders been lifted, so to speak, but it has become increasingly evident that the populations which anthropologists study no longer can be viewed *in vacuo* vis à vis the rest of the world. Thus, more recent studies of ethnic phenomena — (e.g. Wagley and Harris' (1958) treatment of ethnic minorities in the New World; Harris' (1964) analysis of race relations in the Americas; Kunstadter's (1967) overview of tribal minorities in Southeast Asia; or Kuper and Smith's (1969) analysis of pluralism in Africa) — disclose a sense of problem orientation that is not particularly obvious in most earlier works. This new sense of problem orientation has thrown open for discussion the utility of many of the conceptual and methodological devices which anthropologists have used to harvest their data.

Nevertheless, a cursory review of the recent literature on ethnic phenomena leaves the general impression that anthropologists, not to mention other social scientists, have not built very carefully upon the accumulated knowledge of their predecessors. If early ethnologists confounded such notions as society, culture, ethnicity, race, tribe, nation, and the like, it is not at all evident that these and related concepts have been completely sorted out by more recent investigators. Moreover, a great deal of the current research on ethnic and racial phenomena continues to be informed by assumptions that seem somewhat beyond the acceptable limits of naïveté. Related to all of this is the fact that even the more contemporary theoretical orientations of anthropologists remain too diffuse and ambiguous to be productive of systematic comparative research.

In light of these considerations, the recent work by Fredrik Barth (1956, 1964a, 1964b) and his colleagues (cf. Barth 1969) must be viewed as a substantial contribution toward the advancement of comparative ethnic studies. Explicit in much of this work (cf., particularly, Barth 1964b; Haaland 1969; Knutsson 1969; Siverts 1969) is the view that the genesis and persistence of ethnic boundaries, the incorporation of ethnic populations, and the organization of inter-ethnic relations are generally related to factors affecting the competition for environmental resources. The presentation of this thesis remains couched in troublesome conceptual and epistemological ambiguities and, as of the present, research is too limited to sort out and model all of the variables that may be involved. Still, the data presented in support of this view have been sufficiently persuasive to warrant its further consideration. The IXth International Congress of Anthropological and Ethnological Sciences provided the occasion for such an undertaking.

In preparation for the Congress, a small number of scholars were invited to prepare papers with a view toward focussing comparative attention on the relationship that might exist between the genesis and persistence of ethnic boundaries, the political incorporation of ethnic populations, the organization of inter-ethnic relations, and the competition for environmental resources. The papers that comprise this volume of *World Anthropology* are the product of this inquiry.

Although little significance can be attached to the order in which individual papers appear, a brief note of explanation is appropriate. The opening paper by Harmannus Hoetink is clearly the most general. Drawing upon his sociological investigations of New World socioracial phenomena, Hoetink relates varying patterns of resource competition to a typology of socioracial stratifications. In doing so, Hoetink seeks to clarify variables that are operative in respect to the maintenance of ethnic boundaries and the dynamics of inter-ethnic relationships.

The second paper, by Regina E. Holloman, relates resource competition to the dynamics of boundary maintenance among the San Blas Cuna of Panama. Holloman describes how the Cuna have contrived various mechanisms by which they reinforce ethnic boundaries in order to secure competitive advantage, vis à vis non-Cuna, in respect to certain resource domains. This has not precluded changes in the Cuna way of life. However, the overall pattern of Cuna - non-Cuna relationships is not unlike the forms of internal colonialism which Whitten and van den Berghe, respectively, describe for Ecuador and Peru.

Because it serves to further illuminate processes that are but lightly touched upon in Holloman's treatment of the San Blas Cuna, the paper by Norman E. Whitten, Jr. would seem to follow logically in the order of presentation. Briefly, Whitten explains how various lowland population aggregates in Ecuador have assumed, at one level, a Quechua identity while, at another level, they are developing an Indian identity. Within an internal colonial context, the manipulation of these boundaries serves to secure and expand important resource domains that are under competition from mestizos and blancos.

In the following paper, Pierre L. van den Berghe suggests that the competitive distribution of resources has ordained a highly stratified system of social classes in Peru. While less rigidly drawn, ethnic boundaries persist in reference to various population segments. As these boundaries serve to facilitate or deny access to important resource domains, a system of stratified ethnic groups also obtains. These two systems are related. On the one hand, ethnicity accentuates the stratification of social classes while, on the other, social mobility assumes the form of ethnic passing.

Following van den Berghe, Leo A. Despres examines how the competition for resources in Guyana has ordered ethnic populations in a system of unequal status and power. This system of status ascriptions has not precluded the development of class strata. While these two status systems are entangled, they are not coterminous. Accordingly, ethnic identities and status claims enter selectively into the domains of inter-group relations and individual transactions, imparting to both domains a segmentary character. In concluding, Despres presents several hypotheses regarding the conditions that seem to favor the genesis and persistence of ethnic boundaries, the political incorporation of ethnic populations, and the organization of inter-ethnic relations.

The first five papers of this volume are drawn primarily from studies of New World populations. These are followed by two papers which inquire into the relationship between ethnicity and resource competition among African populations. The first of these, by Onigu Otite, presents data derived from field investigations carried out in the Western and Mid-Western States of Nigeria. Otite examines how the persistence of ethnic boundaries and the organization of ethnic populations confer competitive advantage in respect to particular environmental resources. In reference to three case studies, he also shows that different patterns of resource competition correspond to varying patterns of inter-ethnic relations.

In a more sweeping analysis of poly-ethnic systems in Africa, Elliot P. Skinner suggests that almost by definition ethnic groups are competitive for the strategic resources of their respective societies. In reference to pre-colonial, colonial, and post-colonial political regimes, he emphasizes that the nature of ethnic groupings and the competitive strategies they employ are a function of the type of society in which they develop as well as the resources over which they seek control. In concluding, Skinner notes that the problem confronting poly-ethnic systems is that the very processes which give their constituent groups competitive advantage in one techno-politico environment make it difficult for such groups to adjust to changes either in their societies or in the kinds of resources for which they compete.

It seems rather obvious that migrant populations of one type or another have often contributed to the organization of poly-ethnic systems not unlike some of the systems discussed by Skinner and other contributors. However, less obvious are the processes by which these systems are formed.

Thus, following Skinner, Melvyn C. Goldstein examines some of these processes in reference to a culturally heterogeneous population of Tibetan refugees who have organized an agricultural settlement in South India. Briefly, Goldstein describes the strategies which these refugees have successfully employed to secure the resources necessary to their economic rehabilitation in an alien environment. He also describes how these strategies have contributed to the development of ethnic boundaries both within the Tibetan community and between it and the larger society of which it is now a part. In concluding, Goldstein suggests that these ethnic strategies will be problematic in the long run: they depend upon a very delicate balance of intra- and inter-ethnic relationships in respect to the competition for limited environmental resources.

By way of further introduction, it should be emphasized that NO statement of problem beyond that previously outlined was circulated with the original invitation to participate in this special session of the Congress. In other words, the contributors to this volume were not asked to reflect upon a pre-established conceptual framework in respect to the problem under consideration. Rather, it was suggested that they pursue the inquiry independently and in reference to data that they were known to command as a consequence of their own field research.

It was anticipated that, in reference to the problem under consideration, individual contributors would develop whatever conceptual framework they deemed necessary to interrogate the data they had collected. Part of the overall exercise was to determine whether or not a convergence of views would emerge from separate, and independent, analyses. Thus, it was intended that participants prepare their papers for circulation in advance of the Congress, which they did, and that a pre-Congress colloquium would be arranged for their discussion. As it happened, a colloquium did not materialize for lack of funds, and several contributors were unable to attend the Congress at all.

Nevertheless, apart from their substantive contribution, the papers that comprise this volume are not devoid of important theoretical discussion. However, without the benefit of a pre-Congress colloquium, the synthesis and evaluation of this discussion have fallen almost exclusively upon the editor and they form the subject of the final paper, "Toward a Theory of Ethnic Phenomena." In regard to this concluding paper, hopefully I have not confounded or misinterpreted the work of individual contributors, but I trust the reader may determine that for himself.

REFERENCES

BANTON, MICHAEL
  1967   *Race relations.* New York: Basic Books.
  1970   "The concept of racism," in *Race and racialism.* Edited by Sami Zubaida 17–34. London: Tavistock.
BARTH, FREDRIK
  1956   Ecologic relationships of ethnic groups in Swat, North Pakistan. *American Anthropologist* 58:1079–1089.
  1964a "Ethnic processes on the Pathan-Baluch boundary," in *Indo-Iranica.* Edited by G. Redard. Wiesbaden.
  1964b Competition and symbiosis in North East Baluchistan. *Folk* 6(1).
BARTH, FREDRIK, *editor*
  1969   *Ethnic groups and boundaries.* Boston: Little, Brown.
EVANS-PRITCHARD, E. E.
  1940   *The Nuer.* London: Oxford University Press.
FORTES, MEYER
  1945   *The dynamics of clanship among the Tallensi.* London: Oxford University Press.
HAALAND, GUNNAR
  1969   "Economic determinants in ethnic processes," in *Ethnic groups and boundaries.* Edited by Fredrik Barth, 58–73. Boston: Little, Brown.
HARRIS, MARVIN
  1964   *Patterns of race in the Americas.* New York: Walker.
  1968   *The rise of anthropological theory.* New York: Thomas Y. Crowell.
KNUTSSON, KARL ERIC
  1969   "Dichotomization and integration," in *Ethnic groups and boundaries.* Edited by Fredrik Barth, 86–100. Boston: Little, Brown.
KUNSTADTER, PETER, *editor*
  1967   *Southeast Asian tribes, minorities, and nations,* two volumes. Princeton: Princeton University Press.
KUPER, LEO, M. G. SMITH, *editors*
  1969   *Pluralism in Africa.* Berkeley and Los Angeles: University of California Press.
LEACH, E. R.
  1954   *Political systems of Highland Burma.* Cambridge, Massachusetts: Harvard University Press.

MASON, PHILIP
1970   *Patterns of dominance*. London: Oxford University Press.
NARROLL, R.
1964   On ethnic unit classification. *Current Anthropology* 5:283–312.
SCHERMERHORN, RICHARD A.
1970   *Comparative ethnic relations: a framework for theory and research*. New York: Random House.
SHIBUTANI, TAMOTSU, KIAN M. KWAN
1965   *Ethnic stratification: a comparative approach*. New York: Macmillan.
SIVERTS, HENNING
1969   "Ethnic stability and boundary dynamics in southern Mexico," in *Ethnic groups and boundaries*. Edited by Fredrik Barth, 101–116. Boston: Little, Brown.
VAN DEN BERGHE, PIERRE L.
1967   *Race and racism: a comparative perspective*. New York: John Wiley and Sons.
1970   *Race and ethnicity: essays in comparative sociology*. New York: Basic Books.
WAGLEY, C., M. HARRIS
1958   *Minorities in the New World*. New York: Columbia University Press
ZUBAIDA, SAMI, *editor*
1970   *Race and racialism*. London: Tavistock.

Resource Competition, Monopoly, and Socioracial Diversity

HARMANNUS HOETINK

In what follows I shall consider group competition, and other mechanisms by which resources are allocated to ascriptive groups, and their effects on stratification. Second, I shall discuss the generation and maintenance of ascriptive group boundaries, mostly in regard to Western Hemisphere societies.

The term "group competition" is commonly used if two or more groups try to limit each other's access to scarce resources or positions. "Free" competition presupposes a sociological market situation in which the contenders are of roughly the same strength and power. A drastic change in this equilibrium would convert it from a "market" into an "organization," in which the allocation of resources and positions no longer is the outcome of a contest between "freely" contending forces but is the result of monopolistic mechanisms. Once a stable competitive relationship has been established, the competing groups will tend to develop structural similarities within their sectors of competition.

Because a competitive equilibrium within one society implies, as it were by definition, that the lines of division between the main contending groups are vertical rather than horizontal (the groups exist next to, rather than above, each other), we might consider in the Western Hemisphere such societies as Guyana and Surinam as approximations of such equilibriums. Here, the East Indian and Afro-European population groups tend to perceive each other as competitors for resources and positions and have organized themselves in similar ways to enhance their competitive efficiency. In both countries this competitive relationship has existed only for a few decades: i.e. since the East Indian group changed its earlier subordinate position into a competitive one.

In Guyana and Surinam, ethnic competition takes place within one political unit, and there are certain previously accepted rules and limitations set to the competitive game. This implies a modicum of collaboration and consensus between the contending partners. The question is whether such a recent and delicate equilibrium will lead to an increasingly interdependent and institutionalized cooperation and division of labor between the component groups; or whether competition will lead to conflict and thus to a weakening of national political ties or even their rupture; or whether one of the groups will succeed in imposing itself on the other, thus reestablishing the earlier horizontal line of division; or, finally, whether a process of amalgamation will in due time blur or even eradicate the divisionary line. All this depends, on the one hand, on factors that influence the power relationship (e.g. differences in economic ethos, in demographic growth, and in external support), and, on the other hand, on factors that hinder or foment the maintenance of the cultural and/or somatic attributes of the contending groups.

The concept of competition implies that within one social context there are groups in which membership and internal cohesion are determined by noneconomic, ascriptive criteria. In societies where group solidarity is predominantly determined by economic considerations, competition between economically equivalent groups is impossible by definition. It follows that group-competition presupposes: (a) that in certain types of society ascriptive loyalties are predominant over economic ones and (b) that in these societies two or more ascriptive groups are sufficiently equal in power to engage in a competitive relationship.

Competition further implies that the disputed resources (and positions) are "scarce" and that their access and attainability are limited. Of course, all economic goods are scarce in an objective sense, yet, a sparsely populated area may provide its inhabitants with a subjective notion of abundance of land for agricultural purposes; it is this latter notion that determines group action and not the former. Also, "scarcity" can be manipulated. As a result of existing mechanisms of allocation and distribution in a particular society, one and the same resource may be abundant for some members of society, scarce for some others, and inaccessible for the rest. Ideally, then, scarcity refers to resources that are limited both objectively and subjectively. However, in respect to such resources, the existing mechanisms of allocation and distribution do not open up or close completely the avenues of access. All of this is to suggest that, for analytical purposes, "scarcity" must be conceptualized in the middle of an axiomatic continuum between "open" and "closed" resources.

In his classic work *Slavery as an industrial system*, Nieboer (1900) tried to establish a correlation between the occurrence of slavery and the availability of "open resources" (land) in societies with a technological level that demands only simple skills and tools for its agriculture. Later, Nieboer's main thesis was amended and declared valid for all systems of unfree labor (Fahrenfort 1943; Kloosterboer 1960) in clearly stratified societies (Köbben 1967: 13). In many societies, then, in which agricultural land is abundant and needed skills and tools are within the reach of every able bodied man, Nieboer observed a mechanism of social manipulation by which part of the population is tied by force and/or law to existing agricultural enterprises; such a manipulation prevents an exodus to the virgin lands and a subsequent lack of labor. As seen by Nieboer, a system of unfree agricultural labor is nothing but a device of the propertied and employer classes to keep the untapped land resources artificially unattainable for part of the population in order to maintain a sufficient labor force.

Nieboer's thesis leads to the paradox that "open resources" easily produce (if the technological level is low) a situation in which virtually all mobility is denied to part of the population. Where one would expect an absence of individual competition because of an abundance of resources, Nieboer observes instead the rise of a system of compulsory labor. While unfree labor and multiracialism were, of course, not causally linked in the Western Hemisphere, the slaves were, *grosso modo*, somatically different from the masters. This historical coincidence explains why some authors want to present the characteristics of present-day multiracial societies — such as the United States — as the result and continuation of their earlier systems of slavery.

Yet, it would seem more accurate to locate the origin of the present multiracial stratifications of the New World in the mechanisms that allocated positions and resources to the first NONSLAVE members of the subordinated socioracial groups. The legal and economic constraints of slavery impeded any social mobility of the slave per se, but for those who, through manumission, had been placed outside the institution of slavery and in the "free" society the chances of access to resources and positions were determined by a less rigid system of allocation, controlled by the dominant socioracial group, which allowed for a variety of different socioracial stratifications to emerge. Still, in all these variations, there was and is present a predominant criterion of social selection and control based on the social evaluation of the physical ("racial") attributes of the individuals involved. This factor, which generates and maintains "a categorically different distribution of assets" (Barth 1969: 28), may conveniently be called the racist ingredient in the mechanism of allocation.

Before expanding on this theme, it is useful to discuss briefly the one remaining pole of the resource continuum: the case in which the land resources are "closed." In Nieboer's view, in the absence of available land and at a low level of technology, there is no need for slavery as an economic institution. Where such conditions obtain, the landless laborer is forced by an "impersonal compulsion" (rather than by the "personal compulsion" of slavery) to offer his services to the capitalist or landowner (Nieboer 1900: 423).

It is clear why Nieboer uses the technological level as a second and independent variable in his analysis. It is the combination of "open" resources and easily acquired (yet within the prevailing norms) subsistence which attracts the laborers to such an extent that they "have to" be tied to the property of their employer. Where "open resources" are found in a society in which the level of agriculture demands high skills and costly tools, Nieboer would surely see a lesser need for personal compulsion in the form of unfree labor. Clearly, in those societies where land resources are closed and a high level of skills is needed for an acceptable level of subsistence, it follows that mobility among the unskilled is further diminished. The high general level of technology in modern society and, therefore, the high cost of acquiring skills and tools seem to make unskilled laborers ever more dependent on the arbitration, intervention or direct support of the state.

Nieboer, who mainly discusses "primitive" populations, mentions the Eskimo as an example of a people that require great skills and costly tools for their hunting. In such a society there is no place for slavery; on the contrary, the Eskimo who has lost his dog or sleigh is an "idle hand." Suffering from unremediable unemployment, he is dependent upon the charity of those who will let him feed their dogs in exchange for a minimum of social security. Such a situation may serve as a metaphor of modern technological society with its structural unemployment of the unskilled and its attendant system of social legislation.

Now, if such a modern society is also multiracial and has a "racist" ingredient operating in the allocation of resources and positions, then a disproportionately large part of the unskilled and the unemployed will consist of members of subordinated socioracial groups. Structurally, the position of these groups is entirely different from that of slaves in a society with open resources and a low technological level. In Nieboer's opinion systems of unfree labor are functionally linked to certain economic and demographic determinants; their abolition is hence a "natural" historical process directly related to population density and technological progress. On the other hand, a drastic improvement in the position of racially subordinated unskilled strata in a technologically developed society with closed resources would seem to depend on an artificial (perhaps revolutionary) redistribution of resources, and, ideally, on rendering inoperative the "racist" ingredient in respect to allocation of resources.

In spite of this structural difference between the position of slaves and that of the unskilled laborers in modern multiracial societies, these categories are often compared and suggested to be identical. The reason for this is not only the fact that in several countries it was one and the same socioracial group which underwent the change from the former to the latter position but also the fact that in both cases the chances for upward mobility are minimal. It is paradoxical that both in societies with open resources (and a low level of technology), and in societies with closed resources (and a high technological level), the lowest economic strata are doomed to minimum chances for upward mobility.

Where, as in the United States, these lowest strata consist of blacks and, although proportionately fewer, poor whites (not to mention recent Latin American immigrant groups with which I shall not deal here), groups which so far have not disclosed a sense of common solidarity, one has to conclude that also here ascriptive elements weigh more heavily than the economic in the formation of groups. This is not surprising; for where a "racist" ingredient operates in favor of those who belong to the dominant socioracial group, even the lowest economic strata of this group will cherish the expectation that their chances for upward social mobility are greater than those of members of the subordinated socioracial group(s) who occupy similar economic positions. It is this difference in social expectation which converts the objectively similar economic positions of these strata into subjectively dissimilar ones. Seen in this perspective, one can not speak of a pure competitive relationship between poor whites and poor blacks because the former expect, and generally experience, a selective preference based on their membership in the dominant socioracial group.

These considerations make it advisable to distinguish between socioeconomic and ascriptive stratification. In those cases in which clear inconsistencies between the two stratifications occur — poor whites in the United States, poor ladinos or mestizos in Latin America — we observe a preference by the dominant group for ascriptive over economic criteria in the allocation of positions. This is not to deny that the dominance of one socioracial or sociocultural group in a society ultimately rests on economic power. Every stratification is based on power differences. However, what interests us here are the ascriptive criteria which foster or hinder the acquisition of such power.

At this point, it may be recalled that in societies such as Guyana and Surinam "real" competition between their main population groups is made possible because the dividing line between them runs in a roughly vertical direction. This means that virtually all horizontal socioeconomic strata are cut along ascriptive lines and a competitive relationship is feasible on all economic levels. This is a drastically different situation from that which obtains in the majority of traditional multiracial societies in the Western Hemisphere. In most cases, the socioracial dividing lines are perceived as horizontal and power is mostly concentrated in the hands of one ascriptive group. Instead of a competitive situation, these societies disclose a monopolistic control of the principal resources by the dominant group, and, as in the case of the United States, it is this group that allocates positions in the society as a whole.

In recent decades we have seen how political action of subordinated socioracial groups in several Western Hemisphere societies has led to some changes in their favor. In some West Indian societies virtually all political and governmental functions have even been ceded to the subordinated socioracial strata without, however, jeopardizing the economic hegemony of the dominant group and, generally, without creating inconsistencies between socioeconomic and ascriptive stratifications of such a magnitude as to lead to serious frustration and protest on the part of the lower economic strata of the dominant group itself (though in the United States such frustration and such protest recently did seem to express itself politically).

In less recent times, however, improvements in the economic position of members of ascriptive subordinated socioracial strata seem to have resulted mostly from the scarcity of personnel among the dominant group. Thus, as early as the seventeenth and eighteenth centuries, a lack of white middle-level personnel led to the occupation of middle-range positions by members of subordinate groups in some multiracial societies of the Western Hemisphere. Similarly, we observe the early formation of a governmental bureaucratic elite in Surinam, composed of members of subordinated socioracial strata, who came to fill the gap left by an exodus of whites resulting from an economic crisis in the late eighteenth century. The revolutionary elimination of the dominant group in St. Domingue led to the creation of new elites out of the formerly subordinated groups once the Republic of Haiti was established in 1804.

Still another factor, a scarcity of white marriage partners, probably had a positive effect on the stability of sexual liaisons between white males and females from the subordinated strata, as well as on the extent of educational and economic protection given to their offspring. All of this contributed to the formation of a solid "respectable" elite within subordinated socioracial groups. On the other hand, where the early presence or later immigration of poor whites precluded a scarcity of personnel from occurring, the chances for economic improvement of members of the subordinated groups were proportionately less.

It may be useful to emphasize here that the scarcity of white personnel may have fostered the emergence of economic middle and even upper strata among subordinated ascriptive groups, but this scarcity is not, as Harris (1964) is inclined to believe, the sole causative agent of the variety of horizontal socioracial stratifications that developed in Afro-America. All multiracial societies in that part of the world, with the exception of the United States, acknowledged in the early stages of their colonial history the existence of a separate colored (mulatto) middle group, which was distinguished in administrative, military, and social affairs from both whites and blacks and was generally privileged over the latter, even where no clear simultaneous economic or demographic need for the social recognition of such a separate category can be demonstrated. In fact, the ECONOMIC situation of this intermediate socioracial group often was much worse than would have been expected on the basis of their ascriptive rank. Only in the United States, it seems to me, does Harris' argument fully apply: here, the early and permanent presence of very substantial numbers of poor whites (both "traditional" poor whites in the South and more recent poor white immigrants) acted as a pressure-group — perhaps being in part manipulated by the upper white strata to act as such. This resulted in the maintenance of a two-tier socioracial stratification (white over black), impeding the emergence of a durable intermediate and separate mulatto stratum.

Thus, the United States, with its rigid socioracial dichotomy and its concisely defined boundary between white and black, must be viewed as an exception among Afro-American societies where socioracial stratifications generally took the form of the three-tier (white-mulatto-black) model with characteristically vague boundaries between the latter two categories. Within this large collection of three-tier societies, a distinction must be made between the British, French, and Dutch colonies, which have in common with the United States an emphatic effort of the creole white group to maintain its endogamy, and the societies of Spanish and Portuguese America, where the white creole group has been and still is absorbing individuals who, in the former colonies, would have been categorized as coloreds and as such would have been considered less admissible as marriage partners for whites. This process of absorption has made for a much vaguer boundary between whites and coloreds in the Iberian countries, thus creating an uninterrupted scale of color gradations (Seda Bonilla 1968). This does not minimize the fact that "whiteness," as in all white-dominated horizontal multiracial societies, retained the highest social value.

Accordingly, we have to distinguish between a CONTINUOUS socioracial stratification in the Iberian countries, and a DISCONTINUOUS stratification elsewhere in Afro-America, which latter, acknowledging local variations, can be labelled TRICHOTOMOUS, except in the United States, where the stratification system is DICHOTOMOUS.

If one wants to analyze the emergence and maintenance of ascriptive group boundaries in respect to the various ascriptive stratifications that we have distinguished (ranging from the vertically divided competitive type in Guyana and Surinam to the horizontally stratified types elsewhere in Afro-America), attention has to be given to culture as a possible boundary maintaining mechanism.

In this regard, two concepts of culture, often confusingly identified, have to be defined. First, there is culture as a correlate or result of group position: i.e. the set of value orientations, norms, and expectations considered to be characteristic of the position a group occupies in a given stratification. The other concept of culture emphasizes the morphological distinctiveness of complex behavioral patterns or organizations, such as language or religion. The first concept I shall call sociological culture, the second anthropological — or ascribed — culture. Let me hasten to add that the two concepts, which correspond with those used in the structural and the historical "schools" in the social sciences, are not mutually exclusive, but rather they have to be viewed as poles of a continuum: later in this essay I shall deal more extensively with both concepts.

For the moment it may suffice to note that the attitudes, orientations, and norms which comprise sociological culture are, by definition nonautonomous; they are dependent on a given structural position. A group that changes its position changes, ipso facto, its sociological culture. Anthropological culture, on the other hand, no matter what its positional genesis may be, possesses an autonomous organizational consistency that enables a group to adhere to it in spite of drastic changes in position. It further follows that in every stratification or other power relationship, each stratum or power group engenders its own sociological culture but not necessarily its own anthropological culture.

It is clear that in a hypothetically pure competitive relationship between two groups, their respective sociological cultures will be identical because their position vis-à-vis each other is identical. Hence, our conclusion that the ascriptive loyalties (stronger than horizontal economic solidarities), which hold each of these two competing groups together, must find their origin and basis in pre-existing differences of anthropological culture. In the vertically divided societies of Guyana and Surinam, there are indeed differences of such a nature between the Afro-European group and the more recently immigrated Asiatic group. These differences, as well as existing somatic differences, are intersubjectively viewed as significant and mutually reinforce each other. The competitive dispute may, it is true, lead to cultural innovations. However, though inspired by similar structural positions, these innovations will be imbedded in each group's own anthropological culture. Thus it is the latter which is both functionally and genetically linked to the dispute itself.

In the horizontally layered societies of the rest of the New World, the distinction between sociological and anthropological culture is a much more complex matter. In all these societies, historical accident (conquest, colonization, forced or free migration) made for important and commonly recognized differences in anthropological culture. The question as to the extent to which these original accidental differences have been maintained in the course of time, have been blurred, or have been subjected to a process of cultural blending or creolization from which one common anthropological culture has emerged is a legitimate one. Factors of an ecological, economic, demographic, and political nature, among others, have to account for the wide variety and different intensities of these processes. At one extreme we find the deep and persisting differences in anthropological culture between communal Indians and the white creole population in Indo-America. At the other extreme, we find a remarkable comparative lack of such differences both in the United States and in the majority of Iberian Afro-America. The British, Dutch, and French Caribbean societies find themselves in between as far as the emergence of an all-inclusive creole anthropological culture is concerned. There is no clear correlation between this range of cultural variations and the specter of socioracial stratifications that we discussed earlier: a discontinuous socioracial stratification may go together with a continuity in the anthropological culture (United States); or a continuous socioracial stratification may occur in a society where there is a discontinuity (Haiti, Indo-America) or a continuity (Spanish Caribbean) in the anthropological culture. Obviously, the factors that determine the maintenance, blending, or the emergence of new configurations out of the originally different anthropological cultures within one political unit are not identical with, or of the same intensity as, those that determine the emergence of new socioracial stratifications out of the originally separate socioracial groups. This is a matter of more than academic importance because it can be argued that the strength of feelings of national identity varies considerably, depending on whether or not a continuous socioracial stratification and anthropological culture exist, the former probably being even more essential than the latter (Hoetink 1973).

In the societies under discussion, where ascriptive predominates over economic stratification, sociological cultures correlate by definition with the position occupied by the main socioracial or sociocultural categories in each society. Smith's distinction (1965) of white, brown, and black cultures in Jamaica points to such a correlation in a three-tier stratification. Similarly, the socioracial dichotomy in the United States has led to a distinction between white and black sociological cultures, the latter sometimes called ghetto-culture. The recent efforts of North American blacks to change their position have led to the additional emergence of what may be termed an emancipatory culture with special symbols, value orientations, norms, and expectations closely linked to an anticipation of changed socioracial status.

If one defines an ethnic group as one in which the internal cohesion is based on ascriptive criteria, with the criteria seen intersubjectively as sufficiently crucial to generate a culture with comparatively clear boundaries (see Barth 1969), then it might be argued that each of the main socioracial groups in the United States and the non-Iberian Caribbean deserves such a label. The reason that I have abstained from the use of the term "ethnic group" is that, as defined here, it easily suggests an absence of overlapping ascriptive loyalties and this does not occur in the structurally complex political units under discussion. Thus, in the United States, vis-à-vis the black population, the whites may be said to form an ethnic group; yet, this term is also commonly used for those white groups that entertain ascriptive loyalties based upon a common non-American origin and/or cultural background.

Similarly, all ethnic groups in these societies share, to a greater or lesser degree, feelings of identity with and loyalty toward their present nation or territory. Indeed, nations may also be defined as ethnic groups if one views national identity in terms of the extent to which the historical experiences of the nation are perceived and transmitted as COMMON-experiences which make for common symbols, value orientations, norms, and expectations in their dealings with (members of) other nations. The subjective awareness of a commonalty of historical experiences is clearly fostered by the existence of a continuous socioracial stratification and anthropological culture in a political unit. As previously suggested, common language, religion, and the absence of endogamic exclusiveness foster the belief (however fictive) in a common origin and background (Barth 1969: 13). As Barth notes (1969: 11) the "traditional proposition" that race = culture = language (= nation) is far removed from empirical reality. This is certainly true of the political units under discussion. Thus, it would seem advisable not to subsume the manifold ascriptive loyalties which individuals from these societies may profess under the heading of so many "ethnic groups," but rather to analyze these loyalties in terms of their ascriptive content and in terms of their greater or lesser correlation.

I have suggested that no clear correlation exists between socioracial and anthropological-cultural stratification, while such a correlation does exist between the former and sociological culture, at least in the United States and the non-Iberian parts of Afro-America. This latter limitation is necessary for several Spanish Caribbean societies — Cuba, Dominican Republic, Puerto Rico — where, as elsewhere in Iberian Afro-America, a continuous socioracial stratification exists. The question may be asked whether here, in the absence of clear boundaries between the socioracial strata, the numerous, very subtly and ambiguously perceived scales in the white-black continuum will have generated sociological cultures sufficiently unambiguous and identifiable as to be comparable to those generated by discontinuous socioracial stratifications.

I am inclined to answer this question in the negative and to suggest further that in these societies the sociological cultures resulting from different ECONOMIC group positions are much more definable and delineated than those resulting from different positions in the continuous socioracial stratification. This means that, with respect to these societies, I have to modify my earlier general proposition that in multiracial societies ascriptive (socioracial) loyalties predominate over economic ones. In the Hispanic American societies under discussion, this proposition was undoubtedly valid in the earlier stages of their colonial history. However, a continued process of cultural and somatic creolization led to a situation where neither the initially separate anthropological cultures nor the originally separate socioracial groups have maintained boundaries of such a conciseness as to prevent the development of a strong awareness of national identity or as to predominate over economic loyalties in the formation of sociological culture. To put the matter differently, these societies come close to the "class" societies with which "classical" sociology has mostly preoccupied itself. However, in one respect, these societies differ from class societies: even though the many-graded somatic statuses do not correspond on a one-to-one basis to economic positions, and even though sociological culture is predominantly based on economic class, throughout the socioracial continuum "whiter" keeps being associated not only with "socially more prestigious" and "economically more powerful" but also, and linked to it, with "esthetically more desirable." Such a socially determined esthetic factor influencing social selection and allocation operates, it is true, in all horizontally layered multiracial societies. But the difference is that in the Iberian societies under discussion it can be seen to operate more independently, more on an individual basis as it were, since the socioracial categories do not have the morphological solidity that we find in the non-Iberian societies, especially as regards the boundary between "white" and "colored." In the absence of clear economic or cultural factors, I have elsewhere tried to understand this blurring of the "white-colored" boundary in the Afro-Iberian societies in terms of a greater "adoption-readiness" of the white group, ultimately linked to certain differences in physical type between the original white dominant groups in Iberian and non-Iberian America (Hoetink 1971). It may be argued convincingly that also in classical, class-stratified societies, socially determined esthetic ingredients somewhat influence social selection and allocation. Also in these societies, the more and less esthetically "desirable" individuals are not organized in group-like aggregates. The (considerable) difference with the Ibero-African societies in the Western Hemisphere might then be considered one of degree in this respect.

The foregoing may be summarized as follows. The allocation of resources and positions in societies where ascriptive stratifications prevail ideally corresponds to either of two mechanisms: (1) a competitive mechanism operates wherever the dividing lines between ascriptive groups run vertically, or (2) a monopolistic mechanism operates wherever these lines run horizontally. The number and solidity of the ascriptive strata formed in the monopolistic situation vary greatly and justify efforts toward a taxonomy as presented here. The question as to which of the many overlapping ascriptive loyalties — to "social race," to anthropological culture, to the nation — may be considered to be predominant at a given historical moment, and the question as to which conditions economic solidarity may be said to prevail under, can only be answered by comparative research in a historical context. As Barth (1969) notes, a given "ethnic group" may change the content of its anthropological culture in the course of time, yet retain its internal cohesion as a group. Similarly, such a group may also acquire entirely new notions about its origin and background, shifting its ascriptive loyalty to other criteria. In the process, it will sometimes retain its group cohesion; but it may also lose its original feelings of group identity altogether. In my view, the factors that influence the course of these processes are of an objective nature: they have to do with economics, demography, anthropological culture, and notions of common descent or social race, of which the latter are in a complicated and often indirect way linked to objective data. On the other hand, sociological culture is indeed, as Barth (1969) observes, essentially the RESULT, and not the cause of a particular stratification or power relationship, and as such cannot be given but a secondary explanatory function in an analysis of the emergence and maintenance of such a particular group relation. This observation requires further consideration of the distinction between the concepts of anthropological and sociological culture.

Every stratum in a system of stratification engenders an interdependent system of value orientations, norms, and expectations, directly connected with the position of the stratum in the social hierarchy. The extent to which this sociological culture can be articulated and identified, and its boundaries clearly delineated, depends on and is, in fact, synonymous with the extent of mobility the system allows. If one defines, as some do, this sociological culture as "subculture," then one has to conclude that each social class has its own subculture. The term "subculture" is somewhat confusing here, however, in that it more commonly tends to be reserved for those sociological cultures which, due to the closedness of their stratum, have developed a comparatively easily definable set of norms, value orientations, and expectations and, even, may have created organizational patterns of such a morphological distinctiveness (e.g. an embryonic "group language") as to border on the distinction between sociological and anthropological culture. Morphologically, I speak of anthropological culture when we deal with such a distinctiveness and recognizability of complex behavioral or organizational patterns as to warrant the greatest possible consensus on its identification. Positionally, this morphological distinctiveness gives anthropological culture a social autonomy. That is to say, whereas social position "signifies" sociological culture, anthropological culture "signifies" social position. Anthropological culture may create ascriptive loyalties (and thus "ethnic groups" in Barth's sense), thereby determining one's position in an ascriptive stratification or power relationship, whereas sociological culture is determined by a group's position in whatever type of given stratification. Genetically, isolation is the immediate operative agent in the emergence of anthropological culture. Whether this isolation is spatial or social is inessential: the closedness of a pelagic island society, the exclusiveness of a nobility, or the excludedness of a pariah group all imply similar conditions for the emergence of anthropological culture. The difference between the two forms of isolation only expresses itself in the greater importance attached to boundary-maintaining mechanisms in a stratified system with (emerging) different anthropological cultures than in a hypothetical social system with one anthropological culture geographically isolated. The reason for this difference is, of course, that in the stratified system we deal with allocation of resources and positions on the basis of ascriptive criteria (the mechanisms for this allocation varying between the monopolistic and the competitive type), while in the geographically isolated system such a connection between power and anthropological culture is assumed to be absent. Only when the once geographically isolated unit becomes part of a more extensive power relationship will it (be forced to) "decide" which, if any, of its ascriptive loyalties (to anthropological culture, to its territory, to its notions of common descent) it will retain, and which boundary-marking attributes and mechanisms it will adhere to for those purposes.

The notion of common descent in a geographically isolated system is nothing but the consequence of such isolation. In a rigid horizontally stratified system, however, it is both cause and consequence: there is a functional relation between the monopoly of power allocation and endogamy, as well as between the rigid, outcaste-like exclusion from certain positions and endogamy. Thus, the concept of nobility always entails the notions of privilege in power allocation and of common descent through endogamy. These notions of common descent find their boundary-marking expression through such attributes as names, titles, addressing formulas, flags, coats-of-arms, registers of nobility, and, indirectly, through specific rituals of adoption. Privileges in position and power may express themselves in such attributes as special uniforms and insignia, prescribed types of housing and personnel, etc. As to their function, most of these attributes are ATTRIBUTES OF PRESENTATION; they serve as instant identification, thus establishing boundaries (or affinity) at social encounters. (The register of nobility is an ATTRIBUTE OF VERIFICATION in literate societies.)

Analogous types of attributes are found wherever social boundaries are to be marked, and they do not by themselves inform the outside observer about the type of boundary (ascriptive or nonascriptive) involved. In the case of a nobility, only the attributes of descent are ascriptive: an impoverished nobleman will keep them after he has lost the attributes of power and position. The chances for regaining the latter depend, in fact, on the continued social recognition of the former.

Rigidity of the stratification system and durability of social isolation are among the factors that determine whether or not an anthropological culture may emerge out of the sociological culture of a stratum. Thus, in Java, language (High versus Low Javanese) became an autonomous, ascriptive cultural attribute, whereas in Europe such a discontinuous linguistic stratification did not develop (although the temporary adoption of a foreign language, French, by the upper strata of some countries in the eighteenth century had, if not the same genesis, at least the same function).

Language is both an attribute of presentation and an instrument of communication. It serves as a badge of ascriptive identity, and it also transmits a maximum of messages and emotions, which in turn may strengthen this identity. Somewhat analogous, a religious system has its attributes serving individual presentation and its instruments serving communication between men and the supernatural universe. Religion is a functionally less versatile, more specialized, system of communication than language (hence its often special language: Latin, Sanskrit, Hebrew), but its emotive impact, strengthening "we-feelings," is not necessarily smaller. It is these attributes of presentation and instruments of communication that give to language and religion such a historical importance as criteria of ascriptive, anthropological-cultural identity. They even may be used sometimes to suggest a commonalty of origin of their participants, especially where numerical or ecological conditions have prevented the continued existence of observable attributes of descent or where control over allocation of resources makes frequent adoption of new numbers unavoidable. Hence, also, the importance of language and religion in the historical processes that lead to the formation of new nations.

The colonizers and migrants to the New World easily lost their original sociological culture, the norms, value orientations, and expectations produced by and linked to the social position they had occupied in their society of origin. Their new sociological culture was determined by their position in the new country. The fate of their "old" anthropological culture was determined by entirely different processes having to do with precedence of arrival, power relations, and their influence on the social value and function of special anthropological cultural heritages and with the ensuing processes of assimilation, blending, or the maintenance of cultural boundaries. Earlier we saw that in a horizontally stratified system a functional relation tends to exist between monopolization of power allocation and endogamy. It is clear that in societies, such as those of the Americas, the notion of common descent of a stratum, even in complex and populous societies, is strongly enhanced by the existing somatic variations within the population. Here, somatic traits are both ATTRIBUTES OF PRESENTATION and of DESCENT; they further may have, as we have already noted, a socially determined esthetic value. (A social stigma is nothing but an attribute of presentation with a socially determined strongly negative value.)

We have so far discussed four important ascriptive criteria: (1) territoriality (or nationality), (2) notions of common descent, (3) language, and (4) religion. We have seen how each of these has (or, in the case of language, is) its own attributes of presentation. We noted that these four main ascriptive criteria may evolve in a geographically isolated community. In addition, descent, language, and religion may also emerge in a rigidly stratified system, where desired or imposed social isolation leads to endogamy in order to preserve the existing distribution of power and where the creation of ascriptive cultural anthropological criteria is conditioned by such isolation. Finally, historical "accident" (conquest, colonization) may create (as it were ad hoc) stratified systems, where notions of common descent, language, religion, etc. are present and hierarchically ordered "at the beginning" as it were.

The presence of only one of the four ascriptive criteria mentioned here is necessary to create what Barth terms an "ethnic group." In order to establish a subjective awareness of ascriptive loyalty, it is further necessary for the individuals involved to be engaged in a power relationship of either the monopolistic or the competitive type, so that — contrary to a situation of total geographic isolation — their boundaries become marked and their attributes of presentation functional. It is further probable that in each situation there will be a minimal numerical strength under which no efforts at establishing and defending boundaries can or will be made.

If one of the four mentioned ascriptive criteria is present under conditions that create group loyalty, then a wide internal diversity in all other aspects or sectors of social behavior — including variations induced by ecology or by sociological culture in a stratified group — may be present without necessarily obliterating the boundaries established by this criterion. Barth's example of Northern and Southern Pathans (Barth 1969: 13–14) illustrates this case even to the point where "basic value orientations," elsewhere considered by him to be essential, are lacking (the Southern Pathans finding the behavior of the Northerners "reprehensible" by their basic values). The relative ease of adoption of new members varies with the prevalent criterion of ascription. Similarly the type and number of attributes of presentation used depend on which of the ascriptive criteria is operative. For example, in a nation with a rigid socioracial dichotomy, two individuals of similar economic background, language, and religion, but belonging to a different socioracial group, do not need any other attribute of presentation than their own somatic traits. Conversely, in societies where notions of common descent, language, and religion coincide, the variety of attributes of presentation may be large. While it is undeniable that the precise form the "overt signals or signs" (Barth 1969: 14) will take has the same degree of (un)predictability as most other cultural creations, their classification in terms of the group-forming criterion that they are meant to "signify" gives their occurrence, in terms of number and specific function, a logic sufficiently consistent to remove doubts about any utter arbitrariness.

The intersubjectivity that leads to agreements on criteria of group alignment, boundaries, and attributes is of the same order as that which reaches other types of consensus in a given social context. If these consensuses were such as to defy objective classification and a modicum of predictability, the social sciences would not be able to operate on their present levels of abstraction. Comparative research in sufficient time-depth is needed, as Barth notes (1969: 14), if we are to understand better the emergence of ascriptive group alignments, their different types, their coincidence, their overlapping or separation, and the similarity or dissimilarity of the conditions that make their respective boundaries stronger, weaker, or more complex.

REFERENCES

BARTH, F.
   1969   "Introduction," in *Ethnic groups and boundaries*. Edited by F. Barth, 9–38. Bergen and Oslo.
FAHRENFORT, J. J.
   1943   Over vrije en onvrije arbeid. *Mensch en Maatschappij* 19.
HARRIS, M.
   1964   *Patterns of race in the Americas*. New York: Walker.
HOETINK, H.
   1971   *Caribbean race relations: a study of two variants*. New York: Oxford University Press.
   1973   *Slavery and race relations in the Americas: an inquiry into their nature and nexus*. New York: Harper and Row.
KLOOSTERBOER, W.
   1960   *Involuntary labour since the abolition of slavery: a survey of compulsory labour throughout the world*. Leiden: Brill.
KÖBBEN, A. J. F.
   1967   Why exceptions? The logic of cross-cultural analysis. *Current Anthropology* 8:3–33.
NIEBOER, H. J.
   1900   *Slavery as an industrial system: ethnological researches*. The Hague: Martinus Nijhoff.
SEDA BONILLA, E.
   1968   Dos modelos de relaciones raciales: Estados Unidos y America Latina. *Revista de Ciencias Sociales* 12:4.
SMITH, M. G.
   1965   *The plural society in the West Indies*. Berkeley: University of California Press.

Ethnic Boundary Maintenance, Readaptation and Societal Evolution in the San Blas Islands of Panama

REGINA E. HOLLOMAN

In recent years considerable attention has been focused on questions dealing with the nature and social function of ethnicity and ethnic processes. Using both field and historical data collected in 1966–1967 among the San Blas Cuna of Panama, this study examines the relationships among ethnic identity maintenance, the persistence of interethnic boundaries, related interface institutions, and politico-economic evolution.

The Cuna are of unusual interest because they provide an example which runs contrary to expectations. In this century, innumerable small societies have been incorporated into the political and economic networks of nation-states. Where the indigenous political organization was itself below the state level, one of three outcomes has been usual. In some instances there has been gradual or rapid disintegration of the boundaries of the indegenous societies and, relatedly, of higher-level native institutions. Societal readaptation and ethnic stabilization, if achieved, is usually at the family or extended kin level. Alternatively, what Aguirre Beltrán (1967) has termed "refuge areas" have formed, generally, at the village level. In these cases the village-level ethnic unit develops "hermetically sealed" boundaries; articulation with the greater society is brokered; and developmental-evolutionary change is contained and minimized. A third pattern is found in areas of New Guinea and Africa in which very large tribal populations have been organized as polities and integrated by means of externally introduced institutions. The size of the indigenous populations has had a buffering or boundary-maintaining effect, permitting nativization of the introduced institutions over time. Over time such a population may be drawn into the emerging national economy as a peasant or small-farmer class.

The Cuna case followed none of these paths. During the period of concern, 1903–1967, a regional population of twenty to twenty-five thousand evolved politically from the level of *primus inter pares* local chiefdoms to that of a constitutional confederation, recognized as internally self-governing and with special status under Panamanian law. Local-level institutions were greatly expanded to encompass contact and development-related functions such as public building, the transport and retailing of goods and (in a few cases) the provision of electricity. Schools, although a part of the Panamanian national system, were locally constructed and staffed almost entirely by Cuna teachers, with instruction in Cuna for the first year. The ceremonial cycle underwent change with modification and/ or atrophy of some traditional ceremonies and emergence of new ceremonies and fiestas, typically honoring great chiefs of interisland status or patron saints. At the same time, the matrilocal family and the father-in-law/son-in-law work team remained the basis of household organization, and female dress (including the wearing of nose rings) continued to be conservative in most communities. Signs of stress were apparent at many points. Nevertheless, what was most striking was the extent of internally negotiated change of an evolutionary sort coexisting with highly traditional practices.

The ethnic boundary system (i.e. patterns of contact and interaction and related interface institutions) was also atypical. Politically, the San Blas region was incompletely incorporated into the Republic. The political status of the Cuna differed from that of the several other ethnic groups found in Panama, and this special status was legally formalized. A contraband coconut trade — the basis of the cash economy of the region — was articulated with the economy of Colombia rather than Panama. For lack of a better term, I have characterized this boundary system as a type of suzerainty (where it is understood that Panamanian control of Cuna foreign affairs did not extend to de facto control of trade). As I see it, suzerainty RELATIONSHIPS are the result of PROCESSES of economic and political competition which are characterized by a high degree of autonomy.

This study represents an inquiry into the manner in which this configuration developed and stabilized. It is a case description of an ULTRA-STABLE SYSTEM: i.e. one in which system stability is maintained by means of major alterations in social organization (Cadwallader 1968: 437). It is a case of special relevance for the study of human societal evolution. I do not wish to be misunderstood. My analysis of the sixty-plus years of Cuna history presented here implies nothing by way of a prediction regarding the future stability of the situation as it existed in 1967. On the contrary, it seemed unlikely that the parameters as described would remain un-changed. This does not destroy the value to a comparative science of this particular ethnographic present. The period of focus stretches from the founding of the Republic of Panama (with the transfer of jurisdiction over San Blas from Colombia to Panama) in 1903 until 1967. In 1968, the Panamanian government was overthrown and several aspects of the polit-ical situation were altered. Although the most basic fact of San Blas life — the establishment of the island ecological niche itself — dates from the middle of the nineteenth century, the period selected for examination has a certain historical closure. And it is certainly clear that the major re-adjustments necessitated by incorporation into the world market system and into the Republic of Panama took place within the 1903–1967 period.

In a seminal essay on the nature and significance of ethnicity as a prin-ciple of social organization, Fredrik Barth dealt briefly with the problem of how interethnic boundaries are maintained when a traditional society is incorporated into a nation-state or the international market system (1969: 32–35). He assumes the formation of "new elites" in the traditional society, seeing them as the principal agents of change, and regard their choice of strategy as the critical variable governing interethnic boundary stability.

Barth identifies these alternate strategies: (1) In some cases members of the new elite may drop their traditional ethnicity and become incorporat-ed into the dominant cultural group on an individual basis.[1] This results in a continual draining off of the best-educated and most talented mem-bers of the traditional system, and is a factor in the formation of a con-servative, low-ranking ethnic group within the larger society. (2) In other cases, members of the new elite accept minority status. They participate in the larger system in the open sectors and live the rest of their lives with-in the framework of their ethnic group. (3) In still other cases, members of the new elite may emphasize their ethnic identity, using it as a basis for recruiting support "to develop new positions and patterns and to organize activities in those sectors formerly not found in their society or inade-quately developed for the new purposes" (Barth 1969: 33). Although Barth does not use the term, this latter case is an example of readaptation in the direction of increased complexity — that is, of sociocultural evolu-tion. Such readaptation may result from conscious decisions by leadership within a recognized problem-solving context. The Cuna are of this third type. However, the Cuna innovators were traditionalists and in no sense

---

[1] This is the strategy predicted by Marx (see, for example, Bott 1965: Chapter 12).

were they members of a new elite. They and their supporters acted as an "evolutionary cluster" (Mead 1964: Chapter 9).

Barth notes that the MODE of interethnic organization varies from case to case, but that the historical record shows a general transition from economic articulation (typical of the older polyethnic systems of Asia and Middle America) to political articulation. Smith (1969) has described one such form as a "structurally plural" society. The minority form referred to by Barth, and the suzerainty pattern described here, can be taken as additional organizational types, the result of variation in political and economic processes. Barth predicts that political integration will be inherently less stable than the older form based on economic articulation (i.e. interethnic boundaries will be less likely to be maintained). Presumably he is contrasting the "organic" nature of economic interdependency with the power-based nature of political processes. Where sustained political confrontation DOES occur, the competing groups tend to become structurally similar. This point is consistent with the work of Toynbee and other historians and is compatible with the Cuna data.

Barth believes that this tendency toward structural similarity in the political realm entails a general movement in the direction of intergroup similarities. This, he contends, magnifies the importance of the differentiating criteria chosen by the groups involved as ethnic identity markers. In concluding his essay, Barth reiterates his belief that it is this use of cultural diacritica to mark ingroup and outgroup identification that is of fundamental importance for theory: "... ethnic boundaries are maintained in each case by a limited set of CULTURAL features. The persistence of the UNIT then depends on the persistence of these cultural differentiae..." (1969: 38). That is, although he notes the importance of political and economic processes and transactions, Barth's model is basically psychocultural.

However, the persistence of cultural differentiae is problematic. A generative model, as called for by Barth, must explain why it is that actors continue to see it to their advantage to interact in terms of ethnic identities when and if other options are available.[2] It seems to me that we are at the point where we can grant that the emergence and/or persistence of macrostructure is directly related to the channeling of resources. The actions of individuals are related to their perceptions of options and their anticipations of specific results. If these expectations go increasingly unfulfilled, or if the balance of advantages clearly favors a new strategy, then

---

[2]   Optionless situations — those characterized by extreme power imbalance, institutionalized discrimination, and negligible mobility — are omitted from consideration here.

the statistical profile of interactions will reflect a shift in commitments. This is the situation which we label as structural "crumbling." CULTURAL differences may persist because of population clustering (Smith's [1969] "cultural pluralism"). However, the persistence of significant ethnic ORGA-NIZATION and of interethnic boundaries is always an indication that there is differential access to resources along ethnic lines, and that the assertion of ethnic identity has payoffs with respect to resource access and utilization.

A stable interethnic situation is one in which differential niching is established, although tension at an interface may be evident. The process of stabilization (niche definition and interface system generation) can be expected to be stressful. The outcome will be determined by leader strategy, but only within the framework of the major political and economic parameters which set limits on the possible. The highest-level strategy — that which seeks to affect the parameters themselves — is, of course, the most difficult to implement. The adoption of such a strategy entails a certain amount of internal reorganization. Here is the evolutionary thrust. In democratic-capitalistic state systems two attributes of the national structure itself can sometimes be successfully manipulated by ethnic groups: purchasing power (and the related right to boycott) and bloc voting.

Panamanians and Cuna occupy adjacent territories and are not in symbiotic relationship (a tension-limiting factor). The Cuna have secured exclusive access to the resources of the region for themselves. This particular set of boundary conditions was obtained by them as a result of armed conflict in 1925. They maintain a contraband coconut trade with small-scale Colombian entrepreneurs. Although much of the profit from the trade is channeled into imported consumer goods, in 1967 a significant portion was being reinvested in commercial activities and services within the region. Nothing was drained off in taxes or rents. They have also made effective use of a regional fairprice system for imports and regional pricing on the cash crop, coconuts. For several elections they successfully maintained a bloc vote, although this broke down in the early 1960's. They are outside the municipal district *(municipio)* system obtaining for the rest of the country. And they have the option of accepting or rejecting schools in their villages. The extent of regional autonomy was the single most important variable determining the ongoing pattern of Cuna-Panamanian relations at the time fieldwork was conducted.

In an earlier analysis I dealt with the readaptation of the Cuna as an example of system ultrastability (Holloman 1969). My analysis attributed the success of the Cuna in readapting to the following: (a) the capacity of the system to provide appropriate and accurate information upon which leaders could base decisions; (b) the appropriateness of decisions actually made; (c) the ability of leaders to generate support for innovative decisions: and (d) the success of the Cuna in reestablishing political and economic autonomy, thus securing their capacity to IMPLEMENT their decisions.

Because the focus was on Cuna society itself rather than on the interethnic boundary, the extent to which the emergence of a middle-class lifestyle had been retarded in the region, despite the presence in the area of a significant number of middle-class occupations, was not related to the readaptive process. Approximately 6 percent of all men working and living in the area held middle-class jobs (Holloman 1969: 36). Although attitudinal data reflected the shift to middle-class occupations and educational levels, behavior in several key areas did not. For example, contrary to expectations, a 20 percent household survey revealed only one case of neolocality and no cases of patrilocality. Reflecting upon the data, I now believe that both aspects of San Blas Cuna readaptation — the addition of new and more complex activities and the viability of some traditional activities that were expected to be in a state of disorganization — can be presented within a framework which focuses on interethnic boundary maintenance as related to the capacity of the ethnic system to preserve or enhance its members' competitive advantage with respect to resources.

Interestingly, Cuna regional autonomy was not simply a continuation of premodern isolation: it was lost and then regained. Following the Panamanian revolution of 1903, the newly established national government adopted a policy of incorporation and acculturation with respect to its Indian populations. This policy was supported by some Cuna leaders. Between 1903 and 1925, the direction of change in San Blas was toward the breakdown of political and economic autonomy. An anthropologist would have seen a typical picture of early-stage deterioration of a traditional society. The Panamanian government facilitated economic penetration of the area through franchises, and Cuna decisions to exclude non-Cuna from the region were unenforceable. Panamanian national guardsmen, stationed at several points within the region, and local authorities were unable to control the actions of the guardsmen. The Cuna population itself became divided in its attitude toward Panama and modernization. Four villages reorganized under acculturation-oriented leaders known as the "progressive faction." They reconstructed their villages on the Latin American plaza and grid pattern, abolished traditional ceremonies, forbade the wearing of nose rings, and opened themselves to missionaries and schools. Three of these four villages retained this orientation at the time of fieldwork. The fourth (the principal research site) reintroduced traditional dress in 1925 but remained pro-Panama in its orientation. The other villages can be roughly grouped into moderate and extreme traditionalist factions.

In 1925 Nele Kantule, a traditional leader, organized the villages in his faction (the present moderates) in a revolt against Panama. The success of the revolt was due in part to the intervention of the United States (a United States cruiser prevented Panamanian gunboats from putting down the revolt and the United States ambassador presided at the drafting of the peace treaty).[3] Thus, the ability of the Cuna to restore the status quo ante with respect to these vital parameters was partly an accident of history. Whatever the circumstances which established this decision point, it is significant that the Cuna regained their ability to implement major decisions and that their leadership policy was innovative and evolutionary.

Inter alia, the Treaty of Porvenir which concluded the revolt brought about the dismissal of the incumbent *Intendente* (the *Indendencia* itself was retained); the recall of Panamanian national guardsmen; the agreement by Panama to occupy only the administrative island of Porvenir and to station there only "white married men"; the agreement not to impose schools without consent of the individual villages; acknowledgement of the right of Cuna to possess shotguns (but not high-powered rifles); the promise to set aside a sufficient area as an Indian reservation which would be inviolate and free from exploitation by outsiders; and the right to internal self-rule AND equal rights with all other citizens of Panama. Under these conditions the Cuna recognized the sovereignty of Panama (Marsh 1934: 272–273). The legal status of San Blas remained essentially unchanged until 1954, when an organic law for the organization of the *Comarca* [Reserve] of San Blas was passed, superseding all previous legislation. In this highly-detailed document the government of Panama reaffirmed the autonomy and territorial integrity of the San Blas region, although some modifications were introduced which may be important in the future.[4]

---

[3] The course of events was affected by the presence in San Blas in the early 1920's of Richard O. Marsh, an American who came to Panama in 1923 to explore the possibilities for establishing rubber plantations in the eastern Darien. Marsh became a friend of the Cuna. Although he was not responsible for the revolt itself, he was involved in its military and political strategy, and the United States intervention was due to his efforts.

[4] The Cuna and the Panamanian government continue to come into conflict occasionally. An example of the constraints on each is illustrated in the dealings concerning the introduction of the first major tourist facility into the area, that of W. D. Barton. Around 1965, Barton secured right of access to an islet in separate contracts with the government of Panama (details unknown) and with the owners of the land and the

At that time a system of bloc voting under traditional authority was instituted. For voting purposes, San Blas is considered to be a part of the Province of Colon. The Cuna did not begin to exercise their franchise in significant numbers until the 1940's. In 1960, the total population of the province was 105,416. Of this number, 20,084 were tribal Cuna (*Panama en Cifres* 1963: 17). A politician could be successful by attracting a sizable Cuna vote, and political activity in the region and competition for Cuna votes was intensive until the national coup of 1968. During the multiparty period, the Cuna were not given nominations for deputy, but they were placed on the ballot as alternates. The bloc vote broke down as competition (and largess) increased. Nevertheless, their capacity to manipulate their vote to their advantage is latent in the regular political structure.

It is important in understanding Cuna-Panamanian competition to realize that the San Blas variant of Cuna culture is an adaptation to coastal trade. In the middle of the nineteenth century the Cuna began to move from the interior into the islands for reasons of health and in order to have access to trading boats. Cuna men shipped out as sailors, and coconut trees were planted extensively. Insofar as "traditional" connotes a subsistence economy, the term is misleading in the Cuna case. Cash cropping of coconuts was the basis of the economy in 1903. The key resource in San Blas is land suitable for the production of coconuts. The traditional system operated so as to provide all adults access to both coconut land and land for subsistence farming. The land-to-man ratio at the time of fieldwork was such that all adult men in the region apparently had land, although pressure was mounting as a result of population growth.

Before the 1925 revolt, a number of Panamanian and American companies had been granted franchises in the region. Large amounts of land were diverted from coconut and subsistence production to the cultivation of fruit and rubber. This competition over land ended with the revolt. The political boundary system guarantees that land and the revenue from it will be controlled by the Cuna. The continued operation of a traditional pattern of bilateral inheritance has thus far prevented the emergence of a landless group within the population itself. Income per capita in 1967 was

---

government of the town from which they came. There was conflict between Barton and the Indians, and the resort was burned after I left the field. The operation was then renegotiated and reopened. It is now a Caribbean cruise stop.

Sophisticated Cuna leaders attempted to carry on the principle that Cuna should be included in all levels of operations as tourism developed; this had not been implemented at the time of the fieldwork. Because of the isolation of the area by land (the Darien jungle blocks access) and the lack of patrol boats, political dealings between the Panamanian government and the Cuna were governed by strategy and self-restraint, each party wanting to avoid upsetting the balance between them.

estimated at $99, of which 70 percent came from coconuts (Holloman 1969: 134). Land could be bought and sold in 1967. However, because multiple ownership was usually involved, it was often difficult to reach consensus about sale.

Readaptation in San Blas can be viewed as a problem on how to safeguard the territory and the coconut trade while at the same time adding the new activities necessary to permit the Cuna to compete with Panama and to satisfy new demands of the Cuna themselves, all this without permitting threats to traditional authority or allowing economic inequalities to develop. It is not surprising that because the innovators were traditional leaders, support for the traditional bases of authority was built into the pattern of their solutions. The strength of their concern with the preservation of a homogeneous, consensus-based social system is easily seen in the constitution drawn up in 1945 for a regional confederation. That document deals with three matters: the protection of the coconut trade; the reaffirmation of the authority of the chiefs; and the support of the authority of fathers-in-law and the matrilocal household (Holloman 1969: Appendix I).

The introduction of new activities and services within the society was handled organizationally by two devices — cooperation under the local chiefs and the town meeting, and proliferation of *sociedades*, a voluntary cooperative form loosely inspired by the cooperative work organization of the town. Both of these devices permit the Cuna to cooperate for external competition. At the same time, they contain internal equalizing mechanisms: work is an obligation of *sociedad* membership and paid positions are usually rotated among the members as a whole, or among those with the requisite skills. In all of these activities traditionalists and younger, educated members of the population are in close association, so that much information flows to the traditionalists in this way.

The concept that Cuna culture would have to be modified if it were to survive was successfully introduced by Nele Kantule, leader of the revolt. Many of these organizational innovations have already been mentioned, but it is useful to list them so that the true extent of introduced changes is clear. Nele was directly responsible for the following: the fair-price system for coconut sales; the community or public *sociedad* [cooperative] as a form of agricultural organization; the application of the public *sociedad* form to the ownership and operation of stores, boats, and other enterprises; the standing-committee system of the local town meeting and the communal work system in its present form; founding of organizations on a community-by-community basis among workers in Panama City and Colon; initial organization of the Cuna vote as a bloc; and formation of the first interisland government and wholesale-retail commercial network.

The net effect of Nele's program was to compensate for the disruptive effects of change-associated processes which were well under way. He identified and proposed a solution for most of the imbalances that had developed in the first quarter of the twentieth century. Not all of his attempts were successful, however. The bloc vote was never used to force nomination of a Cuna as deputy, and the so-called Party of the Chiefs did not hold together when Panamanian politicians began to recruit personal lieutenants in the area. The first interisland government (which included only the islands in Nele's faction) fell apart in the early 1930's, but the ideal of unification persisted and the present government was formed in 1945. The wholesale buying network did not survive the collapse of the government, but native-operated retail stores have proliferated, and most goods purchased in Panama are transported on Cuna-owned boats, operated sometimes by whole villages and sometimes by private cooperatives.

The *sociedad* has been perhaps the most important of the innovations. It has been adapted for a wide variety of purposes and has had the effect of channeling small-scale investment within the society while preventing great social distance from emerging between men of conservative and modern orientation.

The major area of change which has not been adequately controlled has to do with the role of younger men. It is now normative for a Cuna man between approximately eighteen and thirty-five to spend large amounts of time away from the Comarca, working in Panama or the Canal Zone. The amount of cash and goods sent to the region by these men is not great; further, the burden of producing food for their dependents falls upon the traditional agriculturalists. For the most part, these are older men who should, under traditional mores, be at the height of their prestige and authority as heads of households. Loss of the labor of the younger men is felt in the village cooperative work system. The rate of family abandonment is high. Even when present, younger men tend not to attend town meetings and to avoid work responsibilities if possible. All attempts to extend communal authority to the cities have failed. The existing worker organizations are mutual aid societies.

Attempts to constrain the emergence of a nontraditional lifestyle within the region itself have been more successful. Monetization of internal relationships has been allowed to occur, but has been controlled in interesting ways. Coconuts are used in lieu of cash. Items such as kerosene and soap are regularly purchased by all households. Labor can be bought and sold. The only nonmonetized sector of the economy covers subsistence food products (principally the staples, platanos and guineos). Prices are such that even a man on a teacher's salary could not afford to buy all of his family's food from what was available for purchase. Control of access to basic foodstuffs is the most important way in which the emergence of a fully middle-class lifestyle (i.e. one divorced from subsistence agriculture) is retarded.[5]

Control over storeowners is guaranteed by the fair-price system and by control on profit making. Stores are regarded as services to the community and are expected to put the community welfare ahead of profit whenever the two values conflict. Business enterprises other than stores are regarded with suspicion if organized by individuals rather than a *sociedad* group. At the time of research, one informant had started to raise chickens in quantity for sale. The town decided that the operation was potentially too profitable and he was ordered to go out of business, which he did. Although the growth of businesses has been restricted in this manner, business remains an area of opportunity for a man who is aggressive. It is the younger, better· ;ducated men who tend to hold the key positions in the successful stores and *sociedades*.

In 1967, some towns showed the effects of disintegration of local authority: paths were dirty, town meetings and cooperative work projects were poorly attended, and there were problems of juvenile delinquency (marijuana-smoking and stealing). For the region as a whole, however, these anticipated effects of contact were NOT extensively in evidence. Chiefs received a government salary and were regarded as the official point of contact in each village. A pass system limited movement within the region. A Cuna who wanted to go from his village to another for any purpose had to obtain a pass bearing the stamp of the chief. Chiefs supported one another in returning individuals who appeared without passes. The pass system was also used to support the authority of the father-in-law. If a man's father-in-law objected to his leaving to work in Panama, he was not issued a pass. Because exit from the area by either boat or plane could be closely monitored, this was an effective control. Once in Panama, however, a man was outside the native authority system. Although middle-class informants always made it clear that they acted simply "out of respect," they too obtained passes.

A final control on those men who might be expected to deviate from the traditional lifestyle was exercised through marriage and residence. Because education for women lagged behind that for men, and Cuna women did

---

[5] For example, the principal of the school on Tupile continued to live with his father-in-law, a traditional agriculturalist who provided the staples for the joint household. The principal contributed money. In effect, such men occupied different "niches" within the household organization and were in close symbiotic relationship.

not until recently travel to Panama; most Cuna women in 1967 were traditional in dress and conservative in outlook. They responded to parental authority. The Cuna have strong feelings about out-marriage and it was therefore not unusual to find a librarian or storeowner whose wife wore a nose ring and whose household was traditional in every way. The lack of available house sites was a further check on the emergence of neolocality.

In retrospect, the retardation of internal status differentiation will probably appear as a "holding action" instrumental in the preservation of minimal consensus during a period of rapid institutional change. Problems of heterogeneity and lack of consensus will have to be dealt with if further development is to occur. Otherwise, selective out-migration is almost certain to develop.

CONCLUSIONS

This study is an attempt to clarify our understanding of ethnicity as a principle in societal organization. I have used the Cuna data as an illustration of one type of interethnic situation — one involving incomplete political and economic incorporation, a form of suzerainty. At the macrolevel the stability of the interethnic boundary is reflective of the way in which the Cuna and non-Cuna have arrived at de facto patterns of access (or lack of them) to political and economic resources. At the micro-level, the Cuna side of that boundary is sustained by internal structures, which simultaneously guarantee rewards adequate to sustain member support of the ethnic system and provide for control of change-related deviant behavior.

This analysis suggests that the boundary will remain stable so long as the ethnic system is able to provide adequate rewards to both the traditional and the modern segments of the population. The Marxist prediction that drainoff or defection of the "new elite" is inevitable seems oversimplified. The possibility suggested by Marx and by Mexican Indian and Appalachian ethnography — that San Blas might become a culturally conservative refuge area — is real but not inevitable. Nevertheless, a prediction in this regard would have to be pessimistic. Past success in readaptation cannot be taken as a prediction of the future. The maintenance of this ethnic boundary is contingent upon many factors over which the Cuna exert little influence: e.g. Columbian government coconut policy; Panamanian government policy toward the Cuna; a spreading coconut blight; the development of the tourist industry; and the dynamics of their own population.

Barth has stressed the importance, for boundary maintenance, of the set of mutual identifications and the communications fields established with them. I have attempted here to push the discussion beyond that point to an investigation of the factors which maintain the identity-commitments themselves, that is, to the macro-organizational patterns which define and perpetuate patterns of access to rewards for various segments of the population. The Cuna revolt of 1925 had the effect of resetting the economic and political parameters of the Cuna ethnic system. Competition over land and trade between Cuna and Panamanians was ended, with the Cuna left in possession of their territory. The internal evolutionary changes in political and economic organization were a conscious response of the leadership to the need to build new functions into the system, in order to counter the pull of Panamanian cities and jobs on the emerging modern segment of the population, as well as to prevent the development of dependencies on Panamanian middlemen.

REFERENCES

AGUIRRE BELTRÁN, GONZALO
  1967   *Regiones de refugion: el desarrollo de la comunidal y el proceso domini-cal en Mestizo America.* Mexico D.F.: Instituto Indigenista Interamericano.
BARTH, FREDRIK
  1969   *Ethnic groups and boundaries.* Boston: Little, Brown.
BOTT, PAUL E.
  1965   *The organization of society.* Englewood Cliffs, New Jersey: Prentice Hall.
CADWALLADER, MERVYN L.
  1968   "The cybernetic analysis of change in complex social organizations," in *Modern systems research for the behavioral scientist: a sourcebook.* Edited by Walter E. Buckley. Chicago: Aldine.
HOLLOMAN, REGINA E.
  1969   *Developmental change in San Blas.* Doctoral dissertation. Northwestern University.
MARSH, RICHARD O.
  1934   *White Indians of Darien.* New York: G. P. Putnam's Sons.
MEAD, MARGARET
  1964   *Continuities in cultural evolution.* New Haven: Yale University Press.
  1963   *Panama en cifres.* Publication of the Bureau of Statistics and Census (November 3).

SMITH, M. G.
  1969   "Some developments in the analytic framework of pluralism," in *Pluralism in Africa*. Edited by Leo Kuper and M. G. Smith. Los Angeles: University of California Press.

Jungle Quechua Ethnicity:
An Ecuadorian Case Study

NORMAN E. WHITTEN, JR.

The Jungle Quechua

The vast majority of aboriginal peoples living in eastern Ecuador (the Oriente) in 1972 belong to one of two cultural divisions: they are either Quechua, or they are Jívaro. The latter are well known to

This paper is based primarily on five months of preliminary ethnography undertaken during the summers of 1970 and 1971. The research is sponsored by the University of Illinois, Urbana, and the Instituto Nacional de Antropología e Historia, Quito, Ecuador, and is funded by the National Science Foundation (Grant No. GS-2999). I am grateful to the Director of the Instituto, Arq. Hernán Crespo Toral, for his constant interest and encouragement in this preliminary field investigation. Considerable thanks also are due five assistants who worked at various stages of the preliminary project: Cynthia Gillette, Nacanor Jácome, Marcelo Naranjo, Michael Waag, and Margarita Wurfl. Michael Waag also commented critically on an earlier draft of this paper. Confidentiality promised to the subjects of research now prohibits me from thanking those who helped the most — the Quechua and Jívaroan close associates now caught up in the international scheme of "becoming" Indian while confronting cataclysmic changes in their environments.

The major result of this preliminary research was a proposal to undertake a year of intensive ethnography with the Lowland Quechua, beginning in late August, 1972. This research, a joint project with Dorothea S. Whitten, is also funded by the National Science Foundation (continuation Grant No. GS-2999) and supplemented by funds for research assistance by the University of Illinois Research Board and Center for Comparative International Studies. The study has three basic aspects. In the first, Dorothea S. Whitten, Marcelo Naranjo, and I continue our study of Jungle Quechua ethnicity and adaptive strategies in the face of rapid change in their natural and social environments. In the second, John P. Ekstrom is completing a year's study of colonist strategies of land acquisition between the Pastaza and Curaray River drainages. The third aspect, designed and now being carried out by Theodore Macdonald, involves continuities in Quechua world view and symbolic domains, particularly as they relate to their position in the indigenous shaman system of highland and lowland Ecuador.

anthropology and are regarded as bona fide indigenes. The former Indians are the largest aggregate, numbering approximately 35,000 or more (Burbano Martínez, et al 1964). They speak Quechua[1] as a first language and live a tropical forest life. Yet they are frequently mentioned only in passing by aunthors describing the Oriente. Within Ecuador they are often lumped as "Quijos," (e.g. Porras 1961; Ferdon 1950; Peñaherrera de Costales and Costales Samaniego 1961), reflecting their presumed tribal-linguistic origin west of the Napo River along the eastern cordillera of the Andes; or, they are lumped as "Yumbos" (Peñeherrera de Costales and Costales Samaniego, et al. 1969; Burbano Martínez, et al 1964), which suggests that they are acculturated highland Quechuas who moved into the tropical forest and there mixed with other groups (particularly the Záparos). When compared to the Cofán, Secoya, Siona (Piojé), Huarani (Auca), Awishiri (Auca), Z'paro, and Jívaroans (Untsuri Shuara — see Harner 1972 — and Achuara), the Quechua of east Lowland Ecuador are usually regarded as sufficiently assimilated to lowland *blanco-mestizo* culture as to preclude careful attention. All indigenous people of Ecuador contrast ethnically with the category *blanco–mestizo* (defined below in the section on internal colonialism).

The Jungle Quechua of the central Oriente may be linguistically divided into three major dialect segments:[2] northwest, northeast, and southern (Orr and Wrisley 1965). The northwest dialect, called Tena, is found on the upper reaches of the Napo River, and its headwater affluent the Jatun Yacu. The dialect continues through the adminis-

[1] I am using a standard, familiar international spelling for the word "Quechua," Ecuadorian usage prefers *Quichua*, or *Kichua*. In Ecuador the term is pronounced "Keéchuwa."

[2] Cultural differences between Jungle Quechua of the southern dialect group and the northern group are extensive, and beyond the scope of this paper to list. Suffice it to say here that the Quechua-speakers of the Bobonaza basin — the "Canelos Quechua" — are Upper Amazonian peoples who have been adapting for centuries to the zone best identified with the Bobonaza River north to the Curaray River and south to the Pastaza River. This is the area carved out as the archdiocese of Canelos. In spite of their proximity to the Andes and their language, they have a fundamentally tropical forest way of life, which they have applied in some areas to *montaña* existence. The Canelos Quechua are, in many ways, more similar to Jívaroan speakers in cultural content than to the Quijos Quechuas (Tena dialect). Ethnic derivation is, in historical times, a merger of Záparoan, Achuara Jivaroan, some Jívaroan proper and more recently, Quijjos Quechua cultures. Achuara and Záparoan are the most important contributors to culture content. Ancient Omagua and Cocama Tupian influence is probable. The exact origin of the Quechua language in this zone is unknown, at this time, but ancient tropical forest derivation cannot be discounted. A general ethnography of ethnic derivation, world view, and contemporary adaptation is now in preparation.

trative towns of Tena and Archidona, and on up the Sierra to near the present town of Baeza. It runs down the Napo to the settlement of Ahuano and south to Arajuno, cutting across the Puyo-Napo Road at Santa Clara. The northeastern dialect, called Napo, goes on down the Napo River, and is spoken on such north-Napo tributaries as the Suno and Payamino Rivers. The southern division, called Bobonaza, begins south of Santa Clara and Arajuno and extends to the Pastaza River. Quechua on the Curaray, Bobonaza, Conambo, and Pindo are all of the southern division, though other further dialectical differences do exist. The territory between the Curaray and the Napo is not inhabited by Quechuas — it is exclusively Auca (Huarani, Awishiri) country.

Culturally, the northern and southern divisions of Quechua territories are distinct, and their relationships with highland and other lowland indigenous peoples are also different.[3] The people of the Tena-Napo dialects and Bobonaza dialect regard one another as different; their aboriginal histories and histories of contact are different, and their present socioeconomic status is quite different, though perhaps convergent. The Tena-Napo groups represent expansions around Catholic mission bases from the sixteenth century on to the present (Oberem 1971). Quechua language clearly came from the missions (cf. Steward 1948: 509–515). Their history is one of continuous serfdom to the missions and *haciendas,* and their present socioeconomic position is analogous to that of the infamous highland *Huasipungueros.* They are generally called Yumbos, Napos, and Quijos. For clarity and convenience I will refer to them as "Quijos Quechua." (For a recent monograph on this culture see Oberem 1971.)

Native people of the Bobonaza, Conambo, and Curaray drainages seem to have been buffers between warring groups of Jívaroans. Záparoans, Awishiris, and others from the time of first contact. Missions may have been built in existing refuge areas, and while such missions may have solidified such refuge zones, it may not be accurate to say that the missions created these zones. Throughout southern Quechua territory internal bilingual and bicultural activities between Quechua and Achuara Jívaroan are maintained by marriage. Intermarriage with the Jívaro proper, "Untsuri Shuara," also exists. This pattern of marriage with otherwise warring Jívaroan groups seems to have at least

---

[3] For example, shamans from the Canelos Quechua are regarded as the most powerful in the world by the Jívaro (see Harner 1972), and highland Indians from near Ríobamba regularly visit Canelos Quechua shamans. But, other highland Indians such as the Salasaca and the Otavaleños generally avoid Canelos Quechua shamans and go directly to shamans and curers in Tena and Ahuano.

a 200–years time depth. Also, on the Curaray, Corrientes, and Pindo Rivers, Záparo–Quechua bilingualism and biculturalism exists — here people in the river bank settlements are "Quechua," but many "become Záparo" in the forest. In the latter capacity not only is Záparoan spoken, but aggressive raids against Huarani Auca households have reputedly been made in the recent past. Some Záparo–Quechua bilingualism still exists on the Rio Bobonaza. Finally, more profound influences on Quechua life in the southern areas have come from the extension of trade network (for furs, gold, medicines, and cinnamon) and from the rubber boom of the late nineteenth century to early twentieth century than from the establishment of *haciendas* as in the northern case.

From this point on, my paper deals with the southern dialect, with the Quechua of the Bobonaza drainage — the "Canelos Quechua."

The people in this southern area REFER to themselves in Quechua as *runa* 'indigenous person'. They also use the term *Alama* 'friend' or 'mythic brother',[4] among themselves to ADDRESS those who come from the Bobonaza or Curaray drainages and are southern Lowland Quechua speakers. In Spanish they use the term *gente* 'People', as a reference for themselves. (When speaking Spanish all Jungle Que-

---

[4] The derivation of the term *Alama* comes from a myth segment, dealing, in various ways, with older brother/younger brother authority and tension. In brief, an older and younger brother were on a huge stone in the middle of a great river, having been placed there by a giant condor. The older brother called a great cayman which came to the rock to help the brothers across, but the younger brother jumped down first, crossed, and by the time the cayman made the return trip for the older brother the younger had disappeared. Walking through the forest, lost, and searching not only for the brother, but also for a lost homeland, the older brother reached out to break off a piece of tree mushrom (*ala*) and as he pinched it the mushroom cried out "ouch, my mythic brother, don't pinch me, real brother" (*aiai alajma ama tiushi huaichu huauqui: aiai* 'ouch', *ala* 'mushroom, mythic brother', *j* possessive, *ma* emphasis, *ama* 'no', *tiushi* 'pinch', *hua* 'to me, *i* command, *chu* negative complement to *ama, huauqui* 'real brother'). On saying this the tree mushroom transformed into the younger brother who rejoined his sibling and they went on to more adventures.

There is more to the *ala* complex than this, for ancient peoples had the ability to send their souls (*aya*) into special rocks and logs when their bodies died, from whence a mushroom would emerge to await a wandering *runa* who, in hunger, would pinch the mushroom and awaken the ancient *runa*. In this way, older and younger statuses can fluctuate, because, although the younger brother was lost, rediscovery of him through this process indicates abilities of soul transformation suggestive of ancient, older status. The term *ala* is used in direct address by all acknowledged male participants in Canelos Quechua culture and is, thereby, a crucial ethnic marker. On being called *ala* or *alaj* one must immediately reciprocate the same term, acknowledging mythic brotherhood, or he must reciprocate a pejorative, negative, ethnic term such as *auca* 'heathen', or *mashca pupu* 'barley gut', 'Ecuadorian intruder'.

chuas use *gente* in contrast with *blanco.)* There is no term other than *Alama* used to differentiate the people of the Bobonaza drainage from other Quechua speakers in highland and lowland Ecuador. In speaking Spanish, though, the Jungle Quechua of this zone use *gente* for themselves, and from that point distinguish themselves as people from both *runa llacta* (literally, 'indigenous land' — which is used as though it were Spanish, when speaking Spanish) and *blancos* (literally 'whites' — including Negroes). Jívaros and some colonists who have been in the area for a generation or more designate the Bobonaza Jungle Quechua as *Alama* (and in Jívaro sometimes as "Aram Shuara"), but this is regarded as mildly pejorative by the Indians when used contrastively by any but southern dialect Jungle Quechua speakers. Very few Indians north of Santa Clara on the Puyo-Napo Road even know the term *Alama*, and no one know its meaning (see Note 4).

When speaking Quechua, the division of ethnic categories and territories is quite clear. The Indians themselves seldom refer to their own referent dialect group, except by implicit contrast, when making the following distinctions. In the west — the Andes — there are two 'lands': *runa llacta* and *ahua llacta*. The former is 'indigenous land' but is used in the area under study only to refer to highland Indian territory — regarded as all of the Andes. The latter term, *ahua llacta,* is literally 'highland' but refers politely to all non–Indian Ecuadorians. The *ahua llacta* term in Jungle Quechua is used as a synomym for the Spanish *blanco.* Neither the designation *gente* in Spanish, nor the designation *runa* in Quechua, is used for the Ecuadorian highland *Blanco–mestizo.*

To the north there are two territories of Quechua which correspond to the two dialect areas, called respectively *Alchirona Llacta* and *Napo Llacta* (representing the northwest and northeastern dialect divisions). (Sometimes *Ansuj Llacta* is added to indicate Quechua settlements southwest of the Napo River, on a feeder river to the Jatun Yacu River.) To the north and south lies *Auca Llacta,* 'heathen lands'. In the north this includes the Cushmas (Cofán, Tetéte, Secoya, and Siona), who are but dimly known by reputation, and the hostile Huarani (called *Llushti Auca* 'naked heathens' and *Tahuashiri* 'ridge people' in Quechua). On the Curaray River, and recently along the Bobonaza as well, distinctions are made between the Huarani or "true" *Llushti Auca* to the west, now clustered on the Curaray above the mouth of the Villano and the Nushiño River, and the *Awishiri (Tahuashiri) Aucas* to the east, who now live between the Cononaco and Tivacuna Rivers. The legendary (in Quechua legend) *Puca Chaqui Auca,* 'red leg heathens' of the Tiputini drainage, are said to constitute a third division, and the Canelos Quechua insist that these unknown people speak another language and use bows and arrows. Oil company observations seem to confirm Canelos Quechua insistence on a *Puca Chaqui Auca* group. Also belonging to *Auca Llacta* in the north are Záparo speakers, most of whom are bilingual in jungle Quechua, and many of whom are trilingual in Spanish as well. Northern Achuara from the Corrientes and Conambo River systems are also part of *Auca Llacta*. (Tessman [1930], Steward [1948], and Steward and Métraux [1948] give historical data supporting these divisions made by the southern dialect group of Quechua–speakers.)

Due east of Alama land, in Peru, live *Andoa Runa* in the most eastern territory of the culture area of the Canelos Quechua. Other *Auca Llacta* are said to exist there, especially the Candochi Jívaroans on the Pastaza, Záparoans from the Marañon River, and Cocama on the Tigre River. Within their own territory the Jungle Quechua identify one another by the administrative center closest to their settlement, unless they actually come from that area, in which case identity is by clan segment and actual residence. From west to east the major identifying settlements are the *Puyo Runa* (sometimes *Pinduj Runa*), which include all people from the Pinduj River south to the Pastaza River, north on either side of the Napo Road for a few kilometers, and northeast to Cabecera de Bobonaza. Canelos Runa includes people from east of Cabecera de Bobonaza to Canelos and from Canelos north to the headwaters of the Villano and Curaray River, east to Chambira, and south to the headwaters of the Copotaza River. *Paca Yacu Runa* includes those around the settlement of Paca Yacu north to Villano, and *Sara Yacu Runa* includes all people there south to the Capahuari River, north to the Conambo River, and east on the Bobonaza River to Teresa Mama. *Montalvo Runa* includes the territory north to the Conambo River, east to Peru, and south to the Capahuari. Each *runa* territory is divided into *llactas,* which have recognized living or dead founders and consist of intermarried segments of clans which trek *(purina)* periodically to identified zones, where they encounter other people from other *runa* territories similarly engaged. Sara Yacu–Canelos is seen as the cultural hearth of contemporary Canelos Quechua culture, but the greatest population concentration is between the Pinduj and Pastaza Rivers. The people themselves see their origin area as somewhere around contemporary Yurimaguas, in Peru.

Because of the designation of Canelos as the stereotypic center of southern Quechua culture, because the people of this zone have so frequently been designated as the "Canelos tribe" in the literature, and because the designation "Canelos Quechua" is becoming increasingly accepted in Ecuador, I shall hereafter refer to the people of the southern Lowland Quechua dialect as "Canelos Quechua." The reader is warned, however, that in the Dominican and administrative site of Canelos, proper, there exists MORE INTRUSION from Quijos Quechua and highland Quechua than with any other area of Canelos Quechua territory, including Puyo. Figure 1 indicates the major geographic and ethnic divisions made by the Canelos Quechua in contrastively defining their position vis–á–vis other non–white ethnic categories in the Ecuadorian Oriente.

Marriage between the Canelos Quechua and both cultural groups of Jívaroan has taken place for at least two hundred years. The Canelos Quechua have virtually absorbed the Záparo speakers in the last fifty years, and marriages with highland Indians, occasionally highland whites, and Indians from both northern dialects today take place. For the Canelos Quechua, *Indígena* 'Indian' or preferably *nativo* 'native' is synonymous with their way of life, and they aggressively insist that the appropriate synonym in Spanish for *Indígena* is *gente*. Incorporation of Jívaroans, usually classed as *Auca* will be discussed below, when presenting some aspects of the Canelos Quechua kinship system.

Although the Canelos Quechua are not homogeneous in their ethnic make–up, they are nontheless a self–identifying, if highly individualistic, indigenous aggregate with clear cultural markers; and as an aggregate they are not merging into *blanco-mestizo* culture. We must understand the expansion of Lowland Quechua ethnicity as a rational response to expanding opportunities in the money economy under the continuance of internal colonialism in Ecuador.

Economically, the staple of Lowland life is *yuca* 'manioc'. *Chagras* 'cleared fields' cover from one to three hectares. Land is cleared with ax and machete by a man, his sons, and sons–in–law, more often than not without help of kinsmen or friends, although *mingas* 'reciprocal labor exchange' may take place. Men plant plantains, bananas, corn, and naranjilla. The same men carry the manioc stems to the clearing; then women do the actual planting, keep the *chagra* clean, harvest the *yuca*, carry it to the house, prepare it, and serve it. Sweet potatoes and some *yautía* are also grown on the *chagra*, and these are also the responsibility of women. Palm shoots, *chontaduros*, *yautía*, a variety of fruits, peppers, tomatoes, and herbs are grown in

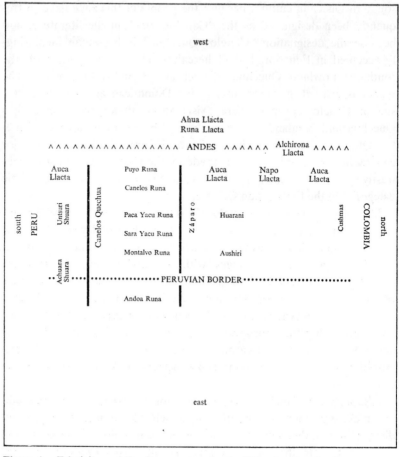

Figure 1.   Ethnicity and Territory as seen by the "Canelos Quechua"

kitchen gardens in back of the house as well as on the *chagra*. Near Puyo the *naranjilla* (Solanum quitoense and several other species) is grown as a cash crop; otherwise, the Canelos Quechua have few crops of cash value, though they are ringed on their western and northern flanks by sugar and tea plantations.

Manioc beer *(chicha* or *asua)* of very low alcoholic content (more of a gruel) is a staple of life, and the making and serving of *chicha* constitutes a focal point of symbolic interaction within the household. The masticated *yuca* is stored in large pottery jars, *(tinajas* or *asua churana manga)* and served in thin, finely decorated bowls *(muca-huas)*. All pottery is made by coiling. Women make their own *tinajas* and *mucahuas* and guard small secrets pertaining to color, design, and ways to get the thinest possible sides and rims. Knowledge and techniques are passed from mother to daughter or from mother to son's wife. The pottery is fired without a kiln. This is the finest pottery made today in the Ecuadorian Oriente, and most, if not all, pottery sold in the highlands as "Jívaro pottery" comes from the Canelos Quechua. Indeed, some Jívaros marry Quechua women and bring them to their own houses in order to have a better pottery than the Jívaro women can provide.[5] Black pottery cooking pots *(yanuna manga)* and eating dishes *(callana)* are also made, sometimes with thumbnail decorations *(sarpa manga)*.

Fine decorated pottery for intra-household use is not disappearing with the introduction of metal pots and pans, but the black pottery is rapidly dwindling. People buy the new goods, or trade other things to obtain them, but they maintain at least one or two *tinajas* for *chicha* storage and at least one *mucahua* for serving.

Several fish poisons, such as *barbasco,* are grown in the *chagra* to be used during relatively dry times of the year, when the rivers run quite low and clear. Hallucinogens such as *Ayahuasca* (three Banisteriopsis species) and *Huanduj* (several Datura species) are grown, together with *Huayusa,* tobacco, and a large variety of medicinal and magical herbs. Men fish with spears, traps, weirs, lines, and nets, and hunt with traps and blowguns. Although many Quechua men make curare poison, using some forty or more plant and other substances, more powerful curare for the blowgun darts comes along trade networks originating in the east. Peruvian Achuara bring poison to Conambo, Montalvo, Copotaza, and Sara Yacu, and Copotaza Achuara or Conambo Achuara carry it on westward. Muzzle loading shotguns are also used for small game, and cartridge guns are becoming available. Long treks *(purina)* to gather turtle eggs, to hunt for large quantities of meat, to catch and dry large fish, to keep a distant *chagra,* and to buy the appropriate black, red, and white clays for pottery decoration are made by a family once or twice a year, sometimes alone and sometimes with a larger kinship or settlement group.

Travel is frequent among the Canelos Quechua, and it is usually by

---

[5] A crucial aspect of Canelos Quechua cultural perpetuity is bound up with the transmission of knowledge and secrets in pottery making. Three souls go to make up each storage jar and drinking bowl: the clay giver soul, the woman's own created body soul, and the household soul. These souls and the knowledge behind each are transmitted generation by generation through women, just as special knowledge of the clan souls acquired through psychedelic experiences are transmitted generation by generation through males. In my future ethnography I will devote considerable time to analysis of such cultural continuity.

foot. The rivers are too rapid and untrustworthy as far as depth goes (sometimes flooded, sometimes quite low) to provide stable avenues for transportation on the Pastaza east to Ayuy or on the Bobonaza east to Canelos. The Curaray, itself, meanders so much that it is about as efficient to travel on foot from one point to another as to make one oxbow turn after another by canoe. Nevertheless, canoes are used when cargo is to be moved, and the Canelos Quechuas are excellent canoe makers and superior boatsmen.

The nuclear family is a very tightly knit unit with man and woman sharing equally in decision making, in spatial mobility, and in upward socioeconomic mobility in some cases. Residence is ideally matripatrilocal but generally bilocal. There is no term for this unit except the Quechua term *huasi*, 'house', and the Spanish terms *familia* and *casa* are used synonymously for *huasi*.

The maximal kinship grouping, and segments of this grouping, are referred to as *ayllu*. The *ayllu,* as the maximal clan, is a stipulated descent system from a common animal ancestor, often a variety of puma or jaguar. Each *ayllu* is today identified with a set of surnames and extends through much of Canelos Quechua territory and on into other culture areas, as well. For people in any clan segment, extended clan (also called *ayllu)* reckoning is from father or father's father back to his father's wife. Within the extended clan there are tightly knit stem kindreds, reckoning from an old, founding shaman. These kindreds are also called *ayllu,* but because of the intertwining of *ayllu* membership through marriage with other *ayllu* segments within a territory, the resulting intermarried segments often refer to themselves by the territorial term, *llacta.*

Each *ayllu* (maximal and extended) maintains its special culture, transmitted to intimate residential in–laws. In this transmission special concentrations of knowledge, or culture, concatenate into the territorial *runa,* which expands and contracts with the *purina* system and fissions across *ayllu* lines in the *llacta* system. In this way shared knowledge embedded in the dispersed *ayllu* of antiquity is transferred repeatedly across *ayllu* boundaries and maintained through conflict and competition in the *llacta* system. *Ayllu* members maintain their *ayllu* ideology, however, through visionary experience, through mythology, and through actual travel. They can re–activate the maximal *ayllu* concept after many generations through the system of shared descent from a common animal ancestor and through shared possession of the souls of the deceased.

In ascending order of kin and neighbor units, a child is born into a *huasi* 'household' unit, in which the woman's cultural maintenance through pottery tradition and the man's maintenance through *aya* 'soul' acquisition assures each newborn of a place in a maximal clan extending back into mythic time. The *huasi* itself exists within a *llacta*, defensible territory, which was established by a founder in alliance with other founders of *ayllu* segments. These minimal *ayllu* segments within a *llacta* are stem kindreds. Beyond the stem kindred is the extended clan, which includes localized and dispersed kinsmen within and beyond a *runa* territory. And beyond the extended clan is the maximal clan, the everlasting system of stipulated descent into mythic time and structure. The ancient relationships among founders of maximal clans, during the time when all animals were human and humans crawled on the ground like babies, are repeated today as myths and are thought to provide the basis for integration of the Canelos Quechua, long before humans came to dominate their sector of the biosphere.

A developmental sequence exists which ties male *huasi, ayllu,* and *llacta* founders to the knowledge of mythical times. On marriage a male must, by taking *huanduj* 'datura' converse with the soul–master, *Amasanga,* and have the soul–master cure him of magical darts *(supai biruti)* sent by jealous suitors of his wife. Also, the bride must visit the wife of the *Amasanga,* the *chagra mama* or *Nunghuí mama,* to get her sacred stones and knowledge to make the manioc grow. If a man wishes to head a stem kindred then he must, through a long period of time, acquire the status of *yachaj* or 'shaman', becoming both curer and potential mystical killer; and when, if ever, he seeks to found a *llacta* he must have made pacts with the various spirits *(supai)* and souls *(aya)* of the territory, in which process he becomes a *potential bancu* 'seat' for the souls and spirits. He usually does not serve as *bancu,* however, because retaliation for the evil done by the spirits and souls through the *bancu* leads many people to attempt to eliminate the *bancu's* social capital — his family, neighbors, and friends — by witchcraft and assasination.

As the process of soul aquisition and making pacts with spirits goes on, something else also occurs due to the constant outward movement of affinally related clan segments: A MAXIMAL CLAN EVOLVES WITHIN A TERRITORY. This maximal clan is often named after a given area. Terms such as Puyo Runa, Canelos Runa, Sara Yacu Runa, etc. then take on another meaning, for not only do the territories exist as interrelated clan segments, but certain clans come to dominate, and knowledge of the *runa* territory suggests the dominating clan. The territorial clans represent a process of "social circumscription" (Carneiro 1970) overlaid with territorial circumscription. Segments of extended clans do cut through these territorial boundaries, however, as do alliances formed through intermarriage. Such cross–cutting of the circumscribed territorial clans suggests an evolution toward an incipient, as yet acephalous, ethnic state of southern Jungle Quechua.

All maximal clans of the Canelos Quechua include Achuara Jívaroans as members of Quechua extended clans. Also, in many of the maximal clans there is one Achuara or even Untsuri Shuara local group *(caserío)* which insures intra–indigenous ethnic contrast (Quechua versus Jívaroan) WITHIN the maximal clan itself. This ethnic contrast between two very different indigenous peoples, together with the countervailing complementarity through cross–cutting intermarriages, is an essential element in the definition of Canelos Quechua ethnicity and social structure and is a key to continuity of indigenous identity during times of rapid change.

The term *ayllu* may refer to the *caserío* when this local group consists of only one segment of the extended clan; otherwise it refers to the speaker's own descent group within the *llacta,* or *caserío.* If the speaker has no descent group members in the *caserío* he will use *ayllu* to mean members of the descent group of his wife, or deceased wife. *Ayllu* is regularly used to denote extended clan and, when involved in territorial disputes with Jívaroans or with colonists, *ayllu* as maximal clan is invoked. In this latter sense indigenous ethnicity is stressed over intra-indigenous divisions, and the concept of common, INDIGENOUS DESCENT, together with the acknowledgement of extensive networks resulting from stipulated clan intermarriage, is used vis-à–vis outsiders. Such a process of assertion of common descent of otherwise contrastive Indian ethnic identities is well under way in several parts of the Oriente, one of which is the Comuna de San Jacinto, near Puyo.

The Jungle Quechua call themselves Christians, and so distinguish themselves as opposed to all other Indians, except the highland Quechua. Practices such as genuflecting and kissing the hand of priests and nuns are ubiquitous. There are few churches in the *caseríos,* and where these exist a priest (or evangelist) may visit a few times a year, on the occasion of special *fiestas.* More generally, the central church for the Lowland Quechua is in a major town, or outlying post (Puyo, Canelos, Sara Yacu, Montalvo, Jesús Pitishca). Everywhere, though, other worlds associated with the sky and an inner earth, and other spirits, creatures and souls associated with the tropical forest and treacherous stretches of rivers, are talked about and visited with the aid of hallucinogens.

THE COMUNA DE SAN JACINTO DEL PINDO

The Comuna de San Jacinto del Pindo was established by executive decree in 1947 by the then national President, Dr. José María Velasco Ibarra. This decree was necessary due to the extreme conflict between colonists and Indians in and around the town of Puyo. Puyo is only nine kilometers east of Shell Mera, the town founded by Shell Oil Company in its explorations beginning in 1937. Indians were inhabiting the area around Puyo (along the Pinduj — now Pindo–Puyo — Rivers) and at the mouth of the Pindo where it joins the Pastaza long before 1899, when a priest (Alvaro Valladares) and some Indians (Jívaroan and Quechua) arrived from Canelos. Long a trading site for furs, gold, cinnamon, and wood, Puyo began to expand rapidly as a national frontier town when Shell Company completed the Baños–Shell Mera Road in the mid–1930's.

There followed about fifteen years of highland colonist settlement in Puyo, which meant squeezing out the Indians, who were apparently vociferous in making their land claims known as more and more settlers moved onto their *chagra* plots and began to raise sugar cane for the production of *aguardiente* 'rum'. The 1947 Presidential decree supposedly was made not only due to Indian-highlander conflict, but also due to growing national attention to the Indian plight in this area, stemming from explorers' accounts. One of the most important guides to the Oriente lived near Puyo, and Velasco Ibarra himself was supposedly respectful of this guide and the others of his extended clan (including one of the many powerful shamans of the area — see Eichler 1970: 109). This guide presumably had enough important contacts among prominent Ecuadorians to force some attention to Indian problems among colonists and traders. Also, it seems, many highlanders seeking to exploit the Oriente were sorely in need of Indian guides and labor, and they turned to the Puyo Runa for such help. It benefited all to have a permanent Indian aggregate with marginal dependence on Puyo's money economy but able to subsist on its own when labor was not needed.

Whatever the specific historical causes, the *comuna* was established just south of Puyo. Its 16,000 hectare territory is bordered on the east by the Puyo River, just after its junction with the Pindo-Puyo, and on the west and south by the Pastaza River. The northern pinnacle begins at the Caserío San Jacinto (the oldest official *caserío* on the *comuna)* and runs southwest to where a bridge now crosses the Chinimbimi, a branch of the Pastaza. Today, eleven official *caseríos* of from 25 to

120 people and at least two other dispersed *llactas* ring the *comuna,* and throughout the *comuna* people also live separately, on particular *chagras,* but with identity claimed to one or two *llactas.* The estimated population of the comuna de San Jacinto during 1973 is 1,600.

The *comuna* is ringed by sugar and tea plantations on all but the eastern flank, and one road cuts the *comuna* en route to the tea plantation south of the Pastaza. This road cuts through a rocky, fertile alluvial plain called *La Isla* 'the island' (because the Chinimbimi fork and Pastaza River enclose it). Here, along the road, there are more than 150 colonists illegally settled, almost all in conflict with the *comuna* members generally, while many form cooperative dyadic relationships with particular individuals from all of the *caseríos.* At the terminus of the road (Puerto Santa Ana) there is an all colonist *(colono)* settlement at the base of a hill, with an all Untsuri Shuara Jívaroan settlement on top of the hill.

In spite of cash cropping around the *comuna,* the *comuneros* only recourse to cash is the *naranjilla* and sale of forest products (including medicines, wood, furs, and a variety of off–and–on products bringing little cash, such as pottery, tourist lances, beads, and live animals). Basically, the *comuneros* farm their manioc and plantain *chaqras* and supplement their diet with poultry, wild birds, fish, and small game. The major change in this has been the impact of cattle during the past eight years.

The *comuna* is loosely governed by a *cabildo,* with elected president, vice president, secretary, treasurer, *síndico* 'lawyer', and a *vocal* 'spokesman,' from each of the *caseríos.* The election is held annually, and thus far has resulted in officials who are bilingual and bicultural, but who are the children of prominent or high ranking, extended clans, or the male affines attached to prominent, high ranking clans. Deals made by the *cabildos* with prominent *colonos,* including the governor of the province, have improved their financial standing; a stratified system of high ranking *cabildos,* having differential access to money through public officials in need of *comuna* land and/or labor, has occurred. However, the intra–*comuna* prestige game involves conspicuous giving (Erasmus 1961), with rank accruing to the giver. Ranking on the *comuna* leads, usually, to uneven access by the *cabildos,* which in turn places them in a position of economic betterment vis–à–vis most other *comuneros;* but the need for conspicuous giving within the *comuna* tempers this class system, and suggests one of ranking evolving into stratification (see Fried 1967). Thus far there is no whole clan of Quechuas on the *comuna* with differential access, though in-

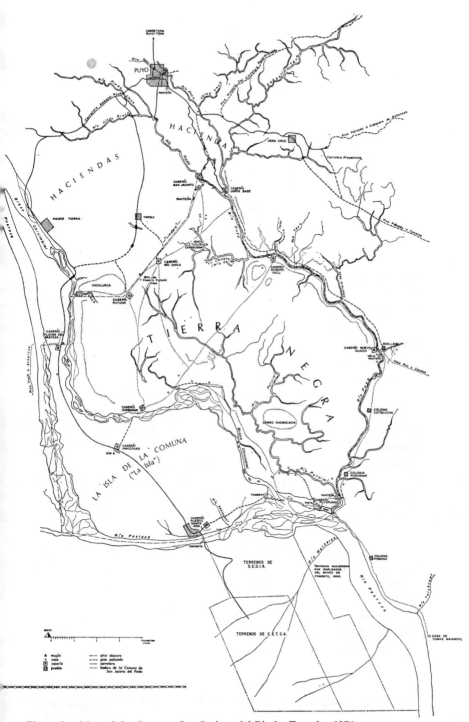

Figure 2.   Map of the Comuna San Jacinto del Pindo, Ecuador 1971

dividuals from high ranked clans do manage to place themselves in a position of differential access to local power domains channeling national resources.

Every single *comunero* is concerned with male fertility and female fecundity. Families are generally very large — ranging upward from one or two children when the parents are eighteen or nineteen to a dozen or so by the time the parents reach their forties. Some fathers continue to sire children into their seventies or eighties. This rational serious concern with exploding the population of the Puyo Runa is tied directly to the political economy. The *comuneros* want to totally populate their territory and other territories, knowing full well that this plan depends on gaining increased access to the money economy.

The strategy adopted is to build new *caseríos* only on the border of the *comuna,* as territorial holding units, while at the same time entering into contractual arrangements with colonists who are attempting to gain a foothold on the island. By "renting" land to *colonos,* and using the money to buy cattle off the *comuna,* the people of this area are trying to build capital resources (cattle, marketable land areas) while acquiring new land and at the same time protecting their *comuna* holdings.

In order to do the latter, constant protests are lodged against colonists renting *comuna* lands. This must be done in Quito, at the Ministerio de Previsión Social, for this is the governmental department established to administer the *comuna* system. Since there is no local agent of the Ministerio it is also necessary to depend on local officials, the governor and political heads *(teniente político, jefe político)* of the adjacent administrative units. In dealing on the national level the *comuneros* enter one power domain (Adams 1970), where only conflict with *colonos* is stressed and where superior power and support is sought. In dealing with the local or regional level of the same domain, conflict AND cooperation with officials and colonists must be stressed; economic support and expansion of promised facilities (e.g. a road in another part of the *comuna)* are requested *often with the result of loss of ground on original grievances.*

More will be said about power domains (national and local) in an ensuing section. Suffice it to say at this point that pro tem transfers of authority from the Ministerio de Previsión Social to the IERAC (Instituto Ecuatoriano de Reforma Agraria y Colonización) are sometimes made in order to bring a local level competitive domain to the Indians. When this is done, though, *the Indians lose their strategic dual-*

ity of national–regional domain manipulation. They then must cope through a unified national–regional domain — one that has as its charge furtherance of COLONIST EXPANSION and, hence, INDIAN DISEN-FRANCHISEMENT AND TERRITORIAL ENCAPSULATION.

The expansion of *caseríos* on the *comuna* is taking place rapidly, and is accompanied by local level clamor by the Indians for national facilities on the larger *caseríos*. For example, there is a Catholic church at San Jacinto and a Protestant one at Puyo Pungo. There are now schools at Unión Base, Rosario Yacu, Río Chico, Chinimbimi, Puyo Pungo, Amazonas, and Playas del Pastaza. Children are taught or preached to in Spanish. In the schools, teachers are recruited from various parts of the nation. They live in the schoolhouse, and teach there for about eight months of the year. The sixth grade is the highest, from which some children go on to school in Puyo, this being paid for by their families.

The experience of the Comuna de San Jacinto del Pindo is being copied by a number of other people in definable *runa* territories that are becoming bounded by colonizing non–*runa* from the highlands. East of the Puyo–Napo Road there are two other *comunas* (San Ramón and Arajuno), and still more are talked about. The *comuna* at Canelos has now become quasi–official by executive decree, and there is talk all down the Bobonaza of establishing *comunas* at the sites of the various administrative towns. In fact, the term *comunero* is being increasingly applied to all Indians, whether or not they live on the *comuna,* and many, if not most, *blanco–mestizos* knowing anything at all about the residence of Indians think that *comuna* means *caserío* and are surprised, or even bewildered, to find that *comuna* refers to the grouping of maximal clan segments in a given area. The Indians always explain their social–territorial structure to non–Indians in kinship terms, noting the intersection of extended clans in the past. When pushed, for example, by curious *blancos* in Puyo as to why there are many families from different backgrounds and with different origins, the reply is that such families were previously related in grandparental generations through marriage, so that *all present comuneros are descended from a common, ethnically diverse, breeding population.* By invoking this rule of stipulated ethnic descent the *comuneros* become, in their own eyes, a distinctive race — different from all *blanco–mestizos* and generally related, but nonetheless distinct, from all other Indians.

I will say more about the Comuna de San Jacinto after setting forth more of the relevant social environment of the Jungle Quechua by reference to internal colonialism, expanding infrastructure, colonization, and the relationships between power domains in this frontier cultural ecological setting.

INTERNAL COLONIALISM

Internal colonialism refers to situations "... where an independent country has, within its own boundaries, given special legal status to groups that differ culturally from the dominant group, and created a distinct administrative machinery to handle such groups" (Colby and van den Berghe 1969: 3). The plural nature of Ecuadorian society has been documented repeatedly (see Jaramillo Alvarado 1936; Whitten 1965; Burgos 1970). What is usually assumed, though, is that expanded economic opportunities will result in the breakdown of plural segments and the establishment of a "mixed" or "mestizo" national ethnic category. Pareja Diezcanseco sums up a prevalent intellectual view on contemporary Ecuador:

Ecuador is not a country inhabited by white folk, for as an ethnic minority they only add up to scarcely one-tenth of the total population. Neither is it a country of Indians, for in that case its history would be one of regression, or else, of stratification ... the nation is *Mestizo* ... Once the Indians enter civilized life ... *the Mestizo part of the population will be more homogeneous* (1970: 88. Emphasis added.).

The swelling of the *"mestizo* part" of the country is seen by many, within and outside of Ecuador, as part of a growth of ethnic homogenization and a basis for the cultural and social revolution that will do away with a caste system where political and economic control rests with the very few *blancos*. But a large percent of the nation is Indian, and a small, but concentrated, percent is black (not mulatto). The national concept of *mestizo* contains a denial of *blanco* (white) supremacy and affirms roots to Indian and (sometimes) Negro, or at least Moorish–mulatto, ancestry. Such an IDEOLOGY OF MIXTURE allows for considerable EXCLUSION OF THE NONMIXED, including Highland and Lowland Indians, and ethnically distinct black communities in northwest, north, and southwestern districts. Furthermore, economic and political integration of Ecuador is taking place through internal colonization, particularly through an expansion of highland *mestizos* to lowland areas inhabited primarily by Indians in the east and blacks in the northwest (see Whitten 1965, 1968, 1969a, 1969b, 1974).

Casagrande, Thompson, and Young (1964: 281–325) and Gillette

(1970) give preliminary analyses of colonization in Ecuador. The former state:

The theoretical interest in studying colonization lies both in the processes whereby an already established sociocultural system is extended, replicated or reintegrated, and in colonization as a CREATIVE PROCESS, since colonists frequently must accomodate themselves to a new ecological situation, and to novel sociopolitical and economic arrangements (Casagrande, Thompson, and Young 1964: 282).

In an earlier work (Whitten 1965), I also took this approach to the predominantly black population of San Lorenzo, a northwest coastal rainforest town. I gave primary attention to the internal social and political structure of black *costeños* and thought of colonists as having to adapt to the new, local scene. But, in the view taken here, another important creative process must be stressed. This is the process of colonization from the high Andes to tropical lowlands. The process is characterized by a transposition of *blanco* ethnic values, reinforced through demographic shifts, causing local peoples classed as *negro* or *indio* to face a socioeconomic environment with an effective, continuing, ideational blockage to strategic resources exploited within their territories.

As highland *mestizos* descend the Andes they enter zones which lack members in the contrasting, upper-class, *blanco* category, and, it seems, in the absence of such *blancos* they assume membership in the *blanco* category themselves. As a consequence, those who would be *cholo* or *mestizo* in the *Sierra* become *blanco* on the coast and eastern slopes. *"Blanco*–ness" is reinforced by generalizing the non–*blanco* ethnic contrast — lumping black *costeños* into one pejorative category and lowland Indians into another. In eastern Ecuador, Indians have again and again had their residences forced completely out of the commercial and administrative towns, while economic dependence on these towns continued to increase.

It seems to me that the process of breaking up specific Indian linguistic-ethnic units ("tribes") is leading not to increased assimilation of Indians to "*mestizo* ways" but rather to an expanding generalized category "Indian" *(Indio)* to which *mestizos contrast themselves for virtually all purposes, when new opportunities in the money economy arise.* National and labor policies designed to speed up change in the *mestizo* sector, then, increasingly retard opportunities for those classed as *Indio*.

The crucial environmental factor for the contemporary Lowland Quechua is the expanding, contrastive ethnic category *blanco,* which includes the *mestizo* in the absence of upper-class *blanco* culture bearers. *Blanco-mestizo* ethnicity forces Quechua ethnicity to intensify, and the strategies played in the arena of expanding and generalizing ethnicity have powerful economic consequences for both ethnic categories, *particularly when one ethnic category (the Jungle Quechua) is encapsulated by national policies of "Indian protection" while the other* (blanco–mestizo) *is given wide powers through the national policy of colonization.*

By "ethnicity" I mean *patterns of human interaction which form the basis for categorical social relations with observable, or projected economic consequences.* Categorical social relationships are characterized by stereotypic criteria, as distinct from structural relations which are characterized by group membership or network relationships which are characterized by extant exchange patterns between interacting individuals (see Southall 1961: 1–46; Mitchell 1966: 52–53; Banton 1967; Whitten and Szwed 1970: 43–48; Whitten and Wolfe 1973). Land access is intimately tied to the economic consequence of ethnic status.

In Ecuador today, Indian lands can only be legally protected from invasion by colonists with the formation of *comunas Indígenas* 'native comunes'. The formation of *comunas* is Indian–initiated but depends for administration on the Ministerio de Previsión Social; special laws pertain to the actions of Indians (and colonists) on the *comunas* (see Peñaherrera de Costales and Costales Samaniego 1962). The Instituto Ecuatoriano de Reforma Agraria y Colonización (IERAC), by contrast, is established to not only do away with *latifundia* holdings in the highlands, but also to encourage as rapid a penetration as possible of colonists into the Oriente, particularly in the zones where oil exploration is underway and where the pipeline and access roads are being built. Colonists are by definition *blanco* in the Oriente in contrast to all people classed as *Indio*.

All Oriente people classed as Indio *or* Indígena, *fall into a national power domain which is essentially static. It must await Indian protest before it will even investigate infiltration and invasion of legitimate Indian land. All people classed as* colono (blanco) *in the Oriente fall under a domain of national expansion and dynamic bureaucratic manipulation aimed at opening new land claims for non–Indians.* More will be said about the domains in the ensuing section.

In terms of oil exploration, Indians are generally regarded as "hunters" of the interfluvial zones and so are hired primarily to set up camps, to stay in the forests, and to work only "on the line" for the oil companies. *Blancos*, by contrast, are seen as new potential agriculturalists, are employed near camps and near towns, and are regarded as the proper spokesmen for all workers (including the Indians).

Quechua has long been the national trade and work language for communicating with all lowland Indians, while Spanish has been used primarily for the *blancos*. Today special bilingual line bosses (mostly recruited from the Summer Institute of Linguistics school teachers) are hired to deal with real and potential "Indian problems," while problems of labor organization, minimal wage, etc., are regarded nationally as a strictly *blanco–mestizo* concern.

EXPANDING INFRASTRUCTURE AND POLITICAL ECONOMY

An infrastructure is the network of transportation facilities enabling economic expansion, together with the administrative and educational apparatus, which establishes a bureaucratic–information system facilitating the expansion based on transportation networks. Hegen (1966) provides a good base for the study of infrastructure expansion in the Upper Amazon up to the mid–1960's. In his study Hegen makes a dramatic, if unrealistic, statement related to colonists (pioneers), which draws our attention to the nation as a whole:

Pioneering creates sociocultural demands and establishes a tax source which in turn will supply funds to satisfy these demands. It will stimulate the establishment and growth of trade, manufacturing and service industries, and the general exchange of goods, based upon a money economy. It will lead to regional specialization, fulfilling thereby the requirements of the demand-supply complex. Above all ... pioneering will revolutionize the static social and political life of the people by integrating them into the responsible, decision-making processes of a modern democracy (1966: 36).

Although apparently writing his conclusion prior to the events themselves and making enormously overgeneralized statements about a political economy which is now in the hands of foreign companies and national military dictatorship, Hegen does direct attention to the expanding infrastructure itself and its importance in opening previous frontier zones to national bureaucratic controls. The official, national expanding infrastructure "follows" the *blanco* settlements, which mark the first results of the colonization programs. Pioneer settlements are not distributed willy–nilly around the jungle, nor are they necessarily first established in the best river–bank agricultural zones. They tend to cluster in areas where resources of value to international commerce exist, at a given time, as well as in the areas already targeted for national development. Not surprisingly, the two areas — those designated for development and those of special interest to foreign concerns for resource extraction — often coincide.

Regardless of the strategic importance of *colono* settlement to national planning, however, one inescapable need must be met — the colonists must find a stable food supply. And they are usually totally ignorant of tropical agriculture. Where Indian settlements exist, the *colono* food supply becomes the native *chagra*. To understand the informal aspect of an expanding infrastructure, we must put native peoples of the Oriente into the picture and carefully note the cycle whereby new lands are "opened" by *blanco* pioneers muscling into Indian *chagras*. By the time an official agent of a responsible bureaucracy arrives via plane or helicopter to an area to investigate alleged irregularities, the colonists are in control of major manioc plots, planted by Indians but claimed by colonists, and the stereotype of Indians as hunters is used to force the natives away from their own productive agricultural lands. This forces the Indians to open new territories to be later exploited in the same manner, unless effective counter–strategies are concurrently enacted. The Lowland Quechua seem remarkably effective in devising counter–strategies that are peace–producing and accommodating in terms of warding off destruction of their population.

Good land for growing crops within any given *runa* territory is limited, and the Jungle Quechua often opt to remain near enough to the national infrastructure tentacles to press early claims during times of invasion. This gives them more opportunity for social network maintenance within a known geographic zone than is characteristic of other Indian groups. The Lowland Quechua are particularly effective in losing one thing to gain something else vis–à–vis colonists and in maintaining strength vis–à–vis various quasi–sympathetic and relatively helpful brokerage agencies (Catholic and Protestant missions, military bases, powerful *hacendados,* land speculators, and even some Peace Corps volunteers). This allows them to not only survive in such a situation of replacive colonization, but to actually expand under such an impress. But the price of their expansion is often peonage, in one form or another, to one of the patronage "helpers."

If we were dealing with nineteenth century and early twentieth century exploitation of natural resources (as we are when dealing with the history of the Jungle Quechua), we might by now be able to construct an adequate model of Indian–*blanco* relationships. Steward (1948: 507–512) did just this, though the many new data turned up will demand a reexamination of his model sequences. But the penetration in the last five years of foreign oil companies (Texaco–Gulf in the north, Anglo and Amoco in the central *Oriente,* together with subsidiary exploration companies and subcontracting companies) and their new technologies, make it clear that the frontier itself falls within an expanding technological sphere superior to, and guided by, agencies more powerful than Ecuador's political economy. *Blancos* and Quechua alike fall into power domains of national bureaucracies and, also, supranational domains reflecting new levels of politico-economic integration (Wolfe 1963). These latter domains are most productively considered as competitive to national interests.

Richard N. Adams (1970) presents us with an exhaustive and highly productive model and methodology for the study of dynamic structure of power in contemporary nations. He defines "power domain" as

... any arrangement of units wherein two or more units have unequal control over each other's environment. Wherever there is a distinctive difference in the relative power exercised by two units with respect to each other, there is a domain, and the two units pertain to different levels of articulation. Units in confrontation at one level will usually pertain to distinct domains. (Adams 1970, p. 56).

Regarding the expanding infrastructure itself, a bit more needs to be said. The Puyo–Napo–Tena Road has moved to Cotundo east of Tena, and the Papallacta–Baeza Road (from the Sierra toward the Oriente) opened in 1971. The Baeza–Cotundo section is underway. The oil pipeline constructed by Texaco Gulf in late spring, 1972, runs from just south of Esmeraldas up the western Cordillera and moves from just south of Quito to Papallacta and follows the Papallacta–Baeza Road. It swings north from Baeza following the Quijos River and Coca River northeast to the Agua Rico River and then due east to Santa Cecilia and south to Coca. The Coca–Santa Cecilia section is completed, with access road, and oil is now being pumped for foreign consumption. The construction of this roadway virtually obliterated the Cofán, Secoya, and Siona Indians in this area (see Robinson 1971).

REFUGE, STRATEGY, AND ETHNIC DISENFRANCHISEMENT

In the area around Puyo the infrastructure expansion is taking place in large part by foot and by plane. From a small airport at Shell Mera, which used to see a maximum of two flights a week, there were over 100 per day until around February, 1973. Most of these fly cargo to the oil camps, but many flights fly colonists and food for colonists. Neither the Jívaro nor the Quechua of this zone intend to let *blancos* invade their territory or take over their land. But they are perfectly willing to exchange usufructory rights to land on a temporary basis for cash that will allow them to expand their own territories. Quechua and Jívaro, as well as *colonos,* want to be near the loci of national interaction — the airports, the proposed roadways, and the basic walking trails. Because the terrain along the Pastaza and Bobonaza is very rugged, it is not clear that there will be roadways in the foreseeable future, though many are on the planning boards. This means that the Indians have a temporary refuge area from Puyo due east, even though the Puyo area is itself the most developed in the current Oriente.

But this refuge area will not last for long. Recently an airport has been opened at Canelos, and Montalvo appears to be the central Oriente analog to Santa Cecilia in the north. The Canelos–Quechua are increasingly hemmed in, and maximal clan segments and *purina* treks are cut in their fringe areas by *blanco* penetration settlements. Their rational, firm desire, to participate in the expanding Ecuadorian economy results in dynamic adaptive strategies which are contingent on national acceptance for success. Practically, I think, they must be "allowed" to continue their legal *comuna* formation, while at the same time fully participating in *colono* expansion.

This mixed strategy, which insists on both boundary establishment and land acquisition, also demands a duality of ethnicity — Indian and bicultural. The former stresses communal ownership of property and the latter individualism. Such a mixing of survival requirements and their strategic presentation to representatives of different national bureaucracies may seem paradoxical, but from the Quechua perspective it is the only way to avoid being further hemmed in and bounded by "protective" measures which establish rigid *comuna* boundaries. The national concept of *comuna Indígena* suggests a reservation complex governed from afar as a total institution. It is supposed to be locally maintained by internal primitive democracy through total agreement by all indigenous members, themselves ideally living in blissful, child–like, ignorance of their treacherous external social environment. Since, of course, no such group of Indians exists on or off any *comuna,* it is easy for developers and those seeking patronage roles to decide that the Indians are too disorganized to maintain "their" *comuna* structure and to use such a rationale to take an even heavier hand in rigidifying Indian territorial boundaries.[6]

The national concept might even now be transformed to reflect the Lowland Quechua notion of *comuna* as a corporate *holding company*. By this perspective the corporation allows for the carrying out of united extended clans' subsistence pursuits, while at the same time allowing people to variously employ their individually and familistically held land and social "stock" to give backbone to expansionist, colonizing functions of their own, eventually increasing the assets of the *comuna* holding corporation. I frankly doubt that Ecuadorian non–Indians will allow this to happen. They will probably continually seek to contain indigenous expansion. Indians themselves will probably continue to attempt to use the *comuna* corporation established through *blanco* containment strategies to break out, economically, politically, socially, and symbolically, unless all their energies are taken up in simply protecting their *comunas* from very real *blanco* invasion.

The well–known international process of Indian disenfranchisement and exploitation, as a complement to ethnic annihilation, rushes on in the Ecuadorian Oriente. The fixing of blame on the disenfranchised by the invocation of an "Indian problem" exacerbates Lowland Quechua territorial consolidation and leads to heightened ethnic awareness, to *blanco* discrimination against Indians, and to *blanco* patronage of those people who are socially and politically disenfranchised.

A pamphlet on Ecuadorian ethnocide (Robinson 1971) is receiving some justifiable attention in Latin America. The very real annihilation of surviving native groups in countries such as Ecuador cannot pass without such attention, concern, and hopefully remedial action. The focus here of my own preliminary report on Jungle Quechua ethnicity seeks to anticipate the complementary problem of total disenfranchisement and structural confinement of the survivors of national ethnocide.

---

[6] One floundering United States Peace Corps project recently gave "motivational training" to a valiant group of *comuneros* fighting for their very lives to hold their territorial boundaries against a massive onslaught of territory-hungry land-grabbers. At the same time, the Peace Corps saviors helped land-grabbers from the highlands to formalize their land claims on institutionalized Indian territory and even offered courses in new agricultural skills to the exploiters. The rationale behind the motivational training was that the Indians had not yet learned to live "communally" on their *comuna*!

POSTSCRIPT, AUGUST, 1973

From our work over the past year, I see the following as unfolding. As the pressures from the militaristic Ecuadorian government, Gobierno Nacionalista Revolucionario del Ecuador, working with the ideology of a "political culture *(cultura politica),"* increase on the Canelos Quechua, these valiant people seek more and more ways to adapt their lifeways to new exigencies in their environment. At one level, they enter a domain of rapid change, but at another they intensify traditional beliefs and practices which give the only meaning possible in a biosphere experiencing chaotic stimuli. As national planners observe the rapid change they assume that the Canelos Quechua are plunging toward *mestizo*–ship in the political culture. But the Indians are increasingly expanding their self–identification system at one level, and becoming more and more "Indian conscious" at another level.

It is apparent to any Ecuadorian or foreign planner, evaluator, or administrator that the Canelos Quechua have a dynamic set of lifeways which is puzzlingly nonnational. But because these people have fewer and fewer overt signs of stereotypic Indianness (they wear clothes, eschew face painting and feather wearing in the presence of *mestizos,* and speak a language which many Ecuadorians understand), differences are attributed not to cultural continuity but to disorganization resulting from rapid change. Our posit that people who survive, expand their population, and consolidate their social system in the face of chaos have a clear, nonanarchistic, social structure is generally dismissed, perhaps because it is too destructive of national and international ideology aimed at simplistic models of how the poor should behave.

I think the following two complementary positions regarding jungle peoples are the only allowable ones in Ecuador today: (1) We must mourn their passing, make great noises about ethnocide, condemning those who destroy indigenous peoples, and do much self-searching to see if, somehow, we are all guilty of the destruction of native life, and (2) We must respect the *mestizo* all the more, for he is the last living embodiment of nativeness; the native has become a national with civilized *blanco* values, and in the new *blanco–mestizo* lifeway lies both the future and the past of national consolidation.

Again, the complementarity of ethnocide–mourning, plus heightened *blanco–mestizo*-ness, establishes a basis for considering the contemporary Jungle Quechua as a flagrant contradiction to national ideology. Perhaps this is why so much contempt is heaped upon these people, even by those nationals and nonnationals who cry loudly for Indian rights. I suspect that all over the world there is a complementarity in the expansion of ethnic culture and its denigration by those who seek to mourn the passing of other traditional cultures and to "help" the expanding ethnic cultures reach a new, "nondifferent," position within the nation. The problem with such help, given the rationale sketched above, is that it is probably a force equally as destructive as planned ethnocide, for it grows from the same source and serves the same national purpose.

REFERENCES

ADAMS, RICHARD N.
  1970   *Crucifixion by power: essays on Guatemalan national social structure, 1944–1966.* Austin: University of Texas Press.
BANTON, MICHAEL
  1967   *Race relations.* New York: Basic Books.
BROMLEY, RAYMOND J.
  i.p.   Agricultural colonization in the upper Amazon basin: the impact of oil discoveries. *Tijdschrift voor Economische en Sociale Geografia.*
BURBANO MARTÍNEZ, HECTOR, LUIS ANTONIO RIVADENEIRA, JULIO MONTALVO MONTENEGRO
  1964   "El problema de las poblaciones Indígenas selváticas del Ecuador." Paper presented at the Quinto Congreso Indigenista Interamericano, Quito, Ecuador, October, 1964.
BURGOS, HUGO
  1970   *Relaciones interétnicas en Ríobamba.* Instituto Indigenista Interamericano Ediciones Especiales 55. Mexico.
CARNEIRO, ROBERT L.
  1970   A theory of the origin of the state. *Science* (August 28): 733–738.
CASAGRANDE, JOSEPH B., STEPHEN I. THOMPSON, PHILIP D. YOUNG
  1964   "Colonization as a research frontier: the Ecuadorian case," in *Process and pattern in culture: essays in honor of Julian Steward.* Chicago: Aldine.
COLBY, BENJAMIN, PIERRE VAN DEN BERGHE
  1969   *Ixil country.* Berkeley: University of California Press.
EICHLER, ARTURO
  1970   *Snow peaks and jungles.* New York: Crowell. (Reprint of 1955 edition with new introduction by Alfredô Pareja Diezcanseco.)
ERASMUS, CHARLES J.
  1961   *Man takes control: cultural development and American aid.* Minneapolis: University of Minnesota Press.

FERDON, EDWIN N., JR.
  1950   *Studies in Ecuadorian geography*. Monographs of the School of American Research 15. Santa Fe.

FRIED, MORTON
  1967   *The evolution of political society: an essay in political anthropology*. New York: Random House.

GILLETTE, CYNTHIA
  1970   "Problems of colonization in the Ecuadorian Oriente." Unpublished M.A. thesis, Washington University, St. Louis.

HARNER, MICHAEL J.
  1972   *The Jívaro: people of the sacred waterfalls*. Garden City: Doubleday, Natural History Press.

HEGEN, EDMUND E.
  1966   *Highways into the upper Amazon basin: pioneer lands in southern Colombia, Ecuador, and northern Peru*. Center for Latin American Studies Monograph 2. Gainesville: University of Florida Press.

JARAMILLO ALVARADO, PIO
  1936   *Tierras del Oriente*. Quito: Imprenta Nacionales.

MITCHELL, J. CLYDE
  1966   "Theoretical orientations in African urban studies," in *The social anthropology of complex societies*. Edited by Michael Banton. New York: Praeger.

OBEREM, UDO
  1971   *Los Quijos*. Memorias de Departamento de Antropología y Etnología de América. Madrid.

ORR, CAROLYN, BETSY WRISLEY
  1965   *Vocabulario Quichua del Oriente del Ecuador*. Mexico: Instituto Lingüístico de Verano.

PAREJA DIEZCANSECO, ALFREDO
  1970   "Introduction," in *Snow peaks and jungles*. By Arturo Eichler. New York: Crowell.

PEÑAHERRERA DE COSTALES, PIEDAD, ALFREDO COSTALES SAMANIEGO
  1961   Llacta runa. *Llacta* 12. Quito.
  1962   Comunas juridicamente organizadas. *Llacta* 15. Quito.

PEÑAHERRERA DE COSTALES, PIEDAD, ALFREDO COSTALES SAMANIEGO, *et al.*
  1969   *Los Quichuas del Coca y el Napo*. Escuela de Sociología de la Universidad Central, Serie de Documentos y Estudios Sociales 1. Quito.

PORRAS G., P. PEDRO I.
  1961   *Contribución al estudio de la arqueología e historia de los valles Quijos y Misaguallí (Alto Napo) en la región oriental del Ecuador, S. A.* Quito: Editora Fenix.

ROBINSON, SCOTT S.
  1971   *El etnocidio Ecuatoriano*. Mexico: Universidad Iberoamericana.

ROBINSON, SCOTT S., MICHAEL SCOTT
  1971   *Sky Chief*. Thirty-minute color documentary film.

SCHEFFLER, HAROLD W., FLOYD G. LOUNSBURY
  1971   *A study in structural semantics: the Siriono kinship system*. Englewood Cliffs: Prentice-Hall.

SOUTHALL, AIDAN
  1961   "Introductory summary," in *Social change in modern Africa.* Edited by Aidan Southall, 1–82. London: Oxford University Press (for the International African Institute).

STEWARD, JULIAN H.
  1948   "Tribes of the Montaña: an introduction," in *Handbook of South American Indians,* volume three: *The tropical forest tribes.* Edited by Julian H. Steward, 507–534. Smithsonian Institution Bureau of American Ethnology Bulletin 143. Washington, D.C.

STEWARD, JULIAN H., ALFRED MÉTRAUX
  1948   "Tribes of the Peruvian and Ecuadorian Montaña" (sections entitled "The Jívaro," "Zaparoan Tribes," and "The Quijo"), in *Handbook of South American Indians,* volume three: *The tropical forest tribes.* Edited by Julian H. Steward, 617–656. Smithsonian Institution Bureau of American Ethnology Bulletin 143. Washington, D.C.

TESSMANN, GÜNTER
  1930   *Die indianer nordost-Perus: grundlegende forschungen für eine systematische kulturkunde.* Hamburg: Cram, De Gruyter.

WHITTEN, NORMAN E., JR.
  1965   *Class, kinship, and power in an Ecuadorian town: the Negroes of San Lorenzo.* Stanford: Stanford University Press.
  1968   Personal networks and musical contexts in the Pacific Lowlands of Ecuador and Colombia. *Man: Journal of the Royal Anthropological Institute* 3(1):50–63.
  1969a Strategies of adaptive mobility in the Colombian-Ecuadorian littoral. *American Anthropologist* 71(2):228–242.
  1969b The ecology of race relations in northwest Ecuador. *Journal de la Société des Americanístes* 54:223–235.
  1974   *Black frontiersmen: a South American case.* Cambridge: Schenkman.

WHITTEN, NORMAN E., JR., JOHN F. SZWED, *editors*
  1970   *Afro-American anthropology: contemporary perspectives.* New York: Free Press, Macmillan.

WHITTEN, NORMAN E., JR., ALVIN W. WOLFE
  1973   "Network analysis," in *Handbook of social and cultural anthropology.* Edited by John J. Honigmann. Chicago: Rand McNally.

WOLFE, ALVIN W.
  1963   The African mineral industry: evolution of a supranational level of integration. *Social Problems* 11(2):153–163.

Ethnicity and Class in Highland Peru

PIERRE L. VAN DEN BERGHE

Throughout the world, the practical import of ethnicity is intimately linked with the unequal distribution of power and wealth. Put in different terms, the relationship between ethnicity and class constitutes the key to an understanding of ethnic conflicts. The rather embarrassing lack of success of social scientists in grappling with problems of ethnicity at the theoretical and, even less, at the practical level, may be explained in part by our intellectual heritage.

Until recently, anthropologists tended to study ethnic groups in isolation from each other, and hence to neglect the field of ethnic RELATIONS. In sociology, ethnic relations have long been studied, but the functionalist mainstream in the United States largely failed to put ethnic relations in their political and economic context, and thus failed to understand the nature of ethnic conflicts. In the Marxian tradition scant attention has been devoted to ethnicity, except as a policy problem.

Happily, in the last ten to fifteen years an increasing number of sociologists and anthropologists have studied group relations in the colonial or postcolonial societies of Africa, America, and Asia (Aguirre Beltrán 1957; Balandier 1955; Barth 1969; Benedict 1965; Colby and van den Berghe 1969; Despres 1967; Hoetink 1966; Kuper 1967; Kuper and Smith 1971; Mayer 1961; Smith 1965; van den Berghe 1967b, 1971). The comparative treatment of ethnicity has greatly increased in sophistication, as witnessed by a spate of recent textbooks on the subject (Banton 1967; Mason 1970; Schermerhorn 1970; Shibutani and Kwan 1965; van den Berghe 1967a). The emergence or resurgence of micronationalisms, especially in Europe and Africa, and the bitter conflicts to which they led have challenged social scientists to deal with what a number of us have called plural societies.

Before turning to the specific case of Highland Peru, let me summarize what I consider to be fairly well established parameters of ethnic relations:
1.   Ethnicity and class are interrelated but ANALYTICALLY DISTINCT phenomena.[1] The fact that different social classes most commonly show subcultural differences and, conversely, that ethnic groups living under a common government are more often than not ordered in a hierarchy of power, wealth, and status does not make class reducible to ethnicity, or ethnicity to class.
2.   The specific relationship between class and ethnicity and the relative importance of each are empirical questions to be answered in every particular case. One must, therefore, be wary of any schemes which, from an *a priori* theoretical position, attribute a paramount role to either.
3.   Ethnicity is both an objective and a subjective phenomenon, the interrelation between these two aspects being, once again, an empirical question. Any conception of ethnicity which reduces either the objective or the subjective side of it to an insignificant role distorts reality. (Currently, extreme subjectivist views of ethnicity have supplanted the older objectivist standpoint.) Ethnic groups are defined BOTH by the objective cultural modalities of their behavior (including most importantly their linguistic behavior) and by their subjective views of themselves and each other.
4.   Ethnic conflicts, like class conflicts, result from the unequal distribution of, and competition for, scarce resources. Class and ethnic conflicts are frequently found simultaneously in the same society, but the lines of ethnic and class cleavages are often not the same.

Turning now specifically to the Peruvian case,[2] several conclusions seem to be consensually accepted among Peruvians and foreign social scientists:
1.   Peru is both class-stratified and ethnically diverse.

---

[1]   Here, so as not to burden the text with arguments already stated elsewhere, I am not considering the distinction between social race and ethnicity. While many authors have recently advocated lumping the two under the single label of ethnicity, and treating race as a special case of ethnicity, I have argued in favor of retaining the distinction, on both theoretical and empirical grounds. As phenotypic criteria of group membership are of such secondary significance in Andean Peru, there is no need to elaborate this point here.
[2]   I am doing so with considerable trepidation, as the present paper is being written during the initial stages of a period of fieldwork in the Department of Cuzco. Fortunately, the extensive and excellent literature on Peruvian ethnic relations helped me fill the gaps in my knowledge. In addition to the works cited here, I am also indebted to a number of Peruvian colleagues with whom I discussed these problems orally, and among whom I should like to mention Jorge Capriata, Julio Cotler, Jorge Flores Ochoa, Fernando Fuenzalida, José Matos Mar, and Oscar Nuñez del Prado.

2. There are great regional and even local variations in patterns of ethnic relations.

3. Physical criteria of group membership, while not totally absent, are clearly secondary to sociocultural criteria.

4. Ethnic boundaries between *mestizos* and Indians are fluid, with considerable intergenerational movement into the *mestizo* group.

5. Objective indices of ethnic membership are extremely variable from region to region and from situation to situation and, even in combination, can lead only to loose probabilistic statements. Even language is weakly diacritic, due to the extensive degree of bilingualism in the Highlands of both *mestizos* and Indians.

6. Ethnic boundaries to a considerable extent are defined subjectively, relatively, and situationally, rather than objectively and absolutely. Even at the local level, there is seldom consensual agreement as to who belongs to what ethnic group. The same terms can be used with a wide variety of meanings and of referents. There are, in most cases, no easily identifiable ethnic groups.

7. There is such a considerable degree of overlap between class and ethnic status that frequently it is difficult to disentangle the effect of each; but it is also clear that neither class nor ethnicity can be discounted, and that ethnic and class-based disabilities tend to be cumulative.

Perhaps the most sophisticated attempt to account for the complex interplay of class and ethnicity in Peru is found in the "sociology of dependence" approach to the problem, and more specifically in Fuenzalida's concept of *cadena arborescente*[3] (Bourricaud, et al. 1971; Delgado 1971; Fuenzalida 1970; Fuenzalida, et al. 1970; Matos Mar, et al. 1969a, 1969b, 1971; Quijano 1971). The approach interprets Peruvian social structure in terms of multiple and interrelated chains of dependence between persons or groups of unequal power, wealth, and status. These chains of dependence converge at the apex into the national and, beyond it, the international ruling oligarchy, as the structure of control is extremely centralized. Peruvian social structure is conceived as a multitude of binary relations of dependence and domination based on half a dozen or so interrelated dimensions.

In geographic terms, the countryside is dominated by the town, the town by the regional metropolis, the regional metropolis by the capital city, and the capital city by the great centers of world trade, power, and culture. In class terms, the peasants are dominated by the small-town bureaucracy and petty mercantile class, the small-town bourgeoisie by the elite of the

---

[3] "Branched-out chain" would probably be the most nearly adequate translation of this mixed metaphor.

provincial capital, the provincial elite by the Limean oligarchy, and the Limean oligarchy by the world cosmopolitan elite. Ethnically, the *mestizos* dominate the *cholos* who in turn dominate the Indians. Linguistically, the Quechua or Aymara monolingual is in a position of inferiority vis à vis the Limean cosmopolite who speaks Spanish, English, and French. Educationally, the illiterate, the primary school graduate, the secondary school graduate, and the university graduate form a hierarchy of prestige and power. Administratively, the district is subordinate to the province, the province to the department, the department to the central government in Lima, and ultimately, Peru to the world powers. Like the famous automobile race, "Caminos del Inca," everything of any consequence in Peru begins and ends in Lima.[4]

Besides centralization and inequality, these relations of dependence and domination are characterized by the fact that the closer one approaches the bottom of the pyramid, the more atomized and marginalized people are to national life; and, conversely, as one approaches the apex, the better interconnected and integrated the organs of domination.

Basically, the sociology of dependence framework constitutes the extension of a Marxian binary-conflict model of analysis to a variety of lines of cleavage, including the ethnic one. "Indianness" in Peru, according to this scheme, can be defined as the low end of a dependency chain on nearly all dimensions of unequal relations: the most Indian person is the illiterate, monolingual, rural peasant. This view of ethnicity comes close to reducing ethnicity to class, or at least to one special aspect of class. It conceptualizes ethnicity, not as a matter of a person being EITHER *mestizo* OR Indian, but as being MORE or LESS Indian or *mestizo*. The absence of clear-cut objective criteria which enable one to draw consensually agreed upon ethnic lines leads Fuenzalida, for example, to reject for Peru the concept of plural society, which, to him, implies fairly well-drawn ethnic boundaries.

This sociology of dependence approach to ethnicity has at least four major strengths. First, it anchors the study of ethnicity squarely in the matrix of relations of power and relations of production, outside of which ethnic relations can scarcely be understood. Second, it reacts healthily against the naive cultural determinist approach that the Indians are the heirs to the pre-Columbian civilizations, and the *mestizos* the carriers of

---

[4]   To mention a few trivial but illustrative examples from personal experience, I have had to send to Lima from Cuzco to obtain duplicate Volkswagen keys, to get a minor camera repair done, to develop films, and to find missing screws for a refrigerator door. In no other country in the world, including proverbially centralized France, have I felt so utterly dependent on the telephone and the local airline as lifelines to the capital city.

Spanish culture. Even the most isolated Indian communities have under-gone enough cultural change to make it misleading to consider them linear descendants of pre-Columbian cultures. Especially in the Highlands where cultural syncretism is greatest, the two traditions have sufficiently blended to make any clear-cut objective differentiation of culture traits between Indians and *mestizos* an impossible task. It is sometimes even impossible to determine which is the "native" tongue of a bilingual person. Many Highland people grow up with both Spanish and Quechua spoken at home from early infancy.

Third, the concept of dependence, by relating ethnicity to class, allows for a flexible description of a fluid and complex situation. It stresses the impossibility of dissociating ethnicity from class status and emphasizes their relativity to the persons interacting and, indeed, to the specific situation at hand. Fourth, this approach to ethnicity avoids the trap of extreme subjectivism, which reduces ethnicity almost purely to the mutual perceptions and definitions of the situation by members of the groups present.[5] The dependence approach, links ethnicity to objective relations of power and of production.

The one main shortcoming of the dependence approach, however, is that it tends to submerge ethnicity too much under class, and to under-state the causal impact of culture, especially language, as factors DISTINCT FROM class. To speak of Indians without reference to their position as oppressed peasants is obviously absurd. But to think that one can sub-stitute *campesino* for *indigena* (as the present reformist government with its knack for euphemisms has made fashionable),[6] and thereby gain a satisfactory understanding of the structure of domination in Peru is also untenable.

Once military conquest establishes a situation of gross inequality amongst ethnic groups, cultural differences, and especially language, serve to perpetuate, accentuate, and reinforce the inequalities between victor and vanquished. The inequalities of class and ethnicity become CUMU-LATIVE, and the system of domination becomes doubly oppressive and exploitative. Access to government, to education, and to wealth is impeded by the double barrier of class and ethnicity. It is further incapa-

[5] Barth's conception of ethnic boundaries, while usefully reacting against the naive ethnographic "objectivism" of defining ethnicity in terms of culture traits, goes too far, in my view, in the direction of subjective reductionism (Barth 1969). Ethnicity is always a blend of objective and subjective factors.
[6] Much as the government seems to delude itself that it solved the "Indian problem" by calling Indians "peasants," it eliminated the *barriadas* on paper by renaming these slums *pueblos jovenes*.

citating to be a peasant who cannot understand the language in which he is governed.

The impact of the so-called revolution which has taken place in Peru since the Velasco regime illustrates this point. To be sure, the various reforms introduced by the Revolutionary Government of the Armed Forces did substantially undermine the power of the oligarchy, and agrarian reform did appreciably alter patterns of land tenure. Thus the Velasco regime did, to a limited but not insignificant degree, affect CLASS relations in Peru, but the impact of the change has been most significant at the top of the class order which, in the nature of the case, is non-Indian.

For the Mancha India of Peru – (the heavily Indian southern departments) – it may, I think, be said that the *reforma agraria* did not appreciably affect the position of dependence and exploitation of the Indians vis à vis *mestizos*. Apart from the relative slowness with which agrarian reform is being implemented and the overwhelming technical problems faced by any political revolution trying to improve living conditions with a system of production that is not only exploitative but ARCHAIC, land reform in the Highlands can be said to have failed partly because of the ethnic barriers between the "revolution's" active agents and its supposed beneficiaries.

For ideological and practical reasons the government wants to transform the *haciendas* into cooperatives. Ideologically, cooperatives fit into the romanticized indigenist conception of Inca communalism and into the progressivist-technocratic mentality of the military rulers. Practically, cooperatives are an alternative to distribution of land into supposedly uneconomic *minifundias*. (In a real sense, the whole Andean agriculture and livestock breeding is archaic and low in productivity, whether run on a large or on a small scale; and the case for economies of scale at the footplow level of technology has yet to be made.) The peasants, on the other hand, with a sound understanding of their class interests prefer, by and large, personal land ownership.

With typical bureaucratic arrogance and paternalism, the government through numerous reformist agencies (most notably SINAMOS) tells the people, and especially the Indians, what is good for them. The *salon* radicalism of the young university graduates hired by these agencies is compatible with a profound contempt for the peasants' alleged ignorance and backwardness. The peasants have exchanged their feudal *mestizo* overlords for a multitude of *mestizo* bureaucrats and technocrats. The cooperative *empleados*, as a junta of petty tyrants, have replaced the former grand tyranny of the *hacendado*. In the words of one peasant, "Before, we had one master; now we have ten." From the peasant's viewpoint the main difference between the *hacienda* and the cooperative is that, in the latter, there is more room for corruption and inefficiency and perhaps a little less for personal abuse of power. Exploitation and domination are more impersonal, collectivized, and bureaucratized.[7]

This kind of "democratic centralism" is, of course, extremely common in regimes with socialist or populist inclinations, but, where there is an ethnic as well as a class difference between exploiters and exploited, the system of domination is all the more difficult to shake. Language, illiteracy, culture, geography, and other factors insulate the Andean Indian from the outside world, and, in the last analysis, it is the outside world that counts. His options are either to leave his community, and in effect cease to be an Indian, or to stay and be dependent on *mestizo* or *cholo* intermediaries for his relations with the outside. Under a radical guise the university student politician, the government technocrats, and the Maoist school teachers are a new, emerging class of power brokers manipulating peasant masses to pursue their political and career ambitions. Radicalism is a technique of *arribismo* for the intellectual.[8] The fact that some of them are of Indian origin is of little consequence. In order to achieve power and wealth, they have to cease BEING Indians and peasants, but they must continue DOMINATING the peasant masses in one form or another. Their former "Indianness" becomes a useful legitimation for their political ambition, and their knowledge of Quechua becomes an instrument of manipulation.

In an attempt to formalize the relationship between class and ethnicity, we may suggest three types of situations depending on two main factors. The first factor is the degree of inequality between ethnic groups. The second is the degree of resistance to "passing" from one ethnic group into another.

The first and rather uncommon situation type exists when the ethnic

---

[7] The best evidence for the failures of agrarian reform can be found in official speeches by government officials seeking to refute the attacks of the "enemies of the revolution" of "one extreme or the other." For example, the speech of the Minister of Agriculture reported in *El Comercio* of Lima on October 16, 1972, rejects charges of "presumed abuses in the application of the law on the part of responsible officials," denies that there is any reason for "lack of confidence towards those who belong to the ruling bodies of the cooperatives," denounces those who provoke "confrontations with the technicians whose contribution is indispensable for the success of the enterprises," and denies "rumors to the effect that the government intends to nationalize rural enterprises and that the beneficiaries of the Agrarian Reform would thus be converted into mere wage-earners." There could scarcely be a better summary of the main reasons for peasant discontent with agrarian reform and of the causes for the serious drop in agricultural production in the Highlands.

[8] *Arribismo* means literally the desire to be on top. It could be translated as "careerist ambition."

groups within a society are of relatively equal class status. Such a situation prevails where, as in Switzerland or in recent years in Belgium, the ethnic groups are nearly proportionately represented at all levels of the class hierarchy and in the major educational, business, state, and other institutions. Though conflict and competition between ethnic groups may be intense in such a situation, the ethnic composition of the population remains relatively stable, irrespective of whether there is resistance to "passing" from one group into the other. Some passing may occur through intermarriage or from other causes, but a major incentive for passing, namely improvement in one's social status, is lacking if the ethnic groups are of approximately equal status.

The two other situations of inequality between ethnic groups are far more common. The second type of society, characterized for example by South Africa, Rhodesia, and many former European colonial regimes in Africa, exists when the constituent ethnic groups are unequally represented at the various class levels, and where the dominant group erects caste or quasi-caste barriers to prevent access into it by members of subordinate groups. Such societies are frequently racist, as physical features are an easy criterion for excluding the "lower orders." Such societies obviously have a rigid social order, though considerable CULTURAL assimilation may take place. Thus in both the first and the second type of society ethnic boundaries tend to be relatively stable, albeit for greatly different reasons. In the first type the incentives for change in ethnic group membership are few; in the second type the incentives are great, but ethnic membership change is prevented by force.

The third type of situation is most commonly found in Spanish America, particularly Peru. The ethnic groups are clearly hierarchical, but the culturally dominant group is relatively open to members of other ethnic groups, who become culturally assimilated. Assimilation into the *mestizo* group may and often does take one or two generations, but, by and large throughout Spanish America, an Indian who learns to speak fluent Spanish and who acquires what is regarded as the local variant of *mestizo* or *criollo* culture ceases to be regarded as an Indian. The result is a relatively fluid ethnic situation in which the subordinate group steadily decreases in proportion.

Let us return to the Peruvian case and more specifically to the southern Andean region of Peru where the Indian population is still most heavily concentrated. To students of societies where ethnic boundaries are more sharply drawn, the fluidity and indeterminacy of the Peruvian situation is at first disconcerting. There is often little consensus, even at the local level, as to who is Indian and who is not. Physical appearance is of marginal significance. To be sure, a small percentage of foreigners and Peruvians of predominantly European descent are identified as *blancos* or *gringos*, but they barely account for one percent of the population in the Highlands and perhaps three to five percent on the coast. Between the overwhelming majority of Indians and *mestizos*, physical appearance is not diacritic.

Language, which is in many parts of Spanish America, e.g. in Mexico or Guatemala, the best single indicator of ethnic status, is not a clear-cut criterion in Highland Peru where Quechua-Spanish bilingualism is extremely widespread among *mestizos* and fairly widespread among Indians. Enough people are equally fluent in the two languages from infancy to make language an imperfect index of ethnicity. Other culture traits, such as dress, diet, the use of coca, and so on, are equally unreliable in the broad center of the ethnic spectrum. Perhaps one quarter of the population is consensually defined as Indian and a tenth as *mestizo*, but the majority in between will be variably classified, depending on a wide variety of factors.

More than any other word, the term *cholo* is symptomatic of this indeterminate state of affairs. That term has generated an abundant literature in Peruvian sociology and anthropology, and, broadly, social scientists have given the word *cholo* three kinds of usages. Some scholars have used the word to designate a group of people intermediate in status between Indians and *mestizos*. Some of those would concede that it would be difficult to define a *cholo* GROUP, but think that they can objectively identify individuals as *cholos*. In a few ethnographies of local communities social scientists have even claimed to identify more than three ethnic groups, differentiating between *cholos* and *mozos* or between *mestizos* and *mistis*.

Other sociologists and anthropologists have preferred to use the term *cholo*, or rather *cholificacion*, to designate a process of movement from "Indianness" to "mestizoness"; or a process of syncretism between the two cultures (Bourricaud 1967). Finally, some social scientists have claimed, in my view quite rightly, that the term *cholo* does not correspond to any objective reality at all, but rather that it is used up and down the social scale as a term of derogation toward one's social inferiors. In other words, who is *cholo* is determined not by any objective characteristics a person may possess but by the social distance between the person so designated and the one who does the name-calling.

If relativity and subjectivity of definition characterize the use of the term *cholo*, do they not also apply to the terms Indian and *mestizo*? I would be inclined to say "yes," but to a lesser degree. Philip Mason

(1970) cites cases of town registries where ethnic classifications fluctuate widely according to the inclinations of successive town clerks, so there is obviously a considerable element of subjectivity in defining who is Indian or who is *mestizo*. However, it is clear that this element of subjectivity decreases steeply at both the upper and lower end of the status spectrum.

Let me illustrate the situation with the community of San Jerónimo, some ten kilometers away from Cuzco, which I have just begun studying. The term *cholo* is scarcely used locally, except in derogation, yet, to an outsider, it might seem most appropriate to designate the entire community as *cholo*. A peri-urban district of some 10,000 inhabitants, San Jerónimo is not "obviously" Indian as is, say, Pisac or Chinchero, nor is it big and cosmopolitan enough to be clearly urban and *mestizo*. From the perspective of the middle-class urbanite from Cuzco, at most 10 percent of the population of San Jerónimo could be unequivocally classified as *mestizos*. Yet, if by Indian one means a coca-chewing peasant, who is a native speaker of Quechua, who dresses in homespun clothes, and so on, an even smaller proportion of the population would fit the description.

What are the objective parameters of the local situation? Quechua is the dominant language of San Jerónimo in the sense that practically everybody (with the exception of the author and his family) speaks it fluently, and most people speak it at home in preference to Spanish. Yet, the use of Spanish is also widespread: perhaps one-fourth of the population speak it with facility (though not necessarily flawlessly); one-half speak sufficient Spanish for limited everyday discourse; and the remaining fourth, principally women, speak little or no Spanish. Anywhere between 70 and 80 percent of the population has achieved minimal literacy, and complete primary education is the rule for the younger generation. Secondary education is spreading fast, and quite a few San Jerónimo youths are students or graduates of the University of Cuzco.

Economically, the town is better off than most in the Department of Cuzco. San Jerónimo is a reasonably prosperous market town, providing a wide range of goods and services to Cuzco. It is located on the main Cuzco-Puno road, boasts several bus lines, has a famous weekly meat market, and is the site of the University of Cuzco experimental farm. Though its cobblestoned streets are both rustic and odorous, the town has long had electricity and potable running water. Nearly all houses are built of adobe and tiles, but most have no toilet facilities, indoors or out. The town boasts a good municipal swimming pool, a stadium, one secondary school for boys and one for girls, a fairly modern town hall, a large church with richly decorated altars, a new police station, and a large departmental penitentiary under construction (by far the most modern and best-built edifice in San Jerónimo).

Though extremes in wealth are lacking, San Jerónimo is clearly stratified by class. Few people are destitute, but the great majority live quite modestly in small two- or three-room houses with little patios where they keep small livestock. A great many people own or cultivate small plots of land in or around town, and so combine part-time farming with petty trade or artisan occupations such as tailoring, stonemasonry, carpentry, shoemaking, and the like. The large *haciendas* are all in the process of being expropriated under the land reform program, but a score or so of families are distinctly better off than the rest of the population. They live in larger, better-built houses, own more land, and are better educated; they frequently earn fixed salaries as teachers or employees, or run sizable businesses such as restaurants. A few people own television sets and older-model private automobiles. Usually referred to as *la crema*, this local elite is clearly *mestizo* (but fluent in Quechua). By Cuzco standards, they are middle class rather than upper class, and might be referred to as *cholos* by upper class Cuzqueños.

Below that class level, however, ethnic boundaries are much more ill-defined, and consensus as to who is Indian or *mestizo* disappears. At one extreme is an informant, who, although himself highly educated and completely fluent in Spanish, is the son of illiterate, monolingual Quechua peasants from a remote district. He described all the people of San Jerónimo as *mestizos*, arguing that, because they live in a town, dress in store-bought clothes and have a different life style than peasants, they could not be discribed as *indigenas*. At the other end of the definitional spectrum is a high-status municipal official who classified some 90 percent of the San Jerónimo population as Indian, basing his judgment on a combination of linguistic, economic, and dress-style criteria. Both Indians and *mestizos* who have the necessary economic means assume religious cargos, and do so for much the same mixture of religious and prestige reasons. There are three organized *comunidades campesinas* in town, but these communities are not Indian by any conventional definition. They are made up of small landowners, who, for the most part, live in town, but who own or cultivate plots located in an arbitrarily defined geographical sector of San Jerónimo District. Ethnicity is not a criterion of membership. There are no political authorities, such as *varayoq*, which could be defined as Indian. Educationally, some sons of Indian peasant families are university students, and, conversely, some poorer persons usually described as *mestizo* have only primary education and may be barely literate. Many well-to-do artisans and owners of stores or trucks may be native speakers of Quechua, though they would also be fluent in Spanish. The general consensus is that ethnicity is less important as a distinguishing characteristic than it once was, and that today *"el dinero es que manda."* The economic criterion of status, which is, of course, far from being the only important one, is perhaps the most visible. It finds its symbolic expression in the assumption of religious cargos: the four main *mayordomos* who sponsor *novenas* in honor of the patron saint incur expenses of $1,200 or more (in a country with a per capita income of some $360 a year). This lavish spending at *fiestas* takes the publicly visible and audible form of fireworks, music, food, and drink and is highly competitive.

From the above account it would be easy to conclude that class is all-important and that ethnicity is not, or has ceased to be. Yet the fact remains that Quechua and Spanish as languages are in a clear hierarchy of prestige, power, and wealth, and thus that the degree of fluency in each determines to a considerable extent the status of its speakers. Even locally, where the average level of competence is higher in Quechua than in Spanish, it is a far greater disadvantage to be monolingual in Quechua than in Spanish. Anyone who matters socially, economically, or politically speaks fluent Spanish. Except for the parish priest and the anthropologist it is scarcely a handicap not to know Quechua, but for anyone who seeks class mobility through education, politics, or business, knowledge of Spanish is a prerequisite. There are many people who, though fluent in Quechua, are said to be ashamed to speak it and to prefer struggling through in their limited Spanish.

Of course, San Jerónimo is in no sense "typical" of Peru, or even of the Sierra. Given the wide range of ethnic situations found in Peru, no town could ever be regarded as a microcosm of the country. Within the single Department of Cuzco, a whole continuum can be found. At one extreme are solidly Indian areas like Ocongate, Ocatca, or Chinchero; where the bulk of the population is still monolingual Quechua, where the ethnic line between Indians and *mestizos* is sharply drawn, and where the socio-economic structure corresponds rather closely to that ethnic cleavage. A small bilingual *mestizo* minority controls the political and economic resources as landowners, civil servants, policemen, shopkeepers, labor recruiters, or, more recently, as SINAMOS bureaucrats and technicians. The Indians form the bulk of the peasantry and of the agricultural wage earners. At the other end of the spectrum are urban or peri-urban areas like Cuzco or San Jerónimo, where ethnic lines are blurred and much more complexly interwoven with class, where consensus as to who is Indian or *mestizo* is almost entirely lacking.

The one extreme approaches the ideal type of the plural society, with sharply drawn lines of cultural cleavage that closely correspond to the politicoeconomic hierarchy. At the other end of the continuum ethnic lines are so intertwined with class lines that the two phenomena tend to merge empirically into each other. In neither case, however, is ethnicity simply REDUCIBLE to class. Though ethnicity and language correlate with and partly determine class position, class is also determined by a number of nonethnic factors. Conversely, there are many aspects of ethnicity that are independent of the relations of power and production which constitute the class order.

Analytically, then, it is equally as important to understand the specific relationship between class and ethnicity as it is to keep the two phenomena clearly distinct.

The complex dynamics of cultural and linguistical change can only be understood in relation to class and, particularly, to social mobility. Social mobility in Peru and indeed in much of Latin America is also ethnic passing. Paradoxical though the situation may seem, ethnicity accentuates stratification, but, at the same time, the very inequality of ethnic groups creates a dynamism of social and cultural change. Ignorance of Spanish shuts the Indian population off from participation in the "national" society much more completely than class barriers could. Even the unemployed *lumpenproletariat* of Lima is a more active participant in the mainstream of Peruvian life than the Sierra peasant or shepherd. Yet, the obvious advantage of learning the dominant language and culture generates a continuing process of Hispanization (or, more precisely, in the Sierra, a continuing extension of bilingualism). Clearly Hispanization is much more than a process of cultural change. It is intimately linked with a process of SOCIAL and GEOGRAPHICAL mobility. The monolingual, illiterate Sierra peasant becomes a bilingual, literate, urban proletarian. Through a multifaceted process of ethnic, class, and geographical mobility which typically takes a substantial part of an individual's lifetime, tens of thousands of Indians annually enter the *mestizo* class order.

Much controversy has surrounded the nature of the "open-class" system characteristic of industrial societies. By comparison, CLASS differences in Peru and other Latin American countries are much larger and more clearly marked. On the other hand, Peru and other Spanish American countries lack the rigid ethnic (and racial) boundaries encountered in a number of highly industrialized countries. Peru might be said to have both a highly stratified class system with many remnants of a preindustrial, agrarian order and an "open-ethnicity" system allowing considerable mobility from the subordinate ethnic group to the lower-class echelons of the dominant ethnic group.

REFERENCES

AGUIRRE BELTRÁN, GONZALO
1957 *El proceso de aculturación.* Mexico: Universidad Naciónal Autónoma de México.
1967 *Regiones de refugio.* Mexico: Instituto Indígenista Interamericano.

BALANDIER, GEORGES
1955 *Sociologie actuelle de l'Afrique noire.* Paris: Presses Universitaires de France.

BANTON, MICHAEL
1967 *Race relations.* London: Tavistock.

BARTH, FREDRIK
1969 *Ethnic groups and boundaries.* Boston: Little, Brown.

BENEDICT, BURTON
1965 *Mauritius: problems of a plural society.* London: Pall Mall.

BOURRICAUD, FRANÇOIS
1967 *Cambios en puno.* Mexico: Instituto Indígenista Interamericano.

BOURRICAUD, FRANÇOIS, *et al.*
1971 *La oligarquia en el Peru.* Lima: Instituto de Estudios Peruanos.

CASTILLO ARDILES, HERNÁN
1970 *Pisac.* Mexico: Instituto Indígenista Interamericano.

COLBY, B. N., PIERRE L. VAN DEN BERGHE
1969 *Ixil country; a plural society in highland Guatemala.* Berkeley: University of California Press.

DE LA FUENTE, JULIO
1965 *Relaciones interétnicas.* Mexico: Instituto Naciónal Indígenista.

DELGADO, CARLOS
1971 *Problemas sociales en el Peru contemporaneo.* Lima: Institutuo de Estudios Peruanos.

DESPRES, LEO
1967 *Cultural pluralism and nationalist politics in British Guiana.* Chicago: Rand McNally.

DOBYNS, HENRY F.
1964 *The social matrix of Peruvian indigenous communities.* Cornell Peru Project Monograph. Ithaca.

FUENZALIDA, FERNANDO
1970 *La matriz colonial de la comunidad de indigenas Peruana.* Lima.

FUENZALIDA, FERNANDO, *et al.*
1970 *El Indo y el poder.* Lima: Instituto de Estudios Peruanos.

HOETINK, H.
1966 *The two variants in Caribbean race relations.* New York: Oxford University Press.

KEITH, ROBERT G., *et al.*
1970 *La hacienda, la comunidad, y el campesino en el Peru.* Lima: Instituto de Estudios Peruanos.

KUPER, LEO
1967 *An African bourgeoisie.* New Haven: Yale University Press.

KUPER, LEO, M. G. SMITH, *editors*
1971 *Pluralism in Africa.* Berkeley: University of California Press.

MASON, PHILIP
1970   *Patterns of dominance.* London: Oxford University Press.
MATOS MAR, JOSÉ, *et al.*
1969a *Peru problema.* Lima: Instituto de Estudios Peruanos.
1969b *Dominación y cambios en el Perú rural.* Lima: Instituto de Estudios Peruanos.
1971   *Peru hoy.* Mexico: Siglo Veintiuno Editores.
MAYER, PHILIP
1961   *Townsmen or tribesmen.* Cape Town: Oxford University Press.
QUIJANO, ANIBAL
1971   Nationalism and capitalism in Peru. *Monthly Review* 23 (July-August).
SARFATTI LARSON, MAGALI, ARLENE EISEN BERGMAN
1969   *Social stratification in Peru.* Berkeley: University of California, Institute of International Studies.
SCHERMERHORN, RICHARD A.
1970   *Comparative ethnic relations.* New York: Random House.
SHIBUTANI, TAMOTSU, KIAN M. KWAN
1965   *Ethnic stratification.* New York: Macmillan.
SMITH, M. G.
1965   *The plural society in the British West Indies.* Berkeley: University of California Press.
VAN DEN BERGHE, PIERRE L.
1967a *Race and racism.* New York: Wiley.
1967b *South Africa, a study in conflict.* Berkeley: University of California Press.
1971   *Race and ethnicity.* New York: Basic Books.

Ethnicity and Resource Competition in Guyanese Society

LEO A. DESPRES

Ethnicity and ethnic group relations, often assuming dimensions of racism, are subjects that have received considerable research attention from all denominations of social scientists.[1] Nevertheless, a great many substantive problems remain unresolved even to the point of theoretical clarification. Not the least of these problems is the widespread persistence of ethnicity as an element of structural significance in the organization of societies of varying types. Ethnicity persists most obviously in those societies that have been labeled, inter alia, complex, multiple, multi-ethnic, segmented, heterogeneous, urban, industrial, pre-industrial, or plural.[2] However, quite apart from the problem of their classification, these societies engage processes of social differentiation and incorporation which are evident in societies usually considered more homogeneous from a cultural point of view. And if, following Barth (1969: 13), one defines ethnicity as a categorical ascription presumptively determined by origin and

Some of the data presented in this paper were collected with support provided by the Social Science Research Council in 1960–1961. Thanks to the support of a Fulbright Fellowship, additional research was conducted in Guyana over a twelve-month period in 1970–1971. A very preliminary draft of this paper was presented to the 1971 meetings of the International Studies Association in San Juan, Puerto Rico, where it benefited considerably from critical comments offered by Harmannus Hoetink, Wendell Bell, and Leo Kuper. I also wish to thank Burton Benedict, Pierre van den Berghe, and Melvyn Goldstein for the benefit of their wisdom in respect to subsequent drafts.

[1]   The literature in this field is much too extensive to summarize here. For a general review, see the following: Banton (1967); Schermerhorn (1970); Shibutani and Kwan (1965); van den Berghe (1967, 1970); and Zubaida (1970).

[2]   See particularly M. G. Smith (1969: 416–419). In this context M. G. Smith cites, among others: Radcliffe-Brown (1940); van Lier (1950); Sjoberg (1952); Nash (1957); Speckman (1963); and Hoetink (1967). Also see M. G. Smith (1960, 1965); Despres (1967, 1968); and the work edited by Kuper and Smith (1969).

background, elements of ethnicity may be in evidence at the organizational interface of group relations in some of the most simple societies of
record.[3]

It very well may be that ethnicity and ethnic group relations implicate
problems that override the specificity of particular cultures, historical
circumstances, polities, and ecologies. Indeed, this is suggested in much
of the current literature.[4] Assuming this to be the case, it follows that the
persistence of ethnicity and the various forms of interethnic accommodation that accompany it cannot be explained completely by reference to
conditions or circumstances peculiar to one society or another at a particular historical moment. And, considering the variability of cultures,
institutional systems, polities, ecologies, and demographic circumstances,
typological efforts to disclose the processes involved seem rather misspent
(e.g. van den Berghe 1970: 21–41; Schermerhorn 1970). What is needed
is some set of propositions, even if tentatively derived, giving issue to generalizations of invariant order in respect to the conditions that favor the
selection of ethnic ascriptions and identities for the purpose of organizing
human activities.

Accordingly, the focus of this paper is simultaneously theoretical and
substantive. Substantively, it presents a case study of ethnicity and ethnic
group relations in Guyanese society. In developing this case, it will be
suggested that the persistence, organization, and differential incorporation
of ethnic groups in Guyanese society is very much determined by the competition for material resources that exists among the various populations

---

[3]   M. G. Smith (1969: 106–111) discusses ethnicity in reference to "mobile" societies, a
category that includes collectors, pastoralists, and some agriculturalists. He suggests
that pluralism may not be significantly evident in societies that approximate a pure
form of band organization. However, his definition of ethnicity, giving emphasis to
exclusive units of social and biological reproduction, is much more restrictive than
Barth's. If the more general definition is employed, then clearly relationships between
territorial bands often assume elements of an ethnic character. See, for example, L.
Marshall (1960, 1965) on the Bushmen. To my knowledge, ethnicity is not often
discussed in reference to band populations. However, as Barth has noted, most of the
research done by anthropologists rests upon the assumption that there are relatively
discrete differences between cultures and that these differences correspond to the
organization of groups and societies. Indeed, how these ethnic units might be classified
to facilitate their comparative study is the whole point at issue in an article by Narroll
(1964).

[4]   I interpret the development of a more general theory to be the thrust of Barth's
recent discussion of ethnic groups and boundaries. A more general theory is also the
objective of Kuper and Smith's (1969) comparative effort in respect to pluralism in
Africa. And more recently, to develop a more general framework than is thought to be
suggested by such notions as the "plural society," Cohen and Middleton (1970) have
suggested that these phenomena be subsumed under the study of "incorporation
processes."

that were settled in this area as a consequence of European exploration and exploitation. To further enhance the comparative assessment of this general thesis, by way of concluding, more specific hypotheses will be presented in respect to the conditions affecting resource competition on the one hand and incorporation processes on the other. Thus, theoretical considerations of a more general nature will follow upon the presentation of data.

Regarding the analysis of data, it will be convenient to focus attention mainly on three dimensions of ethnicity and ethnic group relations: first, that pertaining to the overall social system and the persistence of culturally differentiated populations; second, the nature and character of organized ethnic group relations; and third, the role of ethnicity as it affects individual encounters within varying situational contexts. Although related, each of these dimensions may be dealt with separately.

1.   At the level of the overall social system, one must begin by taking note of census data and the much-discussed problem of census classification. Guyana is said to be a lard of six peoples. As of 1964, the population was comprised of: East Indians (50.2 percent), Africans (31.3 percent), Amerindians (4.6 percent), Portuguese (1.0 percent), Chinese (0.6 percent), and white (0.3 percent). For some curious reason, in 1960 the category "European" was dropped in favor of the category "white." A residual population, the mixed (12.0 percent), is also given categorical recognition.

Students of Guyanese society have proclaimed the ambiguity and empirical invalidity of these census categories. Guyanese who count other Guyanese sometimes give note to subjectively asserted ethnic identities for purposes of classification. In other instances attention is drawn to ambiguously defined cultural diacritica that are assumed to be generally standardized: e.g. dress, religion, house form, or style of life. In still other instances, persons are counted in reference to equally ambiguous phenotypical variations, particularly skin color, facial features, or hair texture. All of this underscores the fact that in the final analysis these census categories are stereotypic. Thus, it has been argued, they are inconsistent with the variation in observed institutional and cultural practices and with the actual distribution of phenotypical diacritica.[5]

Notwithstanding the stereotypic nature of census categories, Guyanese

_____

[5]   See, for example, Braithwaite (1960: 816–831); R. T. Smith (1962: 98–143; 1970: 43–76); Lewis (1968: 35–46); and Cross (1968: 381–397). Although some of these works do not treat census categories as such, they do treat the difficulties associated with any effort to categorically differentiate populations in reference to institutional differences or the distribution of racial diacritica.

often do accord identities to other Guyanese that generally correspond to the ethnic categories in question. Moreover, individual Guyanese do this even when they are inclined to reject for themselves the ethnic identities which others accord them. This is to suggest that the categories in question are not entirely devoid of objective significance. Following Barth (1969: 9–38), it would seem that the critical question is whether or not these ethnic categories enjoin imperative statuses and, if so, how these statuses are structured within the overall social system.

There is substantial evidence to suggest that ethnic categories do enjoin imperative statuses in Guyana. As indicated elsewhere (Despres i.p.), unofficially and sometimes officially, these ethnic categories are the foci of differential consideration within the public domain. One recent example of this is provided by the 1965 inquiry into the problem of "racial" imbalance in the public services. The rather exhaustive study made of this problem was commissioned by the government of British Guiana and carried out by the International Commission of Jurists. Quite apart from its procedures and findings, three points need to be emphasized regarding this inquiry. First, the Burnham government of 1965 commissioned this inquiry in order to alleviate political pressure arising from the widespread belief in the East Indian community that an imbalance among Africans and East Indians existed in the public service. Second, the measure of that imbalance was made in reference to population ratios that were derived from the application of the stereotypic ethnic categories under discussion. Finally, the investigation itself, and the circumstances surrounding it, gave implicit expression to a set of norms according to which a great many Guyanese, including some who are important leaders, are inclined to support the view that within the all-inclusive public domain, the structure of Guyanese society should disclose what M. G. Smith (1969: 434–435) has called a "consociational" form of incorporation.

That is to say, many Guyanese are inclined to view their society as one comprised of diverse ethnic and/or racial collectivities of unequal status and power. Paraphrasing a title borrowed from the Prime Minister's recent book (Burnham 1970), to mold from these one people with one destiny, many Guyanese would maintain that these collectivities need to hold equivalent corporate status in the common public domain. Therefore, regarding recruitment into the public service, consideration needs to be given to ascribed ethnic criteria in addition to criteria of individual achievement. At the very least, achievement criteria should not be developed and administered in a manner that would contribute further to the corporate inequalities that are perceived to exist among ethnic populations as a consequence of their former colonial domination. It follows from these views that Africans and East Indians should be given entitlements not only in reference to their numbers, but also in relationship to the inequalities that are thought to exist in respect to their collective status in the overall social system.

Being somewhat relative to the ethnic population with which one is most generally identified, the definition of corporate inequalities among ethnic populations in Guyana contains a subjective component. But these perceptions also are not entirely without an objective base. If one takes as an objective measure of status inequality the relationship of individuals and groups to the material resources they own, control, or otherwise manage, a definite order of inequality exists among ethnic populations. Moreover, this order of inequality is of such historical depth that the statuses it enjoins are institutionalized and imperative and they correspond to the competition for resources that has obtained among the populations in question The historical data supporting this view have been detailed elsewhere (Despres 1967: 30–67; 1969: 14–44). A brief summary will satisfy the purposes of this analysis.

It is evident that the populations that came to Guyana from Africa, Asia, and Europe differed not only phenotypically but also in their cultural traditions and practices. It is equally evident that other differences developed according to whether such populations were imported as slaves or indentured workers, or whether they arrived as immigrant planters, merchants, public servants, or commercial agents. It is certain also that these differences of origin were modified by early adaptive experiences. Miscegenation occurred, particularly between Europeans and Africans. Languages were lost. And many traditional practices gave way to the agro-industrial demands of an expanding colonial economy.

However, regarding ethnic populations, the process of readaptation in the coastlands of Guyana was itself differentiating. That is to say, while all Guyanese shared the experiences of colonialism and the plantation economy, ethnic populations disclose different historical careers in respect to these influences. More specifically, ordered by the competition for resources that existed within and across varying micro-environments (i.e. plantations, villages, and towns), Europeans have remained dominant in their control of the most productive environmental resources available, particularly land, minerals, employment opportunities, and markets. At the same time, since they were first imported as indentured workers, East Indians have slowly but steadily alienated from Africans the control of those environmental resources that have remained accessible primarily to non-Europeans.

For example, between 1840 and 1900, East Indian indentured workers all but displaced Africans from the labor market which the sugar plantations provided. It is true that following emancipation a great many Africans gravitated away from the sugar plantations. But not all of them did so simply because they wanted to flee the source of their former bondage. On the contrary, the first migratory wave from the estates was created by a general strike in 1842, when the planters attempted to reduce the wages of African workers to the pre-emancipation level in order to help defray the cost of importing more than 50,000 indentured workers. Strikers, it seems, were summarily ejected from estate lands. A more severe strike developed in 1847, when the planters again attempted to reduce wages (Young 1958: 15–21). Except in special job categories such as pan boiling and seasonal cane cutting, Africans could not or would not compete for the wages paid indentures. Thus, by 1911, the African proportion of the estate population had dwindled to 10 percent while the number of East Indians increased to 86 percent. Since 1911, the African proportion has stabilized between 10 and 15 percent.

Similarly, East Indians have displaced Africans from most of the coastal agricultural lands not taken up by the sugar estates. In the years immediately following emancipation, Africans came to occupy virtually all of these lands. Living in villages under various forms of local government organization, they put these lands under ground crops, coconut, and fruit trees. In 1881, only 13 percent of the village population was made up of East Indians and a few Chinese. The African proportion comprised 65 percent and most of the rest was counted as mixed. By the time A. H. Marshall (1955) reported his study of local government in British Guiana, East Indians contributed 54 percent to the village population and the African proportion had declined to 37 percent. In 1960, the East Indian proportion of the rural population (including the population of sugar estates) was 60 percent compared to 25 percent for Africans.

While 93,000 Africans, compared to 379,000 East Indians, continue to live in rural areas, more than half of them are located in the East and West Demerara districts, where the best agricultural lands are occupied by sugar estates and much of the rest by East Indians. Being relatively close to Georgetown and its environs, most of the Africans living in these districts are directly or indirectly dependent upon sources of urban employment for their livelihood rather than agriculture. The agricultural lands they do work provide more by way of subsistence value to children, to the elderly, and to the unemployed than they provide by way of employment in the production of cash crops (Despres 1969: 33–37). Almost all of the coastal agricultural lands in Berbice and Essequibo have been taken up by East Indians.

In the face of these pressures, over the years Africans have turned increasingly to urban employment opportunities in order to secure some sort of resource base. As is shown in Table 1, in 1891 only 21 percent of the African population resided in urban areas, compared to 5 percent of the East Indian population. At the same time, Africans contributed 36 percent to the urban population, compared to the 8 percent contributed by East Indians. By 1960, almost half of all Africans resided in urban areas, and they comprised 50 percent of the urban population. If the mixed population, which sees itself as predominantly African, were to be included in these figures, the proportion of Africans in the urban population would increase to 71 percent.

Table 1. Africans and East Indians in urban population, 1891–1960

Period	Percentage of Africans in urban areas	Percentage of Indians in urban areas	African proportion of urban population	Indian proportion of urban population
1891	21	5	36	8
1911	28	6	42	11
1921	29	6	51	11
1931	34	7	54	12
1946	39	10	54	16
1960[a]	49	14	49	21

[a] In addition to Georgetown and New Amsterdam, figures for 1960 include the Mackenzie-Christanburg-Wismar (Upper Demerara River district) as an urban area. Were this area excluded, the rural-urban composition of Africans and their contribution to the urban population would remain approximately the same (49 percent), but the East Indian proportion of the urban population would increase to 23 percent. In other words, the inclusion of this district significantly expands the urban population base but because East Indians are more concentrated in Georgetown and New Amsterdam, it diminishes their contribution to the total urban population.

It should be noted also that in recent years the East Indian population has experienced considerable change in both size and distribution. Apparently as a result of the eradication of malaria in 1945, a disease that was endemic on the sugar estates, the East Indian population has virtually exploded. Between 1946 and 1960, the proportion of East Indians in the total population increased from 44 to 48 percent (it passed 50 percent in 1964), whereas it had increased less than one percent during the previous fifteen-year census period (1931–1946). At the same time, the African proportion of the total population decreased from 38 to 33 percent. Moreover, not all of this decline can be explained by a shift in African ethnic identity, because the proportion of mixed population increased from 10 to only 12 percent between 1946 and 1960. Attending this growth in the East Indian population has been a change in its distribution, probably related to the widespread unemployment that followed upon technological changes in the sugar industry after World War II. Thus, as shown in Table 1, while the number of Africans living in urban areas increased from 39 to 49 percent between 1946 and 1960, the African proportion of the urban population actually declined from 54 to 49 percent. On the other hand, the proportion of East Indians in the urban population increased from 16 to 21 percent.

All of this is to suggest that the resource competition that had obtained for more than a century between Africans and East Indians in rural areas has now become a feature of urban life as well. Perhaps the magnitude of this competition can be revealed in reference to the public service.

Although the available historical data are inadequate for the precise kind of comparisons that would be most useful, it is quite evident that the public service in Guyana has been a most important source of employment, particularly for urban Africans, during all of this century and much of the last. In 1891, for example, Africans and a few Europeans made up almost the entire teaching profession. As early as 1900, Africans comprised an overwhelming majority of the unpensionable staff in practically every department of the public service. In 1940, they represented 67 percent of all pensionable public servants. And by 1960, they ranked second only to Europeans among departmental heads in the public service. By way of contrast, in 1931, only 12 percent of all Guyanese professionals and public servants (6,202) were East Indians. Also in 1931, East Indians contributed only 7 percent to the 1,397 Guyanese employed in the teaching profession. As late as 1960, East Indians comprised but 16 percent of all pensionable civil servants and only six Indians, compared to twenty-six Africans, could be counted among the fifty-seven departmental heads.

Returning to the previously mentioned study of racial imbalances in the public service, Table 2 presents data indicating the extent to which this resource domain has been invaded recently by East Indians. Considering total employment by the government in 1964, Africans remained in the majority — 50.6 percent compared to almost 40 percent for East Indians. This figure, however, reflects the population of land development schemes in the rural sector, and East Indians comprise more than 85 percent of the population to whom these lands have been allocated.[6] Nevertheless, East Indians have increased their proportion of the public service from 12 percent in 1931 to 33 percent in 1964. They now represent almost 50 percent

---

[6] The allocation of newly developed agricultural lands, particularly to East Indian rice farmers and retrenched East Indian sugar workers, occurred primarily under the Jagan government between 1957 and 1963. In many instances these land development schemes incorporated Crown lands occupied by Africans whose leases had lapsed.

Table 2. Total racial percentages in the security forces, the civil service, government agencies and undertakings and areas of governmental responsibility[a]

Body	European	Portuguese	Indian	African	Amerindian	Mixed	Chinese	Others
The security forces	0.35	0.8	19.9	73.5	1.1	4.19	0.16	—
The civil service	0.29	0.76	33.16	53.05	2.08	9.52	1.15	—
Government agencies and undertakings	0.39	1.05	27.17	62.49	0.14	8.02	0.91	—
Local government	0.06	0.57	49.68	38.89	0.11	10.46	0.23	—
Teachers in primary education	—	1.72	41.27	53.87	1.06	1.46	0.58	0.04
Land development	—	0.4	85.49	13.06	0.17	0.66	0.11	0.11
Percentage of total	0.22	0.88	39.97	50.64	1.16	6.35	0.75	0.03

[a] The data reported in Table 2 have been adapted from figures given in the report of the British Guiana Commission of Inquiry, *Racial problems in the public service* (1965: 33).

of the persons employed in local government and they make up more than 41 percent of the teachers employed in primary education. It should be added that the number of teachers employed in government and government-aided primary and all-age schools is now 5,301, considerably more than the 1,397 employed in 1931. This mobility is even more remarkable when it is considered that most of it has occurred since 1950.

The pattern of mobility, however, has not been confined only to resource domains under the control of government. Still another important resource base for Africans has been the internal marketing system which, in Georgetown, is centered in three large marketplaces: Stabroek, Bourda, and La Penitence. In 1971, a survey of the records kept for persons required to pay rent on market stalls, trays, and the like was made in order to determine the ethnic composition of hucksters, peddlers, and stall proprietors as well as the size and types of enterprises in which they engaged. Comparative data were collected for 1960 and 1970 and, in order to provide some check on the records, an actual census of market operations was made for 1971.

Only some of the data in respect to Stabroek, the largest of the three markets, have been analyzed, but preliminary findings are in keeping with those reported above. In 1960, weekly or monthly rent was being paid on 623 enterprises in Stabroek. Of these, 48 percent were operated by Africans and 52 percent by East Indians. These figures are exclusive of the relatively small number of enterprises operated by Portuguese, Chinese, and others. By 1970, the number of enterprises for which rent was being paid had increased to 755. However, the enterprises operated by Africans had declined from 48 to 33 percent while those operated by East Indians increased from 52 to 67 percent. Perhaps of equal import is the observational impression, yet to be supported by a complete analysis of data, that Africans tend to operate the least substantial of these enterprises. They are more commonly observed operating sidewalk enterprises and selling from trays and boxes than occupying market shops and stalls.

It is clear from these data that, in respect to environmental resources in Guyana, categorically identified populations have been competitively aligned since early in the seventeenth century, when the Dutch West India Company first imported slaves from Africa for the purpose of developing its possessions. The plural character of this system deepened in the nineteenth century when, following emancipation, Portuguese, Chinese, additional Africans, and large numbers of East Indian indentured workers were imported by the British in order to maintain at a low level of cost the manpower resource requirements of an expanding mercantile economy based on plantation agriculture. All of these populations differed in their racial and cultural origins and they continued to differ as a consequence of their particular historical careers. Thus, while the ethnic identities ascribed to these populations are in part stereotypic, they are by no means entirely putative. Accordingly, such identities have persisted quite apart from the subjective inclination of particular individuals to assume a wide range of other social identities. Moreover, in respect to environmental resources, ethnic identities enjoin imperative statuses and these, in turn, disclose an order of inequality among the populations so identified. This order of inequality is no less evident today than at any time in Guyana's history. In support of this view, it is instructive to conclude this portion of the analysis with data revealing the position occupied by ethnic populations in the current Guyanese economy.

Table 3 reports the percentage contribution of various industries to the Gross Domestic Product (GDP) and to the employed labor force for the period 1964-1965. It may be noted from these data that six industries generate approximately 78 percent of the GDP and also contribute 78 percent to the employed labor force. These industries are: sugar and sugar processing, mining, distribution and trade, rice agriculture and mixed farming, services (particularly banking and insurance), and government. How Guyanese stand in relationship to these industries reveals not only that there is an order of inequality among individuals and groups but, more important for our purposes, that the individuals and groups so ordered cluster significantly within the categorical ethnic boundaries under discussion.

Table 3. Percentage contribution to the gross domestic product and employed labor force by industry[a]

Industry	Percent contribution to GDP (1964)	Percent contribution to employed labor force (1965)
Agriculture and food processing:		
Sugar	17.0	18
Rice	5.7	14
Other	5.2	7
Total Agriculture	(27.9)	(39)
Forestry	2.4	2
Fishing	1.9	2
Livestock	2.6	1
Mining	17.1	3
Manufacturing: other than food processing	3.3	5
Distribution	12.8	14
Transportation and communications	6.4	7
Construction	5.1	5
Services: rental, financial and other	10.2	3
Government	10.3	19
Total	100.0	100.0

[a] The data presented here in reference to the Gross Domestic Product have been abstracted from David (1969: 1–42). Data in regard to the employed labor force have been abstracted from various tables presented in the Ministry of Labour and Social Security's publication, *Survey of manpower requirements and the labour force* (1965).

It is difficult to define precisely the collective status which Europeans and other non-Guyanese enjoy by virtue of their relationship to the resources that these industries employ or generate. However, some indication of the situation is provided in an unpublished project proposal circulated by the Agency for International Development at the University of Guyana in 1970. Inter alia, the proposal stated that the importance of foreign control in these areas is indicated by the fact that for 1968 exports of sugar, molasses, rum, bauxite, and alumina totalled $89.1 million, or about 75 percent of total exports. In the same year the "investment income" line item in Guyana's balance of payments showed a net outflow of $17.7 million, largely reflecting the transfer of profits to overseas owners. The report continued: "In the raising and slaughtering of beef cattle, British interests account for about 20 percent of the national herd .... About 45 percent of the insurance business is in foreign hands. The local match company is British owned, and the local flour mill is American owned. Retailing and the import-export trade are both largely in foreign hands." In regard to banking, the report noted: "Except for the new National Cooperative Bank, commercial banking is entirely under foreign control, servicing sugar and distributive trades in an amount equal to about 66 percent of total credit extended to business firms. If credit extended to mining were identifiable, this percentage would, of course, be larger." And finally, the report emphasized: "A 1966 UN survey of manpower requirements indicated that there were about 500 expatriates employed in Guyana in the private sector, concentrated largely in professional and managerial positions." These expatriates and their families comprise a substantial proportion of Guyana's "white" population.

In response to political changes over the past ten years, the employment of Guyanese in the higher echelons of these industries has reduced the number of expatriates in the overall population. Nevertheless, these enterprises remain firmly in the hands of "whites."[7] By virtue of this control, "whites" disclose the characteristics of a corporate economic elite rather than those of a population element in a generalized social class structure. Regarding recruitment into this elite, national, ethnic, and/or racial criteria continue to be important quite apart from criteria of achievement. A variety of epithets — some racial, some ethnic, and some denoting social and political class — are applied by Guyanese to other Guyanese who work and live on the fringes of this elite.

An undetermined but certainly marginal proportion of the resources exploited and produced by these core industries are available to Guyanese, mostly by way of taxes, duties, and wages.[8] Such taxes, duties, and wages serve to differentiate ethnic populations. For example, while the bauxite industry contributes 17 percent to the GDP and only 3 percent to the employed labor force, 95 percent of all bauxite workers are African. Sugar, on the other hand, contributes as much to the GDP, but it contributes significantly more to the employed labor force (18 percent), and 85 percent of all sugar workers are East Indians. While rice agriculture and

---

[7]   The Demerara Bauxite Company is Guyana's largest producer of bauxite and alumina. Owned by Aluminium Ltd. of Canada (ALCAN), this company was nationalized in 1971. The politics of this take-over are extremely complicated but, in the end, the government of Guyana was forced to borrow substantial funds from the United States to maintain the company's inventory and it had to employ a South African marketing firm to gain access to the international bauxite market.

[8]   It is difficult to determine precisely how much the Guyanese actually derive from foreign-owned industries. In the case of bauxite, according to one generous estimate, Guyana realized over a fifty-year period 39 percent of the sale value of bauxite from the Demerara Bauxite Company in the form of taxes, duties, and wages. However, according to Guyana's Prime Minister, the amount quoted represents less than 3 percent of the total profits realized from Guyanese bauxite by Demba's parent firm, Aluminium Ltd. of Canada. The first percent was reported by Demba in the August 27, 1970, edition of the *Guyana Graphic*. The second percent was quoted in a speech by the Prime Minister, as reported in the February 25, 1971, edition of the *Guyana Graphic*. Because bauxite prices are fixed by the parent company according to its own calculations, the true value of the bauxite extracted by this firm may never be known.

mixed farming, including food processing, contribute less than 11 percent to the GDP, they contribute even more than does sugar to the employed labor force (21 percent). As previously indicated, these also are primarily domains of East Indian employment. Still another important source of employment is the distribution industry. It contributes 14 percent to the employed labor force. Much of this employment is taken up by the export-import trade, particulary in bauxite, sugar, and rice, and it provides work for dockworkers, most of whom are African. However, wholesale-retail trade is primarily in the hands of expatriate firms and East Indian merchants and shopkeepers. The latter particularly are inclined to give employment to East Indians.

Considering the imbalance of Indians and Africans employed in these core industries, it is not surprising that Africans comprise a majority of the unemployed in Guyana. It also is not surprising that they define their interests corporately and with particular reference to government. As an industry, the government generates 10 percent of the GDP and contributes 19 percent to the employed labor force. Thus, apart from agriculture, the government is the largest consumer of labor in the country. While all elements of the population look to the government for favors and support, the overwhelming majority of Africans view their control of the government as an absolute prerequisite of their economic survival. As a consequence, competition for the government and for the resources which the government commands is fierce among Africans and East Indians.

To summarize the situation in respect to the overall social system: Guyana has an economy encapsulated within the sphere of European, Canadian, and American domination. Its core industries are foreign-owned and controlled and they leave only a marginal share of the country's material resources unexpropriated and available to Guyanese. The whites who manage these industries are a group apart from the rest of the Guyanese. Over the years, the competitive allocation of Guyana's unexpropriated resources has served to order categorically identified elements of the Guyanese population in an arrangement of unequal status and power. Amerindians are marginal to the whole economy and they exist at the bottom of this stratification structure. Africans, on the other hand, are a sizeable population holding practically no investment in land or commercial enterprises. Outside the bauxite industry, Africans have had little security of employment except in the government service. Thus they have looked, and continue to look, to government for status. Because the East Indian population is made up of businessmen, merchants, shopkeepers, rice farmers, sugar workers, and, more recently, public servants, and in view of its size, Africans are very much inclined to consider the

East Indian population as a threat to their material well-being. East Indians, of course, express reciprocal views. So many racial diacritica attend ethnic identities that most of the mixed population has little choice but to identify with African interests. And finally, because of their number, their racial identity with Europeans, and their threatened position in the economy, the Portugese are of their own accord leaving the country.

2. Inevitably, the structure of inequality among ethnic populations in Guyana has promoted the organization of a variety of special interest groups and associations which, in turn, impart to ethnic group relations much of their political interface. Important among such groups have been the East Indian Association, the Sanatana Dharma Maha Sabha, the Arya Samaj, the Hindu Society, the United Sad'r Anjuman-E-Islam, the Islamic Association, the Muslim Youth Organization, the Sword of the Spirit (Portuguese), the Chinese Association, the Afro-American Association, the League of Coloured Peoples, the Mahatma Gandhi Organization, the Young Socialist Movement (African), and the Progressive Youth Organization (East Indian), to name but a few. Also important in this regard have been various business and professional associations, labor unions, and a variety of special interest organizations, such as the Sugar Producers Association and the Rice Producers Association. And perhaps more important than all of these are Guyana's ethnically based political parties, particularly the Indian-dominated Peoples Progressive Party and the African-dominated Peoples National Congress.

Given the limitations of space and the fact that the political activities of some of these associations are frequently concealed by intriguing alliances and all manner of rhetorical pronouncements, it is not possible to describe fully here the many ways in which such organizations have functioned to promote the exclusive interests of ethnic constituencies.[9] However, perhaps some feeling for the situation can be conveyed in reference to a few examples. Consider, first, the Rice Producers Association.

The Rice Producers Association (RPA) was established by authority of the legislature in 1946 (Ordinance Number 7) to represent the economic interests of rice farmers. In this capacity, the RPA not only negotiated prices for rice with the Guyana Marketing Board, a government-appointed statutory commission, but it secured various subsidies with which rice farmers were provided low cost seed, fertilizer, insecticide, and even gasoline. Although the officers of the RPA were elected by the farmers, invariably they were active members of the Peoples Progressive Party

---

[9] The organization and political activities of many of these associations have been described elsewhere (Despres 1967: 121–176, 221–267).

(PPP). By virtue of the close relationship between the RPA and PPP, the latter was able to secure public resources with which it promoted its political programs in the Indian community. Subsequently, when the Burnham government assumed power in 1965, efforts were made to break this link between the RPA and the PPP.

According to African informants, the Burnham government "bribed" a few Indian rice farmers and with their assistance organized the Guyana Rice Corporation. Ostensibly, as a public company, the Guyana Rice Corporation was designed to supersede the Guyana Development Company, a similar company that had been organized by the colonial government in the 1950's. However, by withdrawing subsidies from the Rice Producers Association and investing them in the new Guyana Rice Corporation, an organization ostensibly run by Indians but controlled by Africans, the resource link between the Peoples Progressive Party and East Indian rice farmers was effectively broken. In the meantime, the Rice Producers Association still negotiates prices on behalf of rice farmers with the government-appointed Rice Marketing Board. However, the RPA has failed to negotiate an increase in the price of rice for more than seven years under the Burnham government. This has driven many Indian rice farmers to give up some of the lands they have occupied, particularly the more marginal lands on which they paid rents. In 1970–1971, the rice industry was in a state of economic depression. Nevertheless, as one informant put it, "... if rice farmers want favors from the government they must learn to share with the Africans. After all, we once had most of the land they now occupy."

Africans in Guyana are inclined to view almost any form of corporate organization in the Indian community as somewhat of a threat to their political interests. This is particularly the case in respect to any association that might disclose ties with the Peoples Progressive Party. Thus, as a general strategy, the Burnham government and the Peoples National Congress have bent every effort to dissolve or otherwise disrupt whatever organizational links might exist between the PPP and various elements of the Indian community. The situation regarding the Rice Producers Association is one example of this strategy. Another may be provided in reference to the Maha Sabha.

The Maha Sabha is a religious association, ostensibly apolitical. However, since the 1950's, its officers have been politically active in the Peoples Progressive Party. In 1970, a power struggle developed within the Maha Sabha between its president and certain PPP activitists who felt the president was too closely associating himself with the Burnham government. Subsequently, the president arranged an election of officers in which only his delegates were allowed to participate. With the help of the police, who kept opposition delegates from invading the meeting, the president succeeded in having himself re-elected. The Burnham government moved immediately to have the president of the Maha Sabha appointed Speaker of the House in the Legislative Assembly. Moreover, contrary to traditional procedure, which is to appoint as Speaker a person acceptable to both the government and the opposition, this appointment was made without the consent of the opposition. As a consequence of these developments, while the PPP continues to maintain its support among the Maha Sabha's membership, it no longer controls the Maha Sabha's corporate offices. However, by virtue of its relationship to the Maha Sabha's president, the Peoples National Congress and the Burnham government have effectively disrupted an organization that once served to join important elements of the Indian community to the Peoples Progressive Party.

One of the most significant ethnic organizations to appear in recent years is the African Society for Cultural Relations with Independent Africa (ASCRIA). The forerunner of ASCRIA is the Society for Racial Equality, essentially a black separatist movement organized by Sidney King (now called Eusi Kwayana) in the early 1960's, when Guyana suffered wave upon wave of racial rioting and killing. As a separatist movement, the Society for Racial Equality sought to have Guyana partitioned into a consociation of three territorial units: one reserved for Africans, one for East Indians, and a third to contain a voluntarily mixed population of whites and non-whites, including Africans and Indians who might not want to live among their own. Failing to win support for this scheme, the Society for Racial Equality incorporated elements of the League of Coloured Peoples and reorganized itself as a black power movement.

To be sure, ASCRIA is militantly black. However, in defining black it combines elements of race, social class, and cultural elements that are visibly African. Membership rules are said to prescribe a six-month course in black studies as prerequisite for full membership status. As one member explained this requirement: "A black who does not think black is a 'redneck' and cannot belong to ASCRIA. A light colored person who thinks black can belong." East Indians, Portuguese, Chinese, Amerindians, or whites cannot belong at all. In keeping with these views, ASCRIA is dedicated to the revitalization of African culture. Thus, it maintains a rather extensive educational program, importing materials and sometimes teacher-volunteers from Africa and the United States. This educational program is based in Georgetown but it reaches into several rural areas of black population concentration. It offers lectures in history, journalism, economics, cooperative organization, and even agricultural practice. It encourages the adoption of African names, values, and dress. It also encourages the use of what are thought to be African rituals in regard to religious practice, weddings, funerals, and other celebrations. And it discourages close associational ties between blacks and other elements of the population, particularly whites.

If ASCRIA were simply a cultural revitalization movement it probably would not be of much concern to other Guyanese. However, this is not the case; ASCRIA is also a political and economic movement with considerable muscle. Its membership is required to be active on many fronts and in 1970 its active membership was estimated to be in excess of 2,000 Africans and still growing. By 1971, at Mackenzie, ASCRIA had assumed such complete control of African bauxite workers that the president of the Guyana Mine Workers Union could not attend a meeting of his own union without ASCRIA's consent. Many of ASCRIA's members are prominently placed in government and in such public corporations as the National Bank of Guyana and the National Co-operative Bank. In 1970–1971, ASCRIA's coordinating elder, Eusi Kwayana, chaired the National Land Settlement Committee and the Executive Board of the National Marketing Corporation. In addition to these and other positions, he also served as a close advisor to the Prime Minister.

Apart from rhetoric and loose ideological pronouncements, ASCRIA's political program is quite clear in its intent and purpose. As ASCRIA defines the situation, all Guyanese have been exploited by British colonialism and American imperialism. In addition, Afro-Guyanese have been further exploited and discriminated against by East Indians and the Portuguese. Because of this, Afro-Guyanese are forced to struggle with poverty and unemployment at the bottom of the power structure. Accordingly, from ASCRIA's point of view, this situation must be changed. Africans have to be re-established on the land, and it makes little difference whether it is land presently occupied, by the sugar industry or by East Indians, or new land in the interior. Africans have to be given an equal share in business, in government, and in other resource opportunities. Again, it makes little difference whether they assume control of enterprises presently owned by Europeans, Indians, and Portuguese, or they are given control of new enterprises developed with government assistance.

In order to accomplish these things, according to ASCRIA, Africans must assert their own independent cultural identity. They must draw upon the historical traditions that are being drawn upon by such contemporary African leaders as Jules Nyerere. They must be educated in the techniques of communal or cooperative management. And above all, at least in the foreseeable future, Africans must retain control of the government.

The close relationship between ASCRIA, the People's National Congress (PNC), and the Burnham government is a source of considerable anxiety among ethnic populations in Guyana.[10] In 1970–1971, many Guyanese would have been inclined to agree with the view expressed by one informant: "Burnham is ASCRIA as much as Eusi Kwayana is ASCRIA. ASCRIA is the cultural and economic arm of the government: the PNC is its political arm." Charges of ethnic and racial discrimination were both prevalent and widespread, particularly in the East Indian community. Thus, in November of 1970, still another association came into being. It called itself the Anti-Discrimination Movement (ADM). Organized and financed primarily by East Indian businessmen and professionals, its leaders held public meetings at which they proclaimed themselves opposed to "gross acts of discrimination and corruption at all levels of the government." The ADM published a weekly, called *Liberator*, which it distributed freely in all parts of the country. By May of 1971, many African political leaders believed that the ADM either was an instrument of the Peoples Progressive Party or that it was in the process of giving birth to a new East Indian political party.

This type of organized interface among ethnic populations can be found in most parts of the society and among virtually all elements of the population. It can be found even among university students. For example, at the end of the 1970 academic year, three groups contested the elections for student government at the University of Guyana. One comprised an all-Indian slate of candidates, another an all-African slate, and the third group presented a carefully balanced slate of Africans and East Indians. As it happened, the all-Indian slate won the election. Subsequently, Africans from the balanced slate accused the Indian candidates with whom they ran of having secretly campaigned in favor of the all-Indian slate. Eventually, a petition was circulated among African students requesting that the vice-chancellor of the university declare the election null and void for a variety of manufactured reasons. The following academic year, 1970–1971, this issue was kept alive and it served to divide the student body for the entire year in respect to every program which the student government sponsored. Student strikes were threatened unless the vice-chancellor moved to resolve the problem. However, his hands were tied

---

[10]   The anxiety which ASCRIA has generated among East Indians is such that even the notable East Indian historian Dwarka Nath (1970: 209–214) felt compelled to address the problem in a postscript to his revised history of the East Indian population in Guyana. Nath considers the relationship between Indians and Africans in Trinidad much less explosive and much less infused with racialism than is the case in Guyana.

by the fact that the election had been properly conducted under the supervision of faculty from the Department of Political Science. In the end, the situation resolved itself when a factional dispute developed within the student government over the misappropriation of funds. This provided the vice-chancellor with an opportunity to remove the student president from office and put the student government in the hands of the university administration until books could be audited and new elections scheduled on the basis of PROPORTIONATE REPRESENTATION.

To summarize, the competition for resources in Guyana has served to order categorically identified populations in a system of unequal status and power. As a consequence, the identities of the populations so ordered have become politically charged. Thus, they have provided a basis for the corporate organization of a variety of ethnically exclusive groups and associations. As these groups and associations seek to secure resources for the constituencies they purport to represent, they must also seek to disrupt the order of inequality that obtains among ethnic populations. In the process, however, such groups not only reinforce the ethnic identities according to which their membership is recruited, but they also serve to align competitively those corporately organized segments of the populations from which their membership is drawn. It remains to be shown how these developments relate to individual inter-ethnic encounters.

3.   It has been noted elsewhere (Despres i.p.) that, viewed from the vantage point of individual encounters, ethnic relations in Guyana assume dimensions that do not make readily apparent the structure of inequality that has been previously described. Social interaction is commonplace among all elements of the general population. In the markets and shops, in government offices, at various places of work, in the schools, at public celebrations, at cricket and football matches or the like, and sometimes in private homes one can observe Guyanese of virtually all ethnic categories interacting, and it does not appear immediately that their behavior is in any way modified by ethnic identities or the imperative statuses that might attach to such identities.

Gradually, however, this general impression begins to change. It may begin with observations at the seawall where people gather to enjoy the evening breezes, or in the Botanical Gardens where couples and families take Sunday afternoon walks. On these occasions, it will be observed that Africans and Indians sit or walk separately and they do not frequently greet one another or join in conversation. Where people dine in public places, particularly where they also dance, but even in the university cafeteria, groups are inclined to be ethnically exclusive. Friends who meet one another at the cinema, the band concert, or on the street are usually of the same ethnic category. So also are the peer groups that walk the streets after school. Then, at the barber shop or some other casual setting where one may be engaged in semi-private conversation, it may be detected how easily the subject swings, without prompting, to matters having to do with ethnic populations and their differences. On such occasions, one may also note how the substance of conversation changes according to who the speaker is and what other persons happen to be in hearing distance. Then, even in private conversation with a doctor, a dentist, a barrister, or a school teacher, the ease with which disparaging remarks are drawn in respect to one ethnic group or another cannot pass undetected.

The observer need not search out these episodes. They will engage his attention at the filling station, the dry-cleaning establishment, the market stall, or the faculty lounge. He will observe them also at the Police Officers Club, the Georgetown Club, the Army Staff Club, the Civil Service Association Club, or at a luncheon meeting of the Rotarians. A casual mention of virtually any subject, whether it be automobiles, cricket, the Mashramani celebration, housing, the cost of living, seawall construction, or even the bloom in the Botanical Gardens, may elicit an unexpected ethnic remark or a drawn out commentary on ethnic politics or the comparative achievement of ethnic populations. For example, a comment on the bloom in the Botanical Gardens caused a filling station attendant to give a five-minute lecture on how the Gardens had deteriorated because the Burnham government had attached a section of the Gardens to the Prime Minister's private residence "for the purpose of entertaining the African masses." Of course, Africans are not the only people the Prime Minister entertains but it is true that his residence incorporates a section of the Gardens which is no longer accessible to the general public.

Clearly, the occasions of inter-ethnic encounters are not only episodic but they are also extremely variable in respect to situation, circumstance, and personnel. This makes their structuring difficult to discern. Nevertheless, as observations are drawn together, it is evident that such encounters disclose a generalized pattern. A few selected examples may serve to illuminate the characteristics of this pattern.

First, in most situations involving non-Guyanese and Guyanese of different ethnic origins, Guyanese of virtually every category tend to obfuscate or submerge their respective ethnic identities in favor of asserting a common national identity. The imperative status that becomes operative under such circumstances incorporates all Guyanese in a manner as to suggest that as a people Guyanese conduct themselves in terms of values that clearly set them apart from non-nationals, particularly Europeans,

Americans, and Canadians. Even other West Indians are given to understand that the Guyanese are nationals to be differentiated from Jamaicans, Trinidadians, or Barbadians. Of course, this national identity, and the imperative status that attaches to it, is reinforced by constitutionally defined legal codes.

In other situations, for example a public meeting sponsored by a new and somewhat radical political group called Movement Against Oppression (MAO), it may be observed that Guyanese of different ethnic origins will merge their respective ethnic identities in opposition to other Guyanese, also of different ethnic origins, who are epithetically labeled as "white niggers," "house slaves," or "red people." This latter group may include East Indians, Afro-Guyanese, Guyanese of mixed ancestry, Portuguese, and Chinese. Collectively, they form a special status category because of their relationship to Europeans or because of their style of life. This group is thought to discriminate against other Guyanese by virtue of their exploitive economic practices and also in terms of their associational proclivities.

What emerges in this instance is an imperative social class status which combines in its definition phenotypical images and cultural diacritica. This is reminiscent of the color-class continuum that has been reported to be widespread in the West Indies (Lewis 1968; R. T. Smith 1970: 43–76; Lowenthal 1972). When it is observed that the distribution of resources is more perfectly correlated with generalized ethnic identities than with specifically defined phenotypical and cultural diacritica, it seems rather difficult to attribute pervasive structural significance to a color-class continuum. For example, at the meeting reported above, there were forty-four people in attendance, including two whites (one Portuguese and one European married to an Afro-Guyanese), seven East Indians, and at least five persons that might easily have been considered mixed. None of these people identified themselves as "white niggers" or "red people," nor were they considered as such by the rest of the group.

These and other observations suggest that elements of a color-class differentiation are perhaps functional, particularly in situational contexts where the submergence of ethnic identities facilitates interaction among persons who have in common something more important than their ethnic differences. More specifically, in the situation cited, ethnic identities were submerged by the assertion of a more generalized "white/non-white" dichotomy which is thought by many Guyanese, including certain ideologically inclined intellectuals, to correspond to a historically derived pattern of economic exploitation in terms of which particular phenotypical images and life styles tend to be associated with certain status groups, particularly Europeans. Thus, the use of such images facilitates interaction among ethnically diverse Guyanese who commonly see themselves apart from such status groups. In other situations, these very same Guyanese may be observed asserting their respective African, East Indian, or Portuguese ethnic identities rather than a generalized identity expressive of their common economic status.

In still other situations, specifically those involving encounters among persons of only two ethnic groups, ethnic identities are asserted to lay claim to special status consideration. The effect of this is to declare the opposition of the group with which one identifies to a third group, no member of which is participating in the encounter. Accordingly, it frequently may be observed that when one or two Africans, or alternatively one or two East Indians, are interacting with non-Guyanese, they will seize the opportunity to assert their African or, as the case may be, their Indian identity by drawing negative stereotypes in reference to a population not represented in the encounter. Similarly, when East Indians have encounters with Portuguese, negative reference may be made to Africans. The variations on this type of episode seem endless but, always, they seem to involve a special status claim for the collectivity with which one identifies.

Invariably, status claims arising from one ethnic identity serve to diminish the claims arising from another. Thus, less commonly observed are situations in which individuals of different ethnic origins counterpose their respective ethnic identities. When such situations are observed, they generally occasion a verbal or a physical quarrel. The exception is when one party to the encounter ignores or dismisses the claim asserted by the other, often in a joking manner. An increasingly common variant on this pattern is when members of militant ethnic associations, ASCRIA for example, seize opportunities to express their militancy. This often occurs in contexts that are organized and, therefore, under control. Under such circumstances, the assertion of conflicting ethnic claims is usually ignored rather than rebutted by persons who might otherwise rise to the offense.

It is evident from these few illustrations that sensitivity to ethnic claims and identities tends to be rather pervasive in Guyana. As a consequence, a rather elaborate code of etiquette has developed in respect to interethnic encounters. The details of this code are imperfectly known but it becomes readily apparent to even the most casual observer that on most occasions it is simply impolite to assert ethnic identities. Such assertions almost always involve claims which diminish the status of one group or another. Thus, unless the situation is appropriate, the assertion of an ethnic identity can be a source of embarrassment to the individual who asserts it. In view of these circumstances, unless observation is more than superficial, it would seem that ethnic identities are more apparent than real and that such identities do not enjoin imperative statuses affecting the interaction of individuals and groups. As suggested here, the opposite is the case.

The question remains: What kinds of situations tend to evoke the assertion of ethnic identities and claims? To answer this, it must be kept in mind that the assertion of such claims establishes a mode of competitive opposition between one ethnic group and another. And invariably, when such a mode of competitive opposition is effected, it reflects upon the fundamental status inequalities that have been previously described. Accordingly, situations which call into question the rights, privileges, and entitlements that are thought to attend the status inequalities existing among ethnic populations, or situations that give issue to the resource allocations from which these inequalities derive, tend to evoke ethnic identities and claims in respect to individual encounters.

The overall pattern that emerges from all of this is one of segmentary opposition. That is to say, some situations evoke national claims which override the claims of ethnic populations. In these situations, the status claims of all Guyanese are joined in opposition to Europeans, Americans, Canadians, and even other West Indians. Some situations bring into focus claims which serve to join Africans and East Indians in opposition to other ethnic and/or racial elements. Still other situations summon forth claims that divide individual Africans and East Indians in opposition to one another. In fact, when some Africans refer to other Africans as "red people," an epithet which combines racial and cultural criteria to define a generalized social class status, it needs to be recognized that some situations evoke identities that serve to divide Africans among themselves. For the most part, this pattern of segmentary opposition corresponds to and reflects both the continuities and discontinuities which the differential incorporation of ethnic populations enjoins in the overall structure of Guyanese society.

4. To summarize the situation regarding ethnicity and resource competition in Guyana, it may be stated that practically all Guyanese declare themselves in support of a political system which defines the rights and obligations of citizenship without reference to ethnic considerations. In fact, such considerations are absolutely proscribed by Guyana's present constitution. However, for reasons that have been stated, this pattern of universal incorporation does not obtain. Rather, since early in the seventeenth century, competition for resources in Guyana has served to order

a system of inequality in terms of which categorically differentiated populations have been joined in competitive opposition. Accordingly, most Guyanese are inclined to view their society as one comprised of diverse ethnic and/or racial collectivities of unequal status and power.

The cultural and sometimes phenotypical diacritica which Guyanese use to identify these ethnic collectivities are stereotypic, but they are by no means completely devoid of historical foundation and empirical significance. The populations to which such diacritica are applied are populations of different origin. During the course of Guyana's colonial history, these populations have been differentially exploited and they have differentially adapted to the conditions of their exploitation. This process of differential adaptation, in turn, has been productive of cultural developments which also facilitate the categorical identity of these populations. Similarly, the inequalities of status which Guyanese ascribe to these ethnic populations are real inequalities when measured against the material resources they command. And it is a fact that both within and across various resource domains these ethnic populations continue to be competitively aligned.

Over the years, the competitive alignment of ethnic populations in Guyana has been productive of considerable tension and conflict. In response to this, and in an effort to achieve stability, particularly in recent times, both colonial and independent Guyanese governments have been inclined to concede to ethnic populations corporate, but equal, entitlements in the public domain.[11] In other words, in the absence of universal incorporation, ethnic populations have been accorded consociational status. However, the definition of what in fact constitutes equal entitlements is a matter on which there exists a great deal of ethnic dissension. This dissension has contributed significantly to the corporate or political organization of the ethnic populations in question.

Thus, existing between the overall structure of Guyanese society and the level of individual encounters is a variety of groups and associations that seek to promote the corporate interests of ethnic populations. These include political parties, ethnic organizations, business and professional associations, religious societies, and in some instances labor unions. The

[11]   One example of this is the constitutional provision for an electoral system based on proportionate representation. This provision was prescribed by the British in Guyana's independence constitution and it has been maintained by subsequent Guyanese governments. Although proportionality is calculated on the basis of votes achieved by political parties and not on the basis of ethnicity, it was the ethnic organization of political parties which prompted the adoption of this electoral system in the first place. Proportionate representation tends to secure a competitive position for the African population which comprises a large minority vis-à-vis the East Indian population.

public interests of some of these groups are avowedly ethnic while the ethnic interests of others are disguised by constitutional charters and public rhetoric. Some of these groups and associations have been more successful than others in achieving their objectives and, therefore, they have been more continuous in their efforts. These groups also vary in the extent of their organization and the size of their active membership. However, quite apart from these variable features, the political and economic activities of such organizations as ASCRIA and the Anti-Discrimination Movement simultaneously bring into sharp focus the corporate interests of ethnic populations and the competition for resources that obtains among them.

It follows from these considerations that ethnicity in Guyana enjoins a system of ascribed statuses of considerable historical depth. This system has been particularly functional in respect to the competition for material resources. However, the persistence of this system has not precluded the development of still another status system according to which individual Guyanese are socially differentiated in reference to their particular achievements. These two status systems are entangled but they are not coterminous. Thus, quite apart from their respective ethnic identities, individual Guyanese may assert a relatively wide range of other social identities. Whether or not particular Guyanese will suppress some or all of these other status identities in favor of asserting claims which attach to their ethnic status is largely a function of the circumstances surrounding different interactional situations.

To state the matter differently, the domain of individual transactions is both situational and episodic but it is not without patterning. Ethnic identities and status claims enter selectively into this domain in that they tend to be asserted whenever circumstances bring into focus the status inequalities that exist among ethnic populations. The pattern is characteristically one of segmentary opposition. It corresponds to and reflects both the continuities and discontinuities between the two status systems under discussion. And it would appear that these two status systems will persist in Guyana as long as ethnicity confers upon individual Guyanese competitive advantage in respect to material resources.

5. It is not the better part of wisdom to generalize too extensively from a single case. However, among anthropologists, it is a *sine qua non* that case studies have heuristic value for comparative purposes. Thus, it is appropriate to conclude this analysis with considerations of a more general nature.

Perhaps the most difficult questions that may be posed regarding ethnicity and ethnic group relations are questions that have to do with the problem of ethnogenesis. Why do populations come to be culturally differentiated in the first place? Why do such differentiations persist? Under what circumstances might we expect ethnic collectivities to become corporately, or politically, organized? What forces tend to promote the differential incorporation of ethnic populations within the all-inclusive public domain? In other words, when and under what conditions will ethnic populations become the object, de jure or de facto, of political discrimination?

At the risk of oversimplification, research in regard to the problem of ethnogenesis is particularly informed by three theoretical orientations which are current in anthropology. Following Barth, one approach directs our attention to the interactional processes by which ethnic boundaries are defined and made operative. The focus of investigation is the ethnic boundary that defines the group and not, as Barth (1969: 15) notes, "the cultural stuff that it encloses." This is not to minimize the fact that ethnic groups only persist as significant units when they disclose marked cultural differences. Rather, it is to emphasize that such cultural differences presuppose a structuring of interaction: they presuppose a relatively stable set of prescriptions and proscriptions governing situations of contact. It is consistent with this approach that ethnic groups cannot be adequately delineated in reference to historically derived cultural systems. Except perhaps for brief historical moments, such systems tend to transcend group boundaries. Moreover, ethnic boundaries often express cultural differences that are more putative than real in an historical sense. Thus, it is also consistent with this approach that the essential feature of ethnicity is its ascriptive character. For example, Barth states: "To the extent that actors use ethnic identities to categorize themselves and others for purposes of interaction, they form ethnic groups in this organizational sense" (1969: 13–14).

A second approach to the study of ethnogenesis may be derived from the work of those anthropologists who have been concerned primarily with the plural features and overall structure of multi-ethnic societies. The conceptions of social and cultural pluralism which inform this orientation are attributed to Furnivall (1939, 1942, 1948), an economist who was struck by the ethnic divisions characteristic of Southeast Asian societies. However, the leading exponent of this approach among anthropologists has been M. G. Smith (1957: 439–447, 1960: 763–777, 1965). Without belaboring conceptual problems that have been thoroughly worked over in the literature, the critical focus of the plural society approach lies in the institutional orders which presumably attend the interactional process of which Barth writes.[12] These institutional orders are taken to be expressive of cultural systems. These systems, in turn, serve not only to differentiate populations which may be called ethnic, but they serve also to delineate the system of relationships that exists both within and across these populations.[13]

Still another approach to the study of ethnogenesis may be derived from the work of anthropological ecologists who have underscored the relationship of material resources to the evolution of cultural systems.[14] In the context of ecological research, cultural systems are viewed as trans-generational behavioral codes, the organization and persistence of which disclose processes of adaptive selection. Regarding the evolution of such codes, it is neither necessary nor logical to assume that those which persist are entirely adaptive or maladaptive, functionally unified, or internally consistent in their institutional organization and expression. Nor is it necessary to assume that these codes are impervious to the influence of individuals. Probably to a significant degree, the adaptive selection of these behavioral codes is a function of factors influencing the extent to which they impede or facilitate the acquisition of environmental resources.

It is not appropriate in the present context to elaborate the merits and limitations of these theoretical orientations. However, assuming a culture to be a set of ways of occupying and using an environment, it follows that a population will become culturally differentiated to the extent that segments of that population differentially exploit whatever resources are available in the same environment. Building upon this assumption, and combining elements derived from each of the three approaches under discussion, generalizations of invariant order may be ventured in respect to the conditions that seem to favor the genesis and persistence of ethnic ascriptions and status identities for the purpose of organizing certain relationships among groups as well as among individuals. Phrased in the form of hypotheses, such generalizations may be stated as follows:

a.   A system of ascribed ethnic statuses will follow the differential adaptation of population segments and persist to the extent that the assertion

---

[12]   For a discussion of these conceptual problems, see M. G. Smith's most recent statement (1969: 415–458).

[13]   It should be noted that M. G. Smith (1969: 427–430) does not equate social and cultural pluralism with ethnic or racial differences, nor does he consider such differences as sufficient or requisite features of social orders based on sectional disjunctions and inequalities.

[14]   The literature on human and cultural ecology is too extensive to relate. However, the views expressed here have been particularly informed by the following: Harris (1964); Alland (1967); Vayda and Rappaport (1968); Geertz (1968); Bennett (1965, 1969); and Vayda (1969).

of ethnic identities serves to confer competitive advantage in respect to environmental resources.

b.   Ethnic identities will tend to confer competitive advantage in respect to resources when (1) the quantity of resources available is severely limited relative to demand and (2) the accessibility of such resources does not require individual command of complex technological skills and knowledge.

c.   Whenever resource domains vary significantly in the complexity of their technological requirements, there will exist corresponding systems of status ascription and status achievement. The coexistence of such systems will engage a pattern of structural continuities and discontinuities according to which ethnic status claims will enter selectively into the domain of interpersonal transactions.

d.   To the extent that phenotypical, rather than cultural, diacritica attend the expression of ethnic identities, boundaries will remain rigid and boundary crossing will be minimized.

e.   The selective advantage of pluralism in a differentiated but relatively stable techno-environment is the reduction of competition among populations for which ethnicity confers competitive advantage.

f.   The corporate or political organization of ethnic populations will follow upon any techno-environmental changes that are productive of increased competition both within and across varying resource domains.

g.   Finally, the differential incorporation of ethnic populations will obtain to the extent that one population segment succeeds in monopolizing control of all resource domains within any circumscribed environment.

Obviously, the validity and comparative utility of these generalizations need to be established. By way of conclusion, and without recapitulating what has been previously summarized, it is suggested that the data in respect to Guyana are sufficiently supportive of these generalizations as to commend their further discussion among social scientists interested in the comparative study of ethnic phenomena.

REFERENCES

ALLAND, ALEXANDER, JR.
    1967   *Evolution and human behavior*. Garden City: The Natural History Press.
BANTON, MICHAEL
    1967   *Race relations*. New York: Basic Books.
BARTH, FREDRIK
    1969   "Introduction," in *Ethnic groups and boundaries*. Edited by Fredrik Barth, 9–38. Boston: Little, Brown.

BENNETT, JOHN W.

1965 "Ecology in anthropological and ethnological sciences: man-culture-habitat relationship," in *Proceedings of the Eighth International Congress of Anthropological and Ethnological Sciences*, 237–241.

1969 *Northern plainsmen, adaptive strategy and agrarian life*. Chicago: Aldine.

BRAITHWAITE, LLOYD

1960 "Social stratification and cultural pluralism," in *Social and cultural pluralism in the Caribbean*. Edited by Vera Rubin, 816–831. Annals of the New York Academy of Sciences 83.

BRITISH GUIANA COMMISSION OF INQUIRY

1965 *Racial problems in the public service*. Report of the British Guiana Commission of Inquiry. Geneva: International Commission of Jurists.

BURNHAM, FORBES

1970 *A destiny to mould*. Trinidad and Jamaica: Longman Caribbean.

COHEN, RONALD, JOHN MIDDLETON

1970 "Introduction," in *From tribe to nation in Africa: Studies in corporation processes*. Edited by Ronald Cohen and John Middleton, 1–34. Scranton: Chandler.

CROSS, MALCOLM

1968 Cultural pluralism and sociological theory: a critique and re-evaluation. *Social and Economic Studies* 18:381–397.

DAVID, WILFRED

1969 *The economic development of Guyana 1953–1964*. London: Clarendon Press.

DESPRES, LEO A.

1967 *Cultural pluralism and nationalist politics in British Guiana*. Chicago: Rand-McNally.

1968 Anthropological theory, cultural pluralism, and the study of complex societies. *Current Anthropology* 9:3–26.

1969 Differential adaptations and micro-cultural evolution in Guyana. *Southwestern Journal of Anthropology* 25:14–44.

i.p. "Ethnicity and ethnic group relations in Guyana," in *Proceedings of the American Ethnological Society*, 1973.

FURNIVALL, J. S.

1939 *Netherlands India: a study of plural economy*. Cambridge: Cambridge University Press.

1942 The political economy of the tropical Far East. *Journal of the Royal Central Asiatic Society* 29:195–210.

1948 *Colonial policy and practice: a comparative study of Burma and Netherlands India*. London: Cambridge University Press.

GEERTZ, CLIFFORD

1968 *Agricultural involution: the processes of ecological change in Indonesia*. Berkeley and Los Angeles: University of California Press.

GUYANA GRAPHIC

1970 Article appearing in the *Guyana Graphic*, August 27.

1971 Article appearing in the *Guyana Graphic*, February 25.

HARRIS, MARVIN

1964 *Patterns of race in the Americas*. New York: Walker.

HOETINK, H.
  1967 *The two variants in Caribbean race relations: a contribution to the sociology of segmented societies.* London: Oxford University Press.
KUPER, LEO, M. G. SMITH, editors
  1969 *Pluralism in Africa.* Berkeley and Los Angeles: University of California Press.
LEWIS, GORDON K.
  1968 *The growth of the modern West Indies.* London: MacGibbon and Kee.
LOWENTHAL, DAVID
  1972 *West Indian societies.* New York: Oxford University Press.
MARSHALL, A. H.
  1955 *Report on local government in British Guiana.* Georgetown: Argosy.
MARSHALL, LORNA
  1960 !Kung Bushman bands. *Africa* 30:325-355.
  1965 "The !Kung Bushmen of the Kalahari Desert", in *Peoples of Africa.* Edited by James L. Gibbs, Jr., 241-278. New York: Holt, Rinehart and Winston.
MINISTRY OF LABOUR AND SOCIAL SECURITY
  1965 *Human resources in Guiana,* volume two: *Manpower requirements and the labour force.* Georgetown, Guiana: Ministry of Labour and Social Security.
NARROLL, R.
  1964 On ethnic unit classification. *Current Anthropology* 5:283-312.
NASH, M.
  1957 The multiple society in economic development: Mexico and Guatemala. *American Anthropologist* 59:825-838.
NATH, DWARKA
  1970 *A history of Indians in Guyana.* London: published by the author.
RADCLIFFE-BROWN, A. R.
  1940 "On social structure," reprinted in *Structure and function in primitive society,* by A. R. Radcliffe-Brown, 184-204. London: Cohen and West.
SCHERMERHORN, RICHARD A.
  1970 *Comparative ethnic relations: a framework for theory and research.* New York: Random House.
SHIBUTANI, TAMOTSU, KIAN M. KWAN
  1965 *Ethnic stratification.* New York: Macmillan.
SJOBERG, GIDEON
  1952 Folk and feudal societies. *American Journal of Sociology* 58:231-239.
SMITH, M.G.
  1957 "Ethnic and cultural pluralism in the British Caribbean," in *Ethnic and cultural pluralism in intertropical countries,* 439-447. Brussels: INCIDI.
  1960 "Social and cultural pluralism," in *Social and cultural pluralism in the Caribbean.* Edited by Vera Rubin, 763-777. Annals of the New York Academy of Sciences 83.
  1965 *The plural society in the British West Indies.* Berkeley and Los Angeles: University of California Press.
  1969 "Some developments in the analytic framework of pluralism," in *Pluralism in Africa.* Edited by Leo Kuper and M. G. Smith, 415-458. Berkeley and Los Angeles: University of California Press.

SMITH, RAYMOND T.
   1962   *British Guiana.* London: Oxford University Press.
   1970   "Social stratification in the Caribbean," in *Essays in comparative
          social stratification.* Edited by Leonard Poltnicov and Arthur Tuden
          43–76. Pittsburgh: University of Pittsburgh Press.
SPECKMAN, J. D.
   1963   The Indian group in the segmented society of Surinam. *Caribbean
          Studies* 3:3–17.
VAN DEN BERGHE, PIERRE L.
   1967   *Race and racism: a comparative perspective.* New York: John Wiley
          and Sons.
   1970   *Race and ethnicity.* New York: Basic Books.
VAN LIER, R. A. J.
   1950   *The development and nature of society in the West Indies.* Amsterdam:
          Royal Institute for the Indies.
VAYDA, ANDREW P., *editor*
   1969   *Environment and cultural behavior, ecological studies in cultural
          anthropology.* Garden City: The Natural History Press.
VAYDA, ANDREW P., ROY A. RAPPAPORT
   1968   "Ecology, cultural and non-cultural," in *Introduction to cultural
          anthropology.* Edited by James A. Clifton, 476–497. New York:
          Houghton Mifflin.
YOUNG, ALLAN
   1958   *The approaches to local self-government in British Guiana.* London:
          Longmans.
ZUBAIDA, SAMI, *editor*
   1970   *Race and racialism.* London: Tavistock.

Resource Competition and Inter-Ethnic Relations in Nigeria

ONIGU OTITE

Marx's theory of economic determinism in human relationships is generally interpreted as a conflict theory of social change. This theory is often analyzed in the context of social classes and with reference to industrialized societies. It is equally legitimate, however, to relate this theory to ethnic stratification as an important form of social differentiation, particularly in the new states of Africa and Asia. There is a strong, though often neglected, case for explaining ethnic relations in the context of Marx's conflict theory.

Although some sociologists argue that conflict, rather than consensus, increases the pace of social change, it is also to be argued that social change causes conflicts. Hence the processes of colonization by which ethnic groups were regrouped arbitrarily into new polities in nineteenth-century Africa and Asia resulted in increased ethnic interactions under a new distribution of power and under discovered differentials in economic opportunities. Differential access to political and economic structures is a feature of plural society, which is nevertheless held together mainly because its ethnic structural elements produce a balance of positive results over the dysfunctional consequences of their separate and conflicting interests.

Plural societies have a diversity of institutions, each of which consists of social and cultural aspects; there is no necessary boundary coincidence between these two aspects (Kuper 1971: 12; Smith 1971: 34–35). Cultural pluralism implies a diversity of culture-bound occupations in varying economic situations and environments. The relation of culture to economic pluralism has been noted by Furnivall (1948: 304) who stated that: "Even in the economic sphere, there is a division of labour along racial lines."

Culture-bound occupations are a tendency particularly among rural peoples (Richards 1956: 22; Otite i.p.), and the incidence of greater ethnic interactions breeds conflicts in social relations owing to scarcity of resources in different economic regions and to adaptations and changes in economic spheres.

These economic orientations exacerbate ethnicity, defined as discriminations and strife based on differences in inter-ethnic symbols. Ethnic differences exist in most countries but these differences would be insignificant if they were not also connected to processes and opportunities for economic survival. Thus ethnicity occurs not because both society and its culture are isolated from others but because frequent interactions sustain sociocultural diversity in a new polity. That is, paradoxically, economy-based conflicts and boundary-breaking activities may lead to ethnic boundary consolidation. Ethnicity is, thus, both the cause and the effect of ethnic boundary formation and maintenance.

The maintenance of ethnic boundaries is a function of changing ethnic ascriptive criteria and group exclusivity. As Barth points out:

Where one ethnic group has control of the means of production utilized by another group, a relationship of inequality and stratification obtains ... [that is] ... stratified poly-ethnic systems exist where groups are characterised by differential control of assets that are valued by all groups in the system (1969: 27).

A study of inter-ethnic relations must therefore account for the unequal access to the sources and opportunities for economic survival. This point is of particular relevance in rural communities in which land is a coveted economic resource.

The above discussion is relevant to an analysis of Nigeria, which is estimated to consist of about 250 ethnic groups (this number is the subject of current research) which were politically incorporated by the colonial powers on January 1, 1914. Nigeria became independent on October 1, 1960. About 80 percent of the members of its ethnic groups live in rural areas, where the primary concern is with agriculture carried on through low-level indigenous techniques.

The remainder of this paper summarizes data relating to ethnicity and resource competition and derived from case studies carried out in the Western and Mid-Western States of Nigeria. Three cases are presented. The first involves Ikale landowners who act as hosts to rural Urhobo immigrants in the Okitipupa Division. The second concerns inter-ethnic relations among the Kwale and Urhobo populations living in Orogun, a rural town located in the Mid-Western State. The third case focuses on the city of Ibadan, where inter-ethnic relations are influenced by the differential access which members of different ethnic groups have to economic opportunities and trade commodities.

THE IKALE/YORUBA AND THEIR GUESTS IN OKITIPUPA DIVISION

The main indigenous people of Okitipupa Division, a rural part of Western Nigeria, are the Ikale, a Yoruba people, who act as hosts to immigrants of several ethnic groups as shown in Table 1.

Table 1.   Ethnic composition in Okitipupa division

Ethnic group/nationality	Total	Male	Female
Nigerians	275,623	139,214	136,409
Yoruba	205,037	103,243	101,794
Urhobo	40,424	20,685	19,739
Ijo	22,663	10,912	11,751
Ibo	2,950	1,886	1,064
Edo	2,408	1,218	1,190
Isoko	859	482	377
Itsekiri	530	261	269
Hausa	349	242	107
Effik	246	156	90
Ibibio	120	104	16
Other Nigerians	37	25	12
Non-Nigerians	22	17	5
Unspecified	64	30	34
Total	275,709	139,261	136,448

Source: *Population census of Nigeria* (1963).

Nearly everyone in Okitipupa Division depends on agricultural work of one form or the other. There are four main categories of workers who are not dependent directly or exclusively upon land resources: the employees of the state local government unit concerned with general administration; the rural shopkeepers, who nevertheless engage in multiple occupations including some farming; the personnel of the local branch of the Ministry of Agriculture and Natural Resources, who advise and experiment on the improvement of agriculture generally; and the employees of the four new oil palm plantations concerned with scientific experiments related to the production and growth of oil palm trees.

There are ethnic occupational specializations in the locality, for example: the Ijo and the Itsekiri fish and trade in open shops by the rivers; the Urhobo and Isoko are concerned mainly with oil palm produce; and the Ikale do farm work. Thus, there is some complementarity in occupations and division of labor. However, the primary resource on which these occupations are based is land. This land is owned and controlled by one ethnic group. The Ikale are the landowners and farmers. The Urhobo, an immigrant group involved in the local oil palm industry, are tenants.

The Ikale are believed to have occupied their present territory by the fifteenth century. Initially land was plentiful and the *Abodi* or an *Oloja*, as the political head and leader of government assisted by a council of chiefs in a town unit, allocated land to his subjects and to strangers. Although the extent of the indigenous town polity is still coterminous with its territorial boundaries, every Ikale family today owns the portion of land which its members have exploited through the generations. As in the past, the political head of each town has no control over how a particular piece of family land may be used or what kinds or quantity of crops might be grown on it.

The earliest recorded immigration of the Urhobo into this area occurred in the late nineteenth century. These early immigrants became attached to lands owned by Ikale after paying a "bush entry" fee of one *naira* each and after striking a verbal agreement to pay a sum of two *naira* (now six *naira*, in 1972) annually to their respective landlords. After paying to their landowner entry fees and rents, wives, other kinsmen, and sometimes friends joined the camps of Urhobo tenants.

The Urhobo immigrants left their homes in Mid-Western Nigeria after their socialization for over fifteen years in their indigenous socioeconomic systems in which the main occupation for livelihood is oil palm produce. When they first arrived in the Okitipupa Division, the Urhobo immigrants found that some of the Ikale people harvested palm fruits from the shorter trees. The Urhobo alone, with their more advanced technology, harvested the taller trees.

A sample of six Urhobo camps/villages revealed an extensive organization of immigrants located in areas of plentiful oil palm trees where stream or well water is available. Each camp, named after the founder who was the first to obtain permission to settle, was inhabited only by Urhobo immigrants. Men, women, and children each played a role in connection with palm produce. Each camp was thus exclusive to the Urhobo immigrants, with mechanisms of social control centered around the camp founder and the heads of the different households. There were thirty-three households in the six camps/villages, having a total population of 240 people. This included forty-one men and their sixty-three wives and children. Although these groups lived among a host society, the Ikale, and although both hosts and guests mixed particularly in market situations, the immigrants maintained their exclusiveness by asserting their cultural symbols, particularly in language, clothing, life style, and basic values. They were different culturally and organizationally.

Having no high formal education as a basis to compete for employment in urban areas, Urhobo immigrants organized around those portions of land granted to them. They had no right to settle or exploit the oil palm trees unless they made their yearly payments. If any one of them wanted to cultivate farm crops, he had to pay extra rent. Accordingly, areas of conflict over land use were regulated by rent requirements.

In spite of the dependency of Urhobo tenants upon Ikale landowners, the latter considered the Urhobo immigrants to be very prosperous. By way of rent, in 1971–1972, a typical Ikale landowner derived a total annual income of 102 *naira* (one *naira* = 100 *kobo*) from an average of seventeen tenants. On the other hand, an average immigrant household of seven people derived an income of 214 *naira* from the production of oil palm produce. Some landlords impressionistically estimated that some immigrant households earned as high as 3,000 *naira* annually. Although there were conflicts arising from these perceived income differentials, particularly whenever efforts were made to increase land rents, such conflicts did not seriously threaten the symbiotic nature of Ikale-Urhobo relationships. Most Ikale agreed that, without the immigrants, no rents could be collected and the taller oil palm trees would remain unexploited by Ikale farmers. Conversely, without the landlords, the basis for immigrant economic activities and organization could not be secured by Urhobo oil palm workers.

Accordingly, real value was derived from the maintenance of exclusive ethnic identities and organizations. In this respect, it was found that 100 percent of the total immigrant parents interviewed would NOT give their daughters in marriage to Ikale landowners and thereby change the pattern of ethnic exclusiveness in the future through filiation and dual local citizenship. Kinship was thus discriminatory not only in terms of ethnic corporateness to exclude nonkinsmen from the free use of land but also in terms of turning migrancy into an exclusive temporary organization geared toward economic gains and survival.

Market and other developments between the 1930's and the 1970's have exacerbated the normal stresses attending Ikale-Urhobo relationships in the Okitipupa Division. During this period, the market price of palm oil increased from 35 *kobo* to 2.5 *naira* per tin and the price of kernel jumped from 2.8 *naira* to 60 *naira* per ton. In response to these market developments, some of the younger Ikale adopted Urhobo technology and turned their attention from farming to the exploitation of the taller oil palm trees. In addition, new economic demands for land also developed. Advised and assisted by the local branch of the Ministry of Agriculture and Natural Resources, collective farms were organized in those areas of the Okitipupa Division where town or ward communities pooled their human and land resources to grow plantations of oil palms, rubber, and citrus.

These new land-based ventures were a further source of conflict between immigrants and indigenes because, in each case, tenants had to be removed from the land that was needed to support these enterprises. In some instances, landowners or their relatives harvested oil palm fruits in respect to which immigrants had already paid rents. In other instances, in order to remove tenants, oil palm trees have been burned and destroyed. When Urhobo tenants objected to these developments, they were usually reminded of their dependent position. This carried into the political sphere where immigrant groups showed apathy in, and acquiescence to, a situation in which they were manipulated almost solely to vote and support indigenous Ikale candidates for political positions in the new state political system. Locally, the Urhobo were regarded as second-class citizens or non-Ikale Nigerians.

Further competition led to a stengthening of exclusive sociocultural organizations. The Ikale landowners asserted their ownership and control of the indigenous government and politics and of the rural economic system. On the other hand, the Urhobo organized their efforts primarily for economic exploitation and the maintenance of their exclusive town and ethnic unions as well as their identification symbols through their language, clothes, and behavior. Immigrant economic and social organizations were geared toward their targets, to obtain money and to return to their rural natal homes or to set up some shopping activities in urban areas, preferably in the Mid-Western State. Of the thirty-three household heads interviewed and "probed" in the six camps/villages, it was found that although 97 percent liked their present camp organization and life while working to achieve their targets, 100 percent would not make any capital investment in their host society; also, 100 percent would return finally to their natal homes in the Mid-Western State. However, they asserted that they might reconsider their position if they had equal access to land and to local citizenship rights.

THE CASE OF RURAL NEIGHBORS

The neighboring rural Urhobo and Kwale (Ukwanni-Aboh) peoples in the Mid-Western State throw a different light on land-based inter-ethnic relationships. The rural town of Orogun (Otite 1971) is inhabited by agriculturalists from both Urhobo and Kwale ethnic groups. Both groups

have access to land in their respective family allotments. There was therefore NO differential access to land resources. Immigrants to this area are
usually kinsmen (near and far) of one group or the other. And both
farmers and oil palm industrialists accept the complementary nature of
their occupations. Thus, although two languages are spoken and two sets
of symbolic systems are present, these are not manipulated for exclusive
ethnic identifications. One group does not control the means of livelihood
of the other group.

This harmony in economic relations has generated harmony in the
governmental and political spheres. The whole town has a single government. Although the town belongs to the Urhobo, Kwale quasi-political
titles such as *Okpara* [ward's eldest patrikinsman], *Okpara-Uku* [town's
eldest patrikinsman, who is also head of the town's gerontocratic govern-
ment], *Onotu-Uku* [foremost leader of the younger age-grade organiza-
tion], and *Okwa-Uku* or *Ekwa-Uku* [Council of Elders] are accepted and
used. These Kwale titles have similar functions among the Urhobo.

Orogun was grouped for colonial administrative convenience as part of
Kwale administration, and this helped to strengthen the use of Kwale
titles in an Urhobo context until 1950, when the town was regrouped with
its Urhobo section in the Urhobo-Isoko Federal Native Authority area.
Although prominent Orogun citizens introduced the Urhobo chieftaincy
titles of *Ohovwore* and *Okakuro* into the Orogun sociopolitical system in
the 1960's, this has not altered the basis of economic relations.

What is crucial here is land and the free and inherited access to it.
Changes in titles in the political sphere have not led to changes in the
system of land ownership and use. Accordingly, the basis of inter-ethnic
harmony remains.

URBAN ETHNICITY

Ibadan, with its population of about 1,300,000 people is stratified ethnically. The town began as a small Egba village and war camp where wandering soldiers and war refugees from the disintegrating states/empires of Ile-
Ife, Ijebu, and Oyo settled in the nineteenth century (Awe 1967: 13–14).
The initial settlement pattern reflected the Yoruba place of origin of these
groups. "Ambitious young men eager to achieve success, craftsmen looking for better opportunities for their trade, and rich men bored with life
in their own towns came there [i.e. to Ibadan]" (Awe 1967: 15). Apart
from the non-Ibadan Yoruba, there are many non-Yoruba ethnic groups
living in Ibadan. These include the Hausa, Ibo, Nupe, and Urhobo.

In Ibadan, immigrant problems are more directly connected with eco-nomic opportunities and types and places of employment than with land. Inter-ethnic relations in Ibadan have been analyzed by Cohen (1965, 1966, 1967, 1969) and others: e.g. Mabogunje (1967) and Okonjo (1967). Cohen concerned himself primarily with the social organization of the Hausa whose exclusiveness in their Sabo settlement (founded in 1916) was a function of their specialization in certain economic enterprises involving kola and cattle, two major trade items, controlled by Hausa "landlords." These landlords also functioned as hoteliers, chief middlemen, and as key figures in a broker network involving the Hausa in relationships with other ethnic groups in the city. Cohen noted that about thirty of the land-lords in Sabo controlled both the employment in the quarter's economy and the housing accommodation. Thus, Cohen noted:

The Hausa of Sabo are associated together on the basis of mutual economic interests and not merely on that of cultural affinity. ... To the landlords, Sabo represents a vast economic establishment in which they have fundamental vested interests. Also, to fulfill their tasks as middlemen between Yoruba and northern Hausa [cattle] dealers, the landlords and their assistants have emphasized their Hausa identity (1967: 122).

This identity related to long-distance and relay trade in cattle from the northern parts of Nigeria. In this trade, Hausa cattle dealers entrusted their cattle only to fellow Hausa middle-men, who retailed the cattle to Yoruba or Ibo butchers. Nearly 75,000 head of cattle were sold in this way annually (Cohen 1965: 8).

It would seem, then, that the Hausa's solution to the various commer-cial and technical problems of the long-distance trade was to develop an "ethnic monopoly over the major stages of the trade" (Cohen 1969: 183). With reference to this monopoly, Hausa cultural symbols were mani-pulated to form a strong basis for the socioeconomic organization of Sabo as a monopoly-control post to prevent encroachment from members of other ethnic groups and to act as a major end of the chain of the cattle trade.

But in the process of achieving such control, the Hausa have come face to face with increasing rivalry, competition, and opposition from various Yoruba indi-viduals and groups. From the very beginning, economic competition led to political encounters with members of the host society. The Hausa, confronting mounting pressure from the Yoruba majority, were forced to organize them-selves for political action (Cohen 1969: 184).

This politico-economic organization had the effect of a double cleavage between the Hausa as cattle sellers and Yoruba as cattle buyers, with the ensuing differences and relationships conceptualized in ethnic terms.

The landlords often talk of the "machinations" and the "treachery" of the Yoruba and the butchers of the "exploitation" and "greed" of the Hausa .... In the same way, the butchers confront the landlords as a tribal group and rely on the support of various other Yoruba groupings in this confrontation (Cohen 1965: 16).

Sabo is also a crucial ethnic organization in respect to the Hausa-Yoruba trade in kola. Yoruba counteraction to the Hausa tightening of the monopoly in kola trade showed up in the 1930's in forms which included several petitions to the colonial government and to local Yoruba chiefs urging that Hausa kola traders be confined to the markets, that is, prevented from reaching the kola farmer directly with carriers and lorries for their purchases. Cohen noted that "... it is evident from the records that whenever a dispute with the Hausa Kola landlords flared up there was an almost instantaneous attack by Yoruba political groupings on the autonomy of Sabo and on its political institution" (1966: 32).

The coexisting and conflicting Hausa and Yoruba identities in the city of Ibadan were thus a function largely of the competition for the economic resources and products of the savannah and forest zones in Nigeria. The Hausa owned and reared their cattle in the savannah region of the northern parts of the country and controlled the trade connected with the cattle, beginning the chain from the north and ending it in the south. The Yoruba grew and owned the kola in their forest environment in the south, and Yoruba middlemen resented the Hausa intrusion in the kola trade at the points of production by Yoruba farmers. Thus conflicts arose as the Hausa organized and bought what the Yoruba owned and as the Yoruba confronted the Sabo organization and landlords while buying the cattle which the Hausa owned. The result of the inter-actions was ethnic monopoly of the various stages and aspects of the cattle and kola economy. In these circumstances, Sabo and the Yoruba in Ibadan acted as separate corporate units in their continuous competition for the control of the cattle and kola trade.

It is to be noted, however, that the sociocultural organization of Sabo is not a replica of that found among the Hausa in the northern parts of Nigeria. "Hausa cultural tradition is thus not the crucial factor in the formation of these Hausa communities in Yoruba towns, even though this cultural tradition is in many ways the basis on which these communities have been established" (Cohen 1966: 19).

Political party activities and the reorganized local government in Western Nigeria cut into Sabo unity and exclusiveness in the 1950's and provided Yoruba business entrepreneurs with an opportunity to challenge Hausa monopoly of the kola and long-distance cattle trade and other

Sabo economic specializations. These developments led to confrontations, however subtle in some circumstances, not only in the economic sphere but also in the religious sphere where the Ibadan Yoruba Chief Imamate organized sustained opposition against Sabo ritual autonomy and exclusive Islamic religious leadership.

CONCLUSION

This paper is an attempt to present a social anthropological analysis of ethnic differences and ethnic group conflict as a function of resource competition in some rural and urban areas of Nigeria. Banton (1957), Rouch (1956), and Gluckman (1961) have drawn attention to similar inter-ethnic relations in other parts of Africa, that is, respectively, with reference to immigrants in Free-Town, Sierra Leone, to the exclusive Hausa immigrant groups in Ghana, and to the ethnic or tribe-oriented groupings of industrial workers in Central African towns. Also, similarly, Maquet (1961, 1967) has analyzed the relationship of the Tutsi (herders) and the Hutu (agriculturalists), showing how ethnic inequality, occupational specializations, and the tribute system form the basis for both complementary and conflictual inter-ethnic relationships in Ruanda.

This paper suggests that political relations also tend to become economic relations. Political positions are thus economic resources exploited in the context of an ethnically stratified society. The impact of the new Nigerian elite in minimizing economy-based inter-ethnic conflicts has not been strong. Drawn from various ethnic groups, the new Nigerian elite generally possess common characteristics obtained through educational, political, and economic socializations and achievements. The new elite are more influential and pre-eminent and are more advantaged than the other members of their ethnic groups in many areas of life. Yet, they share largely the norms of their respective ethnic groups and their behaviors attune to their various cultural systems. In this respect, the new elite are not much different from the rest of the society whose cultural symbols they share. Thus, in spite of their common socialization and education, members of the new elites continue to regard ethnic ties as important.

Therefore, conflicts that occur between ethnic groups also have a strong tendency to divide elites on ethnic lines. Consequently, the new elites can hardly be expected to devise a more acceptable distribution of scarce economic resources among all the members of various ethnic populations, indigenes, and immigrants living in particular areas.

The types of rural and urban economic organizations presented above do not exhaust all forms of inter-ethnic relations based on the competition for resources. They do not, for instance, include an analysis of the consociational efforts of the new states to distribute resources under some centralized system of equity in order to minimize ethnicity and preclude conflict among ethnic populations. This paper has dealt with those areas of ethnic-based control of economic structures and processes which determine largely the nature of inter-ethnic relations in certain areas of Nigeria.

REFERENCES

AWE, B.
  1967   "Ibadan, its early beginnings," in *The city of Ibadan*. Edited by P. C. Lloyd, A. L. Mabogunje, and B. Awe, 11–25. Cambridge: Cambridge University Press.
BANTON, M.
  1957   *West African city*. Oxford: Oxford University Press.
BARTH, F., *editor*
  1969   *Ethnic groups and boundaries*. London: George Allen and Unwin.
COHEN, A.
  1965   The social organization of credit in a West African cattle market. *Africa* 35(1):8–20.
  1966   Politics of the kola trade. *Africa* 36(1):18–36.
  1967   "Stranger communities: the Hausa," in *The city of Ibadan*. Edited by P. C. Lloyd, A. L. Mabogunje, and B. Awe, 117–127. Cambridge: Cambridge University Press.
  1969   *Custom and politics in urban Africa*. London: Routledge and Kegan Paul.
FURNIVALL, J. S.
  1948   *Colonial policy and practice*. London: Cambridge University Press.
GLUCKMAN, M.
  1961   "Anthropological problems arising from the African industrial revolution," in *Social change in modern Africa*. Edited by A. W. Southall, 67–82. London: Oxford University Press.
KUPER, L.
  1971   "Plural societies: perspectives and problems," in *Pluralism in Africa*. Edited by L. Kuper and M. G. Smith, 7–25. Berkeley: University of California Press.
KUPER, L., M. G. SMITH, *editors*
  1971   *Pluralism in Africa*. Berkeley: University of California Press.
LLOYD, P. C., *editor*
  1966   *The new elites of tropical Africa*. London: Oxford University Press.
LLOYD, P. C., A. L. MABOGUNJE, B. AWE, *editors*
  1967   *The city of Ibadan*. Cambridge: Cambridge University Press.
MABOGUNJE, A. L.
  1967   "Stranger communities: the Ijebu," in *The city of Ibadan*. Edited by

P. C. Lloyd, A. L. Mabogunje, and B. Awe, 85–95. Cambridge: Cambridge University Press.

MAQUET, J.

1961   *The premise of inequality in Ruanda.* London: Oxford University Press.

1967   "The problem of Tutsi domination" in *Tribal and peasant economies.* Edited by G. Dalton, 81–87. New York: The Natural History Press.

OKONJO, C.

1967   "Stranger communities: the western Ibo," in *The City of Ibadan.* Edited by P. C. Lloyd, A. L. Mabogunje, and B. Awe, 97–116. Cambridge: Cambridge University Press.

OTITE, O.

1971   On the concept of a Nigerian society. *The Nigerian Journal of Economic and Social Studies* 13(3):299–311.

i.p.   *Rural migrants and economic development: a study of Urhobo immigrants among the Ikale of western Nigeria.*

Population census of Nigeria

1963   Volume two: *Western region*, table 31, page 5.

RICHARDS, A. I.

1956   *Economic development and tribal change: a study of immigrant labour in Buganda.* Cambridge: Heffer and Sons.

ROUCH, J.

1956   Migration au Ghana. *Journal de la Société des Africanistes* (26).

SCHERMERHORN, R. A.

1970   *Comparative ethnic relations.* New York: Random House.

SHIBUTANI, T., K. M. KWAN

1965   *Ethnic stratification.* London: Macmillan.

SMITH, M. G.

1965   "Social and cultural pluralism" in *Africa, social problems of change and conflict.* Edited by P. L. van den Berghe, 58–76. San Francisco: Chandler.

1971   "Institutional and political conditions of pluralism," in *Pluralism in Africa.* Edited by L. Kuper and M. G. Smith, 27–65. Berkeley: University of California Press.

VAN DEN BERGHE, P. L.

1965   *Africa, social problems of change and conflict.* San Francisco: Chandler.

Competition Within Ethnic Systems in Africa

ELLIOTT P. SKINNER

1. One of the major problems facing contemporary African states is the competition between their component ethnic and social groups for the resources of the state (Skinner 1972a: 240–255). This in itself should not be surprising; almost by definition ethnic groups are competitive for the strategic resources of their respective societies. This occurs because ethnic groups are sociocultural entities which, while inhabiting the same state, country, or economic area, consider themselves biologically, culturally, linguistically, or socially distinct from each other and most often view their relations in actual or potentially antagonistic terms (Cox 1970: 317). The nature of ethnic groupings in each society and the competitive short-term tactics and long-term strategies they employ are functions of history and of the resources they seek to control (Fried 1967: 71–72). Groups with more effective tactics and strategies normally gain competitive advantages over the other groups within their societies. Yet this success is not without its liabilities; for the very factors that give groups differential advantages often inhibit their adaptation to changing conditions. The result is that most successful ethnic groups are ill-prepared for change and are often surpassed by formerly less successful groups within the ethnic system.

The ethnic systems of most societies are created by conquests or by migration. Nevertheless, neither military conquests nor migrations automatically produce ethnic systems. In some cases, the conquerors or the conquered absorb each other, and migrant groups either assimilate or are assimilated by their hosts (Skinner 1967: 170–185). Ethnic systems develop when racial, social, linguistic, or cultural groups living in the same society do not merge but retain their own identities. This ethnic particularism most frequently occurs because one or more groups in the system, by remaining apart, derive tactical or strategic advantage in the competition for their societies' resources. They develop what Cox has described as power relations or a system of superordination or subordination with each other, and, through it, control their societies' resources (Cox 1970: 317–318).

In order to enhance their power in an ethnic system, competing groups use any biological, linguistic, and sociocultural characteristics they possess to delineate their groups' boundaries and give them cohesion against their neighbors (Barth 1969). This is especially true of dominant ethnic groups who have more to defend. These latter avoid most types of group interaction which might threaten the identifying characteristics of the group, whether these be biological, cultural, or social. Yet, as I have suggested in another context, groups cannot form ethnic systems without modifying their pristine characteristics (Skinner 1960: 906). Not only do their institutions adapt to each other, but the resulting ethnic system develops characteristics which are more than the sum of the characteristics of the component groups. Moreover, unless they are quite vigilant, the members of the different ethnic groups establish personal linkages which, left unchecked, tend to threaten the cohesion of their respective groups. Naturally, the relative power or importance of the groups involved conditions the adaptation that their institutions are constrained to make.

In colonial situations superordinate groups are usually more autonomous than subordinate ones. Yet even colonizing groups adapt (Malinowski 1945: 12). Colonized groups are less able to protect their institutions and are often more prone to acculturation. As a result of this interaction, in time ethnic systems become characterized by linkages between persons and institutions of the component groups. Moreover, these groups arrive at a consensus about the nature of the ethnic system of their society, and they respect, if not accept, its hierarchy of power and, with that, its differences in access to resources. Their acquiescence obviates the constant use of force by the conqueror or superordinate group to gain compliance. Ideologies are created as substitutes for force, but the potential use of force remains.

There are some complex ethnic systems, especially colonial ones, in which not all the component groups are viewed as integral to them. This may be due to a number of factors: biological, cultural, linguistic, or social. Historical factors are usually the reason why some groups are not viewed as organic to the ethnic system. The one class of groups which is normally marginal to an ethnic system consists of the "strangers." Simmel

(1950: 402–408) theorizes that one of the major reasons for the position of stranger groups in all societies is that they enter pre-existing social systems. As a result they usually establish only transitory relationships with resident groups. Strangers do not subscribe to the conventions of the groups they live among and never become organic members of the system. They tend to remain apart and to confront the system. Moreover, not being a party to the processes by which ethnic systems come into being, stranger groups do not feel constrained by "habit, piety and precedent" to accept the norms of their hosts. Instead, according to Simmel, strangers tend to exploit relationships with their hosts, especially in trade and finance — activities involving the valuable resources of their host societies.

What Simmel failed to realize in his trenchant analysis of the stranger is that no group within an ethnic system, be they strangers or not, can be so "objective or autonomous" that they do not become enmeshed in the nexus of relations within their system. The strangers may not subscribe to all the values of the ethnic systems in which they live, and their institutions may be more autonomous than those of the other groups; yet no group can live within a system unless its institutions adapt to it. Once this happens, stranger groups are heir to many of the same problems of ethnic groups organic to the system. They, too, often find that changes in the society vitiate the effectiveness of the tactics and strategies they use in competition with other groups.

2.   The present competition between social groups in Africa over the resources of their regions is only the latest in a long history of such conflicts on that continent. The structure of the groups in conflict and the nature of the resources they competed for have changed over time. The extremely small-scale societies of tropical Africa cannot really be said to have possessed ethnic groups, and therefore they did not have ethnic systems. Some Pygmy and Bushman groups lived in symbiotic relationship with their more powerful neighbors, but, significantly, these hunters and gatherers exploited different resources than their agricultural and pastoral neighbors. They normally had only intermittent relations with the people of those more complex societies, and despite myths that provided the charters for these relations, the hunters and gatherers were constantly being displaced or absorbed (Turnbull 1962; Thomas 1965). It appears that small-scale groups in prolonged contact with people who exploited the same areas or resources had the tendency to merge or to move away. Despite Smith, small-scale agricultural and pastoralist societies seldom, if ever, formed complex ethnic systems (Smith 1971b: 107).

While some of the more economically complex conquest states in Africa did develop ethnic systems, most of them did not. The tendency was for most of these states to assimilate the populations they conquered biologically, culturally, and socially. Thus, the Swazi of South Africa carried out a policy of intermarriage with conquered groups. They "established a complex network of economic and social obligations, gifts and services in 'in-law' relationship" that merged the diverse elements and "enriched the nation with new ideas, words, rituals and tools" (Kuper 1947: 17). Similarly, the Ambomu, who had migrated into and conquered portions of the southeastern Sudan, amalgamated about "twenty foreign peoples to form the Zande people as the people of the Azande state became known." It was still possible at the time of European conquest to find the foreign elements "at all stages ranging from political absorption and cultural autonomy to total assimilation, both political and cultural" (Evans-Pritchard 1963: 136).

There were apparently limits to the ability of African states to assimilate all groups who were brought into their orbit. Many states in Central Africa and the Sudanic fringe region formed ethnic systems with the conquerors or local ruling groups in superordinate positions. Some subordinate groups in the Sudanese states and in Hima-ruled states in Ruanda and Burundi were incorporated in "castelike" positions with quite limited access to the total resources of these societies. Many of these subordinate groups exploited specific ecological zones or niches or practiced specific occupations. And while myths provided the charters for structuring the "premise of inequality" in these societies, the potential, if not the fact, of physical coercion was ever present (Maquet 1961; Rouch 1954).

There were also African states which absorbed some conquered populations and migrants, incorporated others as subordinate groups, and assigned still others the status of strangers. The invading Dagomba from Ghana quite easily absorbed and assimilated the Ninisi in the Upper Volta region with whom they shared major sociocultural characteristics, with the exception of political organization (Skinner 1964). The result was the Mossi states. The Mossi did not absorb but only incorporated the Fulani pastoralists who, according to tradition, drifted into their country and "submitted voluntarily to the authority of the Mogho Naba (Dim Delobson 1932: 90). These people remained socially different from the Mossi, even though in time they learned the Mossi language and adopted many aspects of Mossi culture (Skinner 1964: 195).

The Mossi were especially hospitable to Yarse (Dioula) and Hausa (Zanguete) refugee traders who settled in the wards of the capital at Ouagadougou. These two groups had their own chiefs and headmen and paid homage to the Mogho Naba as part of the cortege of the Baloum Naba, the Chief Steward of the Palace and "Mayor" of Ouagadougou. A very large percentage of them married Mossi women, including the daughters and sisters of former Mogho Nanamse, and, of course, their sisters and daughters married Mossi men, including the Mogho Nanamse. Nevertheless, these two populations remained distinguishable from the Mossi population by language (all are polyglot), religion (Islam), and especially by occupation, because they remained traders. They were not absorbed because they had the important role of conducting the trade with people of their original homelands who visited Ouagadougou. Their visiting countrymen lived with them in Ouagadougou, and they represented their guests at court if and when there were problems to be resolved. It was, therefore, to the interest of the Mossi political hierarchy that the resident trader populations retain their linguistic and other skills necessary for dealing with foreign traders (Skinner 1964: 194).

The ethnic system that developed within Mossi society had its analogues in other parts of the Sudan. Migrating pastoral peoples were partially incorporated into these states, and foreign traders were incorporated as strangers, but comparable agricultural peoples were assimilated. The strangers in Sudanese towns lived in special wards (sometimes called Zongos) under the control of their own chiefs or headman. Es Sadi described this pattern for Timbuktu as early as 1352. He wrote: "Timbuktu at that time [of the Battuta's visit] was inhabited by people of Mimah and Tawarek (Molathemin), especially Masufa, who had a headman of their own, while the Melle governor was Farba Musa" (Barth 1859: III, 663). In some societies these chiefs and headmen represented their followers at the local courts; in other areas the local ruler appointed one of his officials to deal with the strangers and their chiefs. Comparable data from East Africa suggests that the twelfth century ruler of Sofala welcomed traders from Kilwa to settle permanently in his realm. He also offered them wives to gain their friendship so that they could act as local representatives for their visiting countrymen (Freeman-Grenville 1962: 90). Note, that with few exceptions, the strangers were under the political control of the local African political authorities and stayed on only at the sufferance of their hosts.

3. European contact with and conquest of African societies created many more ethnic systems than had ever existed before on the continent. The commercial activities of the early Europeans stimulated a vast movement of different populations; and subsequent European conquest incorporated different societies within the same colonial territory. During the

heyday of colonialism, many traditional African polities, societies, and linguistic entities were broken up and incorporated with other comparable entities into different colonial territories. Thus the Europeans changed the very structure of the African societies they conquered.

The most important process in the creation of colonial-type ethnic systems was the imposition of European political control over all the groups within their colonies. In some cases the Europeans co-opted the local kings and rulers into a system of indirect rule or created formal leaders for acephalous populations. In other cases the Europeans attempted to rule all the societies directly. But whether the Europeans used indirect rule or direct rule, the result was that the African societies lost their independence and were brought into a colony-wide political organization. Similarly, the African societies were brought into a colony-wide and worldwide economic system, which subordinated their own economic institutions to that of the dominant Europeans. This occurred whether the Africans were forced or induced to work in mines or on farms and plantations, to produce cash crops, or to raise money to pay taxes either by selling their animals or subsistence crops. Thus the Africans also lost their economic independence. Therefore, politically and economically African societies became part of an ethnic system dominated by the Europeans. Later on, by both force and emulation, the other institutions of the subordinate African groups adapted to European rule.

But if the sociocultural institutions of the subordinate Africans adapted to the colonial ethnic system, so did those of the dominant Europeans. In many ways the European institutions changed radically from what they had been before arriving in Africa. For example, the early Dutch Huguenots who settled in South Africa and became mixed farmers bore the sobriquet "Boer," thus emphasizing their differences from the dominant British. Then, as these Boers conquered the Africans and became masters of the land, they called themselves "Afrikaaners" and their Dutch dialect (with its Hottentot words) "Afrikaans." Nevertheless, these very Afrikaaners developed qualities quite different from either those of the local Africans or of the distant Europeans. First of all, they exaggerated an adherence to "Western Civilization" and developed a pride in skin color — a mystique of albinism — unknown to the Europe from which they came. Then, as if to make albinism the natural order in South Africa, the Afrikaaners started to call the Africans, "non-whites" (van den Berghe 1967: 37–46).

Colonial Europeans used the mystique of whiteness or albinism as a symbol of prestige which gave them pre-eminent access to their colonies' resources. Yet, some Europeans had greater access than others. The

European group that controlled the colony, or was dominant in the European metropole that governed the colony, had a higher rank in the colonial ethnic system. In South Africa, the once-ruling white English-speaking ethnic group, vaunting the superiority of its social institutions and culture, controlled most of the resources of that "Union." The subordinate white Afrikaaner group with its distinctive culture, language, and social institutions had to settle for second place. In French colonial Africa, northern and Parisian Frenchmen held better positions and superior status to the Bretons and French of the "Midi." Similarly, the French-speaking Walloons retained the same hegemony over the Flemish in the exploitation of the Belgian Congo as they did over that minority in Belgium. The status of noncolonizing whites normally reflected the power and prestige of their nation-states in world affairs. This was true especially of the Americans. Despite these differences, so important was whiteness for gaining access to power and prestige, that Europeans did not hesitate to repatriate or deny entrance into the colonies to members of their group whose behavior threatened the status of their group.

The Europeans were directly responsible for creating or stimulating the development of many of the ethnic categories found among Africans in colonial and contemporary Africa. In addition to calling the blacks of South Africa, "non-whites," the Europeans in South Africa called them collectively, "Kaffirs," "Natives," and "Bantu." Within the territory that the British called Nigeria, the peoples of the kingdoms of Ife, Oyo, Ilorin, Ibadan, and Ijebu became known collectively as the Yoruba. The people of different Akan-speaking states in the Gold Coast became known as Ashanti; and the SUBJECTS of the Mogho Nanamse of Ouagadougou, Yatenga, and Tenkodogo became known as Mossi. Similarly, in East Africa many of the groups that emerged as identifiable entities during the colonial epoch did not exist as such before. Edel reported from Uganda that the only sense of common Chiga identity came from a common rejection of alien overlordship (Edel 1965). Colson reported that the so-called Plateau Tonga of Northern Rhodesia received their identity "due to circumstances beyond their control." This identity was a function of "Government policy and convenience, and not cultural, linguistic, or political distinctions among the Tonga themselves" (Colson 1951: 95–96).

Government policy, as well as the colonial situation itself, appears to have facilitated the introduction of a number of foreign ethnic groups into almost every ethnic system in Africa. These foreign ethnic groups or strangers not only prevented structural continuity between the rulers and the ruled, but interacted in a particular way with both the dominant Europeans and subordinate Africans. Those "noncolonizer" European groups such as the Lebano-Syrians of West Africa and the Greeks residing in other African areas did not share the colonizers' access to the resources of the colonies. Even though they had biological, social, and cultural characteristics of Europeans, they were not party to the establishment of the ethnic system and had difficulty even securing recognition as "Europeans." Those "colonizing" European groups living in territories not controlled by their nation-state, such as the Portuguese in the Congo (Zaire) and the Afrikaaners in Angola, suffered less discrimination. Nevertheless, both the colonizers and the colonized in these ethnic systems treated them as "strangers."

The Asians who lived in various parts of East and southern Africa exhibited all the qualities of the classic stranger ethnics. Originally from various parts of the Indian subcontinent, and belonging to several ethnic, linguistic, and religious groups, these people helped forge the first link between England and East Africa (Mangat 1969: 25–28). Yet, the British considered them foreign to the ethnic system that arose. The Indians complained that "a deliberate attempt" was made to debar them "from any share in the commerce and agriculture of the country," on account of their race and color (Mangat 1969: 104). In response, the British Governor emphasized the prior rights of the British, and even non-British, whites. He declared that "this East Africa Colony is going to be controlled by our own kith and kin" (Mangat 1969: 104). Ironically, in order to justify the withholding of equal access to the Indian strangers, the British asserted the paramountcy of African rights in the country. While this cynically reversed the previous declaration of European paramountcy, it ensured the continuation of Imperial control in the Colony (Mangat 1969: 126–127). Yet, it was this declaration that was to legitimize the future Africans' right to independence.

4.   Once African groups recognized the nature and importance of the colonial ethnic systems, they, too, started to compete with the Europeans and with other Africans for the available resources of their colonies. The nature of the competition and the relative success of the African groups was a function of many factors: the sociocultural attributes of the African groups, the nature of the resources to be exploited, and the history of their relations with the Europeans. Those Africans who were exploiting resources desired by the Europeans came into open conflict with the invaders or their rulers. In South Africa, because both "the Boers and the Xhosa were pastoralists practicising agriculture 'as a side line' ... the contact between them soon issued in conflict for control of valuable grazing land" (Marais 1937: 333). The Xhosa were beaten in this first "Kafir War"

and driven from their land. Their loss was also a partial gain for other Africans, especially the Fingos. The whites found the Fingos more pliable. They were judged to be

better agriculturalists than the Xhosa and more acquisitive. Because they were broken up into small groups and had no powerful chief, they readily accepted a European leadership which showed itself well-disposed toward them. It is, therefore, not surprising that civilization has made greater progress among the Fingo than among any other Bantu people in South Africa (Marais 1937: 336).

The Kikuyu of Central Kenya suffered the same fate as the Xhosa within the East African colonial ethnic system. Ardent agriculturalists, they were deprived of their land by the Europeans, confined to reservations, or forced to become squatters on their own land (Huxley 1953: I, 86ff.; II, 60ff.). Here again, the Europeans were able to take advantage of the growing conflict among the African members of that colonial ethnic system. We are told that "Luckily — for the British — most other tribes in Kenya, like the Masai and the Kamba, dislike Kikuyus ..." (Gunther 1955: 375). The Kikuyu were not supported by other groups who were themselves seeking rewards within the local ethnic system.

Colonial African groups used various tactics and strategies for gaining the upper hand over others. The highly centralized Baganda helped the British establish control of Uganda, and "continued to serve Britain by helping to administer other parts of the country, whilst their own mon-archial government was allowed to continue its functions with only the lightest supervision from colonial officials" (Hatch 1969: 214). The Baganda leaders obtained other advantages from this type of association: "They were able to entrench their land rights, thus becoming a landed aristocracy, and thereby prevent the British from introducing white col-onists as they did in Kenya" (Hatch 1969: 214). In Nigeria, on the other side of the continent, the Fulani found that "a willingness to accommo-date themselves to European overrule was an essential ingredient in pre-serving their privileges and perquisites as a ruling minority" (Collins 1970: 43).

European rule also facilitated the radical transformation of the relation-ship between preexisting African strangers and their hosts and led to the influx of large groups of African ethnic strangers in many colonies. Hun-dreds of thousands of Africans forcibly or voluntarily migrated to the new or revitalized towns, mines, and plantations to earn money to pay taxes and to obtain the amenities they were learning to need. Certain groups of Africans, such as the Dahomeans and Togolese, emigrated to serve as a subordinate administrative class in the French colonial service throughout Africa (Challenor 1970). And, in almost every case, the African strangers advanced to higher positions in the colonial ethnic system than those occupied by local people — the "sons of the soil."Many strangers, profiting from the colonial system, ignored the moribund indigenous political authorities and actively competed with the local people for jobs in the expanding traditional economies and in the modern economic sectors. The strangers were not above using their "foreignness" as a tactic in competing with local people. Many of them manifested no loyalty to the areas in which they lived. The strangers often owned property where they settled, married, and had children, but considered themselves, and were considered, strangers. They paid more attention to their home countries than to areas where they lived and used their incomes to build up their homelands rather than their adopted countries (Skinner 1963).

There were several reasons for the behavior of the strangers. In many cases, they simply felt and asserted that they were culturally, educationally, physically, or psychologically superior to the local Africans. Second, they often claimed that whereas they willingly adapted to the colonial system, the indigenous people refused or neglected to do so. Third, the strangers often asserted that the local people mistakenly lumped all foreign groups together and discriminated against them. Thus the "Dahomeans" stated that, being really Fon, Savs, and Popos, they differed widely in their reaction to the local people, but all bore the opprobrium shown toward "Dahomeans." The people called "Northerners" or "Ibos" in northern Nigeria declared that they were often "Ibibio," "Calabari," or "Ijaw" and did not all behave alike with respect to the local people. Yet they were taken to be "Ibo" and treated as such. The "Hausa" in the Gold Coast claimed that their group included people from Hausaland, as well as the culturally different Yoruba, Mossi, and Kanuri, some of whom were hostile to the local people. On the Copper Belt of Northern Rhodesia (Zambia), the Chewa, Nsenga, and Kunda often resented being known as "Ngoni" and treated as such. The same was true of the various groups from Nyasaland, who were called Nyasa and allegedly discriminated against. The inhabitants of Tanganyika were said to consider all the Nilotic peoples from Uganda as "Ganda," and blamed all the "Ganda" for the peculiarities of one group.

The stranger groups very often failed to take into consideration the structural reality of the colonial ethnic systems. Regardless of whether they saw themselves as internally segmented or not, they were viewed as monolithic groups by both the Europeans and local Africans. Moreover, they often used both those sociocultural features they had in common with and those which distinguished them from the local people to carve out important social, economic, and even political niches in the colonial ethnic system. Conversely, a comparable process occurred among the populations indigenous to the colonies. They collectively became "sons of the soils," and considered themselves to be the disenfranchised "originaires" of whatever specific colony they lived in. Later, they were to employ this new identity as a tactical and strategic weapon in their fight against the colonial ethnic system.

The non-African strangers in Africa were able to take greater advantage of the colonial situation than the African strangers, and normally they had greater access to the strategic resources of the colonies than the indigenous people. The Lebanese, who contemplated going to West Africa, were so certain of succeeding economically that they believed that "'Those who fail their future in Lebanon search for it in Africa'" (Khuri 1965: 385). Prospective Lebanese emigrants were assured that West Africa was a place "where money making is easy as shovelling in sand, the fun of living is heightened by the easier availability of women, and where harmony and good will among the Lebanese community prevail" (Khuri 1965: 393).

The Lebanese in West Africa could and did make money by considering every African "a potential thief; counting the money received twice to avoid possible mistakes; trying to please all tastes 'by word if not by deed'; never allowing a customer to go empty-handed; selling commodities at the highest price possible" and so on (Khuri 1965: 394). The easily available women were not Lebanese women — few of whom came from Lebanon — but African women whose poverty often led them to prostitute themselves. Many Lebanese became so adapted to the colonial ethnic system that, while considering the African an *Abid* [slave], they fawned upon the European rulers and adopted many of the negative attitudes of these conquerors toward the African people. Nevertheless, their ambiguous position did not win them friends. They were disliked by both Africans and Europeans (Apter 1955: 169n; Winder 1962: 296–333).

The Asians in East Africa had many of the same characteristics as the Lebanese strangers in West Africa. While some of the Asians opposed the colonial ethnic system in which the Europeans were on the top, they came next and the Africans last, and "there was a wide measure of acceptance" of it (Ghai 1966: 11). The Asians, extremely communal-minded, highly endogamous, and devoted to maintaining their culture and their links with their countries of origin, formed a "self-sufficient, ethnocentric community" and wanted to be left alone to make their way in the ethnic system. As long as their economic position was not threatened, the Asians accepted the status quo. Ghai declares that:

It is surprising that there was not more resentment of the superior status and racial arrogance of the European. In a curious way, the Asians had come to believe in the myth of white superiority. The pyramidical racial structure was sometimes taken too much for granted; it was proper and inevitable that in the order of things, the white men should be at the helm. Rather as corollary of this attitude, and partly as a rationalisation of the better economic, social and political status of the Asians compared with that of the Africans, the Asians began to believe that the Africans were inferior to themselves... More subconsciously than consciously, the East African Asian has been a racialist (Ghai 1966: 12).

The Africans, reacting to the attitude of the Asians, grew to dislike them. Meeting the Asians primarily as buyers of produce, shop-keepers, and givers of credit, many Africans grew to feel that the Asian traders had conspired together "to hinder the participation of the Africans in commerce; and that were it not for this conspiracy, the Africans would rapidly and effectively engage in trade" (Ghai 1966: 13; Morris 1968: 143). That this view ignored the problems the Asians were having with the Europeans, as well as the fact that both groups were victims of a colonial ethnic system favoring the Europeans, did not matter. In time, the Asian ethnic stranger group became more hated than the dominant ESTRANGING European.

5.   Conflict and competition between and within all groups in the colonial ethnic systems sharpened as the African nationalism developed. After an initial period of disbelief that their hegemony had been challenged, the Europeans in most nonsettler territories conceded the Africans' right to self-determination. By so doing, the Europeans avoided much tension and bloodshed and were able to retain control of the resources of most African territories. In the settler territories, the situation was more complicated. In Kenya, for example, European intransigence lead to Mau-Mau. Later, when the Europeans sought to come to terms with the Africans, the unity of the whites crumbled. A number of prominent Europeans recommended sharing political and economic control with the other groups. A faction led by Mr. Michael Blundell "advocated a number of liberal measures, including a movement away from tribal exclusiveness, African or European, in the holding of land — hitherto the 'White Highlands' have been sacrosanct — and even an experiment in multi-racial secondary education." These proposals marked the abandonment of the old aims of complete white social and political superiority. Inevitably Blundell's own right wing became indignant (Perham 1970: 168). Similar divisions appeared among whites in the Central African Federation. Garfield Todd and others did advocate some sharing of power, but for most whites in the

Federation, partnership with the Africans was seen in terms of the relationship "between a horse and its rider" (Sithole 1959: 125). The Europeans were unwilling to really share economic and political control with the Africans, even in order to mimimize their losses. They broke up into quarreling factions. The Africans in Northern Rhodesia (Zambia) and Nyasaland (Malawi) finally gained independence. Those in Southern Rhodesia failed to do so. The Europeans in Angola, Mozambique, and South Africa were able to weather the tides of nationalism and still have complete control of African territories.

The prospect of independence, and with it the opportunities to control the resources of their emerging nation-states, engendered conflict among the indigenous Africans and between them and the strangers. Nationalists from the various colonial territories, who had superimposed the identity of AFRICAN over cultural or linguistic identities and had used it as an operational weapon against the Europeans, were constrained to return to older identities and loyalties. These persons found to their chagrin that they could not compete for power using the ethnic identity, African, but had to use parochial ethnic group identities. In Nigeria, Kenya, the Gold Coast, Sierra Leone, and other territories ethnic groups permutated and started to jockey for power. Many such groups had never functioned as corporate entities before or during the colonial period. An observer in the French Congo declared: "We anthropologists thought that tribes were small in this area ... but the rise of local political organization seems to have stimulated the re-emergence of larger tribal associations than we had ever identified" (Carter 1960: 90).

For many individual African political leaders, the need to use parochial loyalties for electoral purposes was traumatic. Persons who had created interterritorial alliances or who had functioned on the territorial level found it humiliating to have to retreat to specific regions or districts where they had the strongest ties in order to be elected. The odyssey of Nnandi Azikiwe is perhaps the best example of this. An early Pan-Africanist who had studied among blacks in the United States, Zik worked as a journalist in both Liberia and the Gold Coast and headed the National Council of Nigeria and the Cameroons. But as Nigeria approached independence, Zik had to seek political support among the "Ibo" communities in eastern Nigeria (Azikiwe 1970). Similarly, Dr. Joseph Conombo, a parliamentarian from Upper Volta, had gained so much respect among the African delegates to the French National Assembly that he was made a minister in the Mendès-France government. With independence approaching, he found to his chagrin that he had to retreat to a political base among the "Mossi" people in his home district.

Ethnic competition among Africans for control of the resources of emerging nation-states was certainly the major cause of conflict in Africa during the late 1950's and 1960's. The conflict in the Gold Coast between Kwame Nkrumah and the chiefs was baldly portrayed as a struggle over the most vital resource of the country. The people of the Ashanti region campaigned under the slogan: "Vote for Cocoa" (Nkrumah 1961). In the Upper Volta, the conflict broke out between "Mossi" and "non-Mossi," and also among "Mossi" of the various pre-colonial kingdoms, for the control of the state. In many cases "Mossi" allied themselves with "non-Mossi" against other "Mossi." Ethnic conflict delayed the independence of Nigeria. This was complicated by the presence of "southern" strangers in the north, and involved competition between the "Yoruba," "Ibo," "Hausa-Fulani," "Beni," and the congery of peoples in the "Middle Belt." In Uganda it was the "Baganda" against the "non-Baganda," and in Kenya there was competition between the Kikuyu-Luo alliance and the Kamba and lesser ethnic groups. The civil strife that broke out in the Congo (Zaire), when the Belgians attempted to retain economic and military control, despite independence, was exacerbated by conflict amongst the Bakongo, Bangala, Baluba, Lulua, and Lunda-controlled "Confederation of Tribal Associations of Katanga" (Turner 1972: 225).

So intense was ethnic conflict for the control of the emerging nation-states and their resources that early attempts at federations quickly failed. In 1959, the leaders of the Senegal and Soudan, hoping to curb the growing fissiparous forces in French Africa, created the Mali Federation. At that time, President Senghor of Senegal asserted that: "We have made a good start in Mali by uniting populations whose natural characteristics — climate, soil and blood, language and customs, and art and literature — are similar. Senegal and Soudan constitute a rather homogeneous and relatively rich economic entity" (Senghor 1962: 152–154). When the Mali Federation did not survive even one year, Senghor explained:

We underestimated the present strength of territorialism, of micro-nationalism [a euphemism for 'ethnicity'] in Africa. We forgot to analyze and understand the sociological differences among the territories of what used to be French West Africa, differences that the colonial administration had reinforced (Senghor 1964: 4–5).

The experiences of the Mali Federation, the Gold Coast, Nigeria, the Belgian Congo, and the other emerging states demonstrated the major importance of political power in the new states. Ethnicity was often used to mobilize political power and to cloud ideological differences. The radical Convention Peoples Party in the Gold Coast was able to mobilize the more numerous non-Ashanti and some Ashanti youth to defeat the United Party composed primarily of Ashanti and the older conservative bourgeoisie. In Kenya the Kenya African National Union (KANU), a coalition of the more numerous Kikuyu and Luo led by the uncompromising Kenyatta and Mboya, defeated the smaller groups, such as the Kamba, in the Kenya African Democratic Union (KADU). The Mouvement National Congolais (MNC) of Lumumba, made up of a multiplicity of small ethnic groups and united with the powerful Bakongo-dominated ABAKO, defeated the smaller Belgian-backed CONAKAT of Moise Tschombe. Later, when the MNC-ABAKO coalition broke, Lumumba's MNC broke up into regional sections composed of local ethnic groupings.

During these power struggles, ethnicity was clearly used as a tactical and strategical operations weapon by a small class of westernized African politicians seeking control of their countries' resources. Ethnicity served political ends. King Baudouin of Belgium may or may not have understood this when he said, in support of Katanga's secession, that: "Entire ethnic groups headed by men of honesty and worth ... ask us to help them construct their independence. It is our duty to respond favorably" (Young 1966: 182). What the leaders of the ethnic groups in Katanga wanted to do was to secede from the emerging Congo nation-state and to control their region's valuable resources. They used CONAKAT, but this new ad hoc coalition of ethnic groups had no traditional or colonial reality, because it was created during the preindependence period. For their part, the heirs of the ethnic system that once was colonial Belgian Congo opposed secession. They viewed Katanga as an organic part of the new state, and refused to accept the loss of its resources to secessionists supported by outside interests. The same Congolese leaders who had opposed Moise Tschombe when he wished to secede with Katanga accepted him as premier of the entire Congo. They viewed him and the "Katangese" as legitimate members of the emerging state.

6. In contrast, the autochthonous peoples of few of the emerging African states, or regions, were willing to consider the "ethnic strangers" as legitimate citizens and, thus, competitors for the resources of their country or regions. A few traditional or pre-European stranger groups, such as the Dioula in the Ivory Coast and the Hausa in Upper Volta, were considered legitimate members of the emerging state system, primarily because they had preserved their links with the local people during the colonial period. The attitudes toward the postconquest stranger groups were quite different. The local people had been often quite disappointed

by the attitudes of these strangers during the colonial period. They had hoped that, whether African or Asian or white, the strangers, as subordinate members of the colonial ethnic system, would have been more considerate of the plight of the truly dispossessed. Instead they found the strangers as exploitative as the estranging dominant European groups. Thus, they often were not prepared to concede to the strangers the same rights as they, the peoples indigenous to the new state or region, had.

Most ethnic strangers in Africa during the period of decolonization also found themselves in an ambiguous position. They had conflicting views about local African nationalism and were quite fearful of the future. For example, many African strangers in the northern region of Nigeria were pro-independence, but their sentiments were viewed with suspicion by the indigenous northern peoples. The latter felt that the southerners had taken the northerners for granted, and they assumed that "in a self-governing Nigeria, the north would in effect be a backward protectorate governed by southerners" (Coleman 1958: 361). The fears of the northerners erupted into anti-southern riots in 1953 and, thus, delayed the independence of Nigeria until 1960.

The African strangers in the Gold Coast were divided in their attitudes toward the contending political parties and sought to maintain their social and, especially, economic positions by playing off one political faction against another (Skinner 1963: 312). This did not succeed, because many local interest groups made their political support of the contending parties contingent upon a reduction in the wealth, power, and prestige of the strangers.

In the nearby Ivory Coast the strangers, including the Dahomeans and Togolanders, did support the fledgling nationalist movement. Yet, so fearful were the local people (Ligue des Originaires de la Côte d'Ivoire) that the "Dahomeans" would retain their important positions after independence, that they rioted against them in October 1958. From Paris, where he was negotiating with the French over the terms of independence, Felix Houphouet-Boigny sent the following message: "In tears, disgraced, I ask you not to proceed with the expulsion of our brothers from Dahomey and Togoland until I shall be with you. Then we shall talk and find a solution to the problem" (*Time* 1958: 42). His appeal failed. The local people expelled the strangers, ending a situation that seemed intolerable to them.

The situation was comparable in the Belgian Congo. In the Katanga towns of Elisabethville and Jadotville the first elections in the Congo's history:

resulted in a clear triumph for the strangers, largely because of ethnic cohesion in their ranks. The four African boroughs in Elisabethville designated burgomasters from outside Katanga, two being Kasai Baluba. Suspicion of favoritism towards Kasaiens by the new burgomasters was widespread in such matters as allocation of public housing and of resident permits; the fear grew among authentic Katangans that unless vigorous action was taken immediately, the social hegemony of Kasai Baluba, reinforced by political leadership, would result in a permanent caste system with themselves frozen at the bottom (Young 1966: 173).

The indigenous people formed the CONAKAT, taking one of the first steps that would lead to chaos in the Congo.

Thus, in all of these cases, the local people felt that the African strangers were not prepared to surrender the gains they had made during the colonial period and were not above seeking to replace the Europeans in the status hierarchy. The result was violence and the attempt to expel them. That these strangers were themselves Africans did not seem to matter. The ethnic identity, African, that had arisen in opposition to the Europeans broke down and was replaced by narrower identities.

The Asian ethnic strangers in Africa faced a terrible dilemma as African nationalism arose. Judging themselves racially superior to the African, "They failed to effectively fight on behalf of the Africans, and later with them" (Ghai 1966: 13). A few Asian leaders did support the Africans, and, during the Mau-Mau emergency in Kenya, sympathized with the rebellion, if not the methods used, by the rebels (Mangat 1969: 176). But by and large the Asians sought their own interests as against those of the Africans. Therefore, when in the late 1950's the political initiative rapidly passed into the hands of the Africans, the latter became more and more unwilling "to accept Asians on equal terms within their nationalist movement." The Africans increasingly resented the position of the Asians within the several territories, and the latter grew fearful for their future (Mangat 1969: 177). This tension and ambiguity surfaced quite dramatically when the question of citizenship in the new states arose: would the Asians opt for local citizenship or for the retention of their British passports? Ghai states, quite unequivocally,

that most Asians living in East Africa could have obtained an East African citizenship. However, large numbers of them did not opt for such citizenship. This has been partly because of much confusion and misunderstanding about the implications of citizenship. Primarily, the decision to retain British or Indian citizenship has been inspired by fear that to give this up would be to give up the right to any kind of protection in the event of confiscation of property or persecution (1966: 15).

This attitude of the Asians further alienated the Africans, who, with few exceptions, further excluded the Asians from important positions in the emerging states. Moreover, the Africans increased their resentment of the economic and social position of the Asians within the several territories (Mangat 1969: 177).

Relations between the Asians and Africans deteriorated rapidly after independence, especially because the Asians made no sustained efforts to bring Africans into their businesses, failed to curb their racial arrogance, and made few commitments to the nation-states now controlled by Africans. As a result, those Asians in Uganda who were noncitizens were expelled and those who were citizens were threatened with expulsion, if they failed to stop discriminating economically and socially against the local people. The Asians in Kenya, Zambia, and in other countries are under pressure to relinquish control of trade and commerce and to change their social attitudes toward the local people or suffer the consequences. Already in Zanzibar a few African leaders have attempted to strike at the root of the racial attitudes of the Asians. They have threatened to imprison any Asian father who refuses permission to his daughter to marry an African man. Thus, the future of the remaining Asians within the ethnic systems of contemporary East Africa may hinge upon whether they can adapt, or will be permitted to adapt, to new realities. "The era of Asian domicile in East Africa is coming to an end," stated the *Kenya Mirror* in August 1972. Some people believe that these views may correctly reflect the sentiments of most East Africans.

The Syrio-Lebanese strangers in contemporary African states have had difficulties, comparable to those of the African and Asian strangers, as the territories in which they lived passed from dependency to independence. Fledgling politicians in the Nigerian House of Representatives sharpened their political tools by urging a restriction on the Syrio-Lebanese in order "to protect the economic prosperity" of their country (Winder 1962: 315). The equally new Ghanaian politicians were urged by the newspapers to stop the Lebanese from calling the Africans *Abid*, a word that means servant in Arabic but with connotations of being a "slave." The leaders were urged to

Tell the local Lebanese traders that we are not prepared to tolerate racial insults. He who sees a free man and calls him "slave" is less than a commodity in the old slave society — he is a brute-simple, a being whose adulterated brains have been eaten up either by excessive money grabbing tricks or merciless greed (Winder 1962: 322).

People in Nigeria complained that "The Lebanese still consider themselves to be superior people; the British used to do this too, but they have changed" (Winder 1962: 318).

Those Syrio-Lebanese, who people believed were seeking to accommo-
date themselves to the emerging political order in West Africa were
accused by competing political groups of trying to protect their economic
interests in the country by buying off the politicians. Attempts by the
strangers to counter these charges were in vain, because many people
believed the charges to be true (Winder 1962: 326–329). By 1958, African
attitudes toward the Syrio-Lebanese had become so charged that Hanna
was constrained to write that "even though in the past 30 years disturbances and open attacks on the Lebanese have taken place, yet the tension
was never so high as at present and the problem was never so acute"
(1958: 463). The coming of independence to many West African states has
resulted in more pressure on the Syrio-Lebanese to modify their relationship with the local economies. The government of Mali curbed the ability
of the Syrio-Lebanese to transfer currency across the state's borders,
except through the state bank. The government of Ghana restricted the
entrance of Syrio-Lebanese as traders and controlled the amount of trade
they could participate in. The government of Liberia has banned the
Lebanese from the rural areas, even though it has resisted the efforts of
some ministers to expel all of these strangers. Almost everywhere in West
Africa the Syrio-Lebanese strangers find themselves suspected of having
an unequal access to the resources of the societies in which they live and
of reaping illegal profits. Thus, the end of the colonial period has brought
with it the end of a colonial ethnic system in which the dominant whites
occupied the highest status position, ethnic strangers were in the middle,
and indigenous groups were at the bottom.

7.   One of the problems that faced the African states after independence
was how to allocate the rights to their resources. Ethnicity had loomed
large during the decolonization period, and then ethnic systems arose
after independence. Ethnic competition for power and money had threatened the national unity of many states. In Sierra Leone "The Mendes
appear to have received more of the political rewards than the Temnes
during the period following independence. This situation laid the foundation for intensive conflict between the political parties which in turn led
to ethnic violence" (Simpson 1972: 179). There was great concern in
Kenya over the "Kikuyuization" of the bureaucracy, with all that that
implied for control of the country's resources. One parliamentarian declared:

Today, when we look at the top jobs in the government, we find that in most
of the ministries, including certain cooperatives, practically all of these have
been taken over by people from the Central Province... If one tribe (Kikuyu)

alone can take over about 72 per cent of the Kenya jobs, and they are less than two million people how can you expect 25 per cent of the jobs to go to more than eight million people who belong to other tribes (Rothchild 1972: 302).

The issue of ethnic inequality in the allocation of jobs and access to Kenya's resources was debated at length in that country's parliament. In 1968, there was a motion calling for "immediate government rectification of the situation and for the distribution of jobs and opportunities so far as possible according to the group's numerical proportion in the total population" (Rothchild 1972: 303). The motion itself was rejected, but not without members drawing attention to the tragic role of ethnicity in the grim events in Nigeria.

The rash of military coups in contemporary Africa is only partly related to ethnic competition for the resources of the various nation-states. The problem is more complex. First of all, the economies of most of these countries are still controlled by Euro-American companies, and little attempt has been made to nationalize them. Second, and a corollary of the first, the African leaders have been unable to fulfill the promises made to the people during the independence struggle that the end of European rule would bring schools, jobs, houses, and other modern amenities. Third, given their inability to make drastic changes in the allocation of their countries' resources, the African leadership class had sought its own welfare and that of its immediate allies. The rural masses, finding themselves taxed to support the modern administrative structure located in the primary cities, increased their migration to these areas. Those elite groups out of power and unable to gain access to positions of wealth attacked the very structure of the nation-states (Skinner 1972b: 1208).

It is quite significant that the very first coup in West Africa — the overthrow of the Olympio government in Togo in 1961 — was precipitated by the President's refusal to raise the soldiers' salaries. He felt that he could not put an unreasonable amount of his country's scarce resources at the disposal of the military. Moreover, he did not think that they had any "greater claim on their home country than any other unemployed Togolese" (Welch 1970: 16). Feeling that they were discriminated against, the ex-mercenaries of France's Indo-Chinese war shot the President and seized control of the state. The numerous coups in Dahomey were due in part to the inability of the government to satisfy the economic and other demands of a civilian administrative bureaucracy, trained for colonial service by the French, but now too expensive to be supported by a poor nation-state (Skurnik 1970: 82). President Kwame Nkrumah of Ghana was overthrown, because many groups in that nation-state, including the military, felt that his socialist plans had ruined the state's economy

(Owusu 1970: 322). The subsequent installation, and removal from power, of a civilian president by the same military had less to do with ethnicity than with the soldiers' views that they could do a better job in government.

The decision of the Upper Volta army to assume its responsibility when Maurice Yameogo lost the confidence of the urban and labor elite of Ouagadougou was unconnected to ethnicity. The political "outs" resented the way Yameogo was distributing the limited resources of that state. The issues in the Nigerian coup that led to the Biafran secession were not that clear-cut. The young and primarily Ibo officers, who initiated the first coup, allegedly felt that they were "stamping out tribalism [ethnicity], nepotism, and regionalism" (Olorunsola 1972: 32). But when the equally corrupt Ibo politicians were not assassinated, when the regions were disbanded, and when an Ibo general was named ruler of a centralized country, there was the suspicion of attempted Ibo domination. The result was a counter-coup, a pogrom against the Ibos, the secession of Biafra over the distribution of the country's resources, and a civil war.

The military regimes that now rule most of the African nation-states have attempted to play down ethnicity as a basis for participation in the affairs of state. The military regime of Upper Volta, profiting from the solidarity that existed in the army among all the officers irrespective of ethnic group, has stressed the determination of the army to develop the whole country and treat its citizens without regard to ethnic group or region. Since 1965, General Mobutu has pre-occupied himself with reducing ethnic and regional identities, restructuring and depoliticizing the regions, and building a national political party. He hopes "to structure competition and the expression of grievances in such a way that expression in ethnic form is not encouraged" (Turner 1972: 265). General Gowon apparently also hopes to restructure the pattern of competition for the resources of Nigeria by creating many more political units and giving their inhabitants greater control over local resources. Moreover, he hopes that by keeping the army in power until 1976, "nonethnic" base interest groups will emerge in the country. In other words, many, if not most, of these African military regimes are attempting to eliminate the ethnic group as the basis for mobilization for competition for the resources of their societies. They are attempting to do so by creating structures and mechanisms to facilitate linkages of people across the present boundaries of ethnic groups. Their fear is that, unless this is done, the fragile African nation-state structure will dissolve into chaos.

CONCLUSION

Ethnic groups arose under specific conditions in the history of Africa. They were based on the differential access that groups had to the resources of their specific societies. In many cases those co-habiting groups had different social and cultural institutions, and they were often biologically and linguistically dissimilar. These differences frequently enhanced the ability of the component groups in an ethnic system to exploit various parts of the total ecology. When necessary, some groups were even provided personnel so that they could more easily exploit their ecological niches. Many of these ethnic systems had myths that provided the ideological basis for their existence and continuation. As a result the participant groups in the ethnic system did not often realize how their own institutions had been modified to fit the ethnic system of which they had become a part. This was especially true of the stranger groups which, not being a party to the initial process by which ethnic systems were established, felt somewhat outside the system and immune to its basic requirements. Nevertheless, all groups within the ethnic systems recognized the element of power, which enabled the societies to persist, and differentiated access to its resources.

The model of "ethnic system," dealing as it does with a pattern of superordination and subordination among ethnic groups living in complex societies, has great utility for analyzing the differential access of groups to their societies' resources. These groups may differ socioculturally, biologically, and linguistically, and these differences can be beneficial to the societies' exploitation of their natural environments. Nevertheless, the ethnic system model insists that groups cannot live within an ethnic system without their basic institutions adapting to each other. The more dominant the group in the system, the less adaptation it may be required to make. Relative power, then, is an important element in any ethnic system. Actual or potential use of force not only governs relations within ethnic systems but also conditions the nature of the access of component groups to their societies' resources.

The ethnic system model is quite different from that of the "plural society" (Despres 1968: 3–26). That model has tended to obfuscate the political factors that determine how complex societies function. It emphasizes the importance of the values and institutions of the various groups in the society and the value consensus that exists between them. It also belittles the role that actual or potential force plays in arriving at the value consensus that permits societies to exist, even in the face of unequal distribution of their resources. There is little appreciation of the dissatisfaction of social groups with their societies. Conflict is ignored or minimized because groups are viewed as getting what they want out of their societies (Kuper 1971: 183).

Any model that deals with complex social systems must deal effectively with the processes by which they come into existence, and how and why they persist. It is quite clear that the institutions of all groups entering a complex system, whether viewed as an ethnic system or a plural society, adapt to the new conditions. But what is significant is that the institutions of the dominant group condition how the institutions of the other groups adapt. Moreover, the dominant group has a more effective boundary-maintaining-and-conserving mechanism to protect its group's interest than the weaker or more exploited groups. Rather than rely upon values to prevent weaker groups within the system from dealing with its dominant institutions, the stronger groups often use force or other control mechanisms (Smith 1971a: 33).

The problem for most groups in ethnic systems is that their position within the system depends upon the use of tactics and strategies that are often difficult to change, despite a changing environment. Dominant groups are especially vulnerable, because success tends to blind them to the fact that acculturation, technical change, or the development of new resources vitiate the effectiveness of their traditional mechanisms for maintaining unequal access to their societies' resources. The Europeans and Asians in the African colonial ethnic system were unable to change their tactics and strategies even though the environment in which they were operating had changed radically. Some of them were not prepared for change and lost power.

Significantly, almost none of the African regimes faced with the task of distributing their countries' resources have opted for a pluralist model, even of the cultural pluralist variety. They believe that the pluralistic model is a sham behind which certain ethnic groups maintain control. The Africans have also not opted for an ethnic system model, because to them the ethnic system model implies a hierarchy of group dominance and subordination. They are using a democratic model which has as its goal the freedom of the individual, unconstrained by ethnic or other ties, to gain equal access to the resources of their societies. The only problem is that, given the limited resources of any state, neither individuals nor groups can gain access without some kind of mobilization around common goals, ideals, or characteristics. The Africans will not be able to get rid of ethnicity as easily as they hope; they undoubtedly have class struggle in their future.

REFERENCES

APTER, DAVID E.
   1955   *The Gold Coast in transition*. Princeton, New Jersey: Princeton University Press.
AZIKIWE, NNANDI
   1970   *My odyssey: an autobiography*. New York and Washington: Frederick A. Praeger.
BARTH, FREDRIK, *editor*
   1969   *Ethnic groups and boundaries: the social organization of culture difference*. Boston: Little, Brown.
BARTH, HENRY
   1859   *Travels and discoveries in North and Central Africa*, three volumes. New York: Harper and Brothers.
CARTER, GWENDOLEN M.
   1960   *Independence for Africa*. New York: Frederick A. Praeger.
CHALLENOR, HERSCHELLE S.
   1970   "Expatriation, discord and repatriation: a study of Dahomeyan strangers in French West Africa as a problem in the colonization and decolonization process." Unpublished doctoral dissertation, Columbia University.
COLEMAN, JAMES S.
   1958   *Nigeria: background to nationalism*. Berkeley and Los Angeles: University of California Press.
COLLINS, ROBERT O., *editor*
   1970   *Problems in the history of colonial Africa, 1860–1960*. Englewood Cliffs, New Jersey: Prentice-Hall.
COLSON, ELIZABETH
   1951   "The Plateau Tonga of Northern Rhodesia" in *Seven tribes of British Central Africa*. Edited by Elizabeth Colson and Max Gluckman, 94–103. London: Oxford University Press.
COX, OLIVER C.
   1970   *Caste, class and race: a study in social dynamics*. New York and London: Modern Reader Paperbacks
DESPRES, LEO A.
   1968   Anthropological theory, cultural pluralism and the study of complex societies. *Current Anthropology* 9(1):3–26.
DIM DELOBSON, A. A.
   1932   *L'Empire du Mogho-Naba: Ciytynes des Mossi de la Haute-Volta*. Paris: Domat-Montchrestien.
EDEL, MAY, ABRAHAM EDEL
   1965   African tribalism: some reflections on Uganda. *Political Science Quarterly* 80(3):357–372.
EVANS-PRITCHARD, E. E.
   1963   The Zande state. *Journal of the Royal Anthropological Institute* 93: 134–154.
FREEMAN-GRENVILLE, G. S. P.
   1962   *The medieval history of the coast of Tanganyika*. London: Oxford University Press.

FRIED, MORTON H.
1967   *The evolution of political society: an essay in political anthropology.* New York: Random House.

GHAI, Y. P.
1966   "Prospects for Asians in East Africa," in *Racial and communal tensions in East Africa.* Nairobi: East African Publishing House.

GUNTHER, JOHN
1955   *Inside Africa.* New York: Harper and Brothers. (Originally published 1953.)

HANNA, MARWAN
1958   "The Lebanese in West Africa: problems and criticism." *West Africa* (May): 463.

HATCH, JOHN
1969   *The history of Britain in Africa, from the fifteenth century to the present.* New York and Washington: Frederick A. Praeger.

HUXLEY, ELSPETH
1953   *White man's country: Loud Delamero and the making of Kenya,* two volumes. London: Chatto and Windus.

ILBOUBO, PIERRE
1966   *Croyances et Pratiques Religieuses Traditionnelles des Mossi.* Recherches Voltaiques 3. Paris and Ouagadougou: CNRS.

KENYA MIRROR
1972   Article appearing in the *Kenya Mirror,* August.

KHURI, FUAD I.
1965   Kinship, emigration and trade partnership among the Lebanese of West Africa. *Africa* 35(4):385–395.

KUPER, H.
1947   *An African aristocracy.* London: Oxford University Press.

KUPER, LEO
1971   "Some aspects of violent and non-violent political change in plural societies: (A) conflict and the plural society: ideologies of violence among subordinate groups, (B) political change in white settler societies: the possibility of peaceful democratization," in *Pluralism in Africa.* Edited by Leo Kuper and M. G. Smith, 153–193. Berkeley: University of California Press.

KUPER, LEO, M. G. SMITH, *editors*
1971   *Pluralism in Africa.* Berkeley and Los Angeles: University of California Press.

MALINOWSKI, BRONISLAW
1945   *The dynamics of culture change: an inquiry into race relations in Africa.* Edited by Phyllis M. Kaberry, xvi-171. New Haven: Yale University Press.

MANGAT, J. S.
1969   *History of the Asians in East Africa, 1886–1945.* London: Oxford University Press.

MAQUET, JACQUES
1961   *The premise of inequality in Ruanda.* London: Oxford University Press.

MARAIS, J. S.
1937   "The imposition and nature of European control," in *The Bantu-*

speaking tribes of South Africa: an ethnographical survey. Edited by
I. Schapera. London: Routledge and Kegan Paul.

MORRIS, H. S.

1968 The Indians in Uganda. London: Weidenfeld and Nicolson.

NKRUMAH, KWAME

1961 I speak of freedom: a statement of African ideology. New York:
Frederick A. Praeger.

OLORUNSOLA, VICTOR A.

1972 "Nigeria," in The politics of cultural sub-nationalism in Africa. Edited
by Victor A. Olorunsola. Garden City, New York: Anchor Books,
Doubleday.

OWUSU, MAXWELL

1970 Uses and abuses of political power, a case study of continuity and change
in the politics of Ghana. Chicago and London: The University of
Chicago Press.

PERHAM, MARGERY

1970 Colonial sequence, 1949 to 1969. London: Methuen.

ROTHCHILD, DONALD

1972 "Ethnic inequalities in Kenya," in The politics of cultural sub-
nationalism in Africa. Edited by Victor A. Olorunsola, 289–331. Garden City, New York: Anchor Books, Doubleday.

ROUCH, JEAN

1954 Les Songhay. Paris: Presses Universitaires de France.

SENGHOR, L. S.

1962 Nationhood and the African road to socialism. Translated by M. Cook.
Paris: Presence Africaine.

1964 On African socialism. Translated and with an introduction by M.
Cook. 4–5. New York: Frederick A. Praeger.

SIMMEL, GEORG

1950 "The stranger" in The sociology of Georg Simmel. Edited and translated
by Kurt H. Wolff, 402–408. New York: Free Press.

SIMPSON, DICK

1972 "Ethnic conflict in Sierra Leone," in The politics of cultural sub-
nationalism in Africa. Edited by Victor A. Olorunsola, 153–188.
Garden City, New York: Anchor Books, Doubleday.

SITHOLE, NDABANINGI

1959 African nationalism. Cape Town: Oxford University Press.

SKINNER, ELLIOTT P.

1960 Group dynamics and social stratification in British Guiana. Annals of
the New York Academy of Sciences 83(5):904–912.

1963 Strangers in West African societies. Africa 33(4): 307–320.

1964 The Mossi of the Upper Volta. Stanford: Stanford University Press.

1967 "Group dynamics in the politics of changing societies: the problem of
"tribal" politics in Africa," in American Ethnological Society. Proceedings of 1967 Annual Spring Meeting, 170–185. Seattle: University of
Washington Press.

1972a "Group dynamics in contemporary Africa: concordance and discord-
ance," in Man for humanity: on concordance vs. discord in human

behavior. Edited by Jules H. Masserman and John J. Schwab, 240–255. Springfield, Illinois: Charles C. Thomas.

1972b Political conflict and revolution in an African town. *American Anthropologist* 74(5): 1208–1217.

SKURNIK, W. A. E.
1970 "The military and politics: Dahomey and Upper Volta," in *Soldier and state in Africa*. Edited by Claude E. Welch, Jr. Evanston: Northwestern University Press.

SMITH, M. G.
1971a "Institutional and political conditions of pluralism," in *Pluralism in Africa*. Edited by Leo Kuper and M. G. Smith, 27–65. Berkeley: University of California Press.

1971b "Pluralism in precolonial Africa" in *Pluralism in Africa*. Edited by Leo Kuper and M. G. Smith, 91-152. Berkeley: University of California Press.

THOMAS, ELIZABETH MARSHALL
1965 *The harmless people*. New York: Vintage Book.

TIME
1958 Ivory Coast: Togolanders go home. *Time* (November 10) 42.

TURNBULL, COLIN M.
1962 *The forest people, a study of the Pygmies of the Congo*. New York: Simon and Schuster.

TURNER, THOMAS
1972 "Congo-Kinshasa," in *The politics of cultural sub-nationalism in Africa*. Edited by Victor A. Olorunsola, 195–283. Garden City, New York: Anchor Books, Doubleday.

VAN DEN BERGHE, PIERRE L.
1967 Language and nationalism in South Africa. *Race* 9(1).

WELCH, CLAUDE E., JR., *editor*
1970 *Soldier and state in Africa: a comparative analysis of military intervention and political change*. Evanston: Northwestern University Press.

WINDER, R. BAYLEY
1962 The Lebanese in West Africa. *Comparative studies in society and History* 4(3):296–333.

YOUNG, CRAWFORD
1966 "The politics of separatism: Katanga, 1960–1963," in *Politics in Africa: seven cases*. Edited by Gwendolen M. Carter, 167–208. New York: Harcourt, Brace and World.

Ethnogenesis and Resource Competition Among Tibetan Refugees in South India

MELVYN C. GOLDSTEIN

Although ethnicity has become one of the most actively studied problem areas in contemporary anthropology, there has been little research on the dynamics of ethnogenesis. This paper examines this process in reference to Tibetan refugee populations who have been settled in an agricultural scheme located in the State of Mysore. The position taken here is that the competition for resources that exists among these refugee populations, and between them and the Indian population, is one of the critical factors underlying the development of ethnic boundaries now operative both within and outside of the Tibetan community.

BACKGROUND

Throughout the nineteenth and early twentieth centuries a permanent Tibetan minority came into existence in India. Darjeeling, Kalimpong, Ladakh, Lahul, and areas of the North East Frontier Agency such as Tawang were incorporated, together with their indigenous populations, into British India. All of these populations, however, were absorbed as parts of territorial units with ongoing social and cultural systems and as such posed no great problem to the Government of India (GOI), which adopted a laissez faire attitude toward them.

I would like to express my appreciation to the American Institute of Indian Studies for supporting my research in India in 1966 and 1967. I would also like to thank the various officials of the DLG and the State Government of Mysore for their aid during this period. In particular, though, I would like to thank Mr. Chamba Tsundru, Representative of His Holiness the Dalai Lama in the settlement, for without his sympathetic aid the research could not have been accomplished.

Beginning in 1959, however, a dramatic new factor emerged. In that year, as a result of internal disturbances in Chinese-controlled Tibet, the Dalai Lama together with many members of his government fled to India and the other Himalayan border states. Unlike the earlier instances of incorporation, these Tibetans were not part of intact territorial and socio-cultural systems. They were an uprooted population and as such presented an immediate problem to the GOI with respect to their subsistence and housing. There could be no laissez faire attitude with respect to these help-less Tibetans, and most of the refugees were initially organized into transit camps. Today there are about 100,000 Tibetan refugees of whom 70,000 to 80,000 reside permanently in India.

The normally grim plight of refugee populations is greatly exacerbated when the refugees manifest either, or both, of the following characteris-tics: (1) a cultural tradition alien to that of the host country, and (2) a lack of special technological skills compatible with the labor needs of the host country.

If, following Goodenough (1970: 99), we take culture to be a "set of standards for perceiving, believing, evaluating, communicating and act-ing," then the impact of the first factor is self-evident. A refugee in a totally alien cultural matrix is like a person wearing the wrong glasses. His perceptions and evaluations of life around him, his norms for behav-ior, and his standards for communication are no longer efficacious. The myriad cues and clues that subtly mediate interpersonal interaction now distort and produce confusion and conflict. When, added to this, refugees do not possess special technological skills, their prospects for successful rehabilitation are very slim indeed. It is not surprising, therefore, to find that the term "refugee" connotes a spectrum of dysfunctional, socially pathological traits such as homicide, suicide, alcoholism, and insanity. Unfortunately, all too often this stereotype is an accurate representation of the reality of the situation.

The Tibetans who entered India in 1959 possessed both debilitating characteristics. With the exception of a handful (mainly aristocrats) who spoke some English and/or Hindi, the refugees spoke only Tibetan. Meat-eating Buddhists from the cold climate of the Tibetan plateau, they found themselves thrust into the sweltering heat of vegetarian Hindu India. The refugees were nomads, monks, farmers, and petty traders, none of which occupations, on the surface, offered any competetive advantages in India. Almost all had no familiarity with modern industrial technology.

The obstacles facing the Tibetans were not just external ones. They came from widely disparate regions in Tibet where they spoke mutually unintelligible dialects, operated under different sociopolitical systems, and were traditionally hostile. Not only could Tibetans not communicate and interact freely with the Indians around them, in many instances they were hard pressed to do so among themselves.

Tibetans, therefore, entered India, a land already overburdened with massive poverty and unemployment, without language facility, without knowledge or understanding of Indian social and cultural systems, and without any potentially useful occupational skills. Their future looked anything but bright. But in point of fact, their initial adaptation to life in India has been very successful. The stereotyped refugee syndrome did not develop among Tibetans, and segments of the refugees have been very successfully rehabilitated, the most successful of the rehabilitation programs being the permanent agricultural settlement. The retention of traditional Tibetan sociocultural patterns in an unabashedly pluralistic adaptation stems from the interplay between traditional structures and new requirements. In particular, the retention of traditional patterns of political hierarchy and authority has afforded Tibetans tremendous competitive advantages in exploiting their new niche.

REHABILITATION

Before discussing the rehabilitation project, however, let me make a brief comment about the Dalai Lama and his "government" (DLG), and the policy of the GOI toward it and Tibetans in general. From the beginning the Dalai Lama and his officials interceded with the GOI on behalf of the Tibetan refugees. They immediately set themselves up as spokesmen for the mass of disparate refugees and even maintained offices in the transit camps. The GOI accepted this and was prepared to work with the Dalai Lama's staff, although only within clearly delimited parameters.

The GOI clearly did not want to recognize the Dalai Lama's organization as a *de jure* "government-in-exile." Even after the 1962 Chinese invasion of India, when the status and authority of the Dalai Lama's "government" soared, the GOI assiduously refused to accord it formal governmental status. In a similar vein the GOI also refused to resettle all Tibetans in one area in north India as the DLG had suggested. What is important to note, however, is that within these parameters the GOI adopted a very liberal attitude toward the administration of the Tibetans.

The GOI early made the fundamental decision to partake actively in efforts to rehabilitate the refugees. The next step obviously was to establish the ideological framework within which such rehabilitation should occur. If we view the options open to it as a continuum running between the two poles of assimilation and pluralism, the GOI clearly opted for a policy which fell toward the "plural" end of the continuum. From the beginning, the policies of the GOI were not intended to discourage or destroy Tibetan cultural institutions and traditions. Working together with the DLG and a variety of foreign aid groups, the GOI launched a program of rehabilitation within a framework compatible with the maintenance of Tibetan culture.

The most successful of the rehabilitation strategies called for the creation of a series of permanent agricultural settlements throughout India. The idea was to resettle Tibetans then living in transit camps or working on road repair gangs and to provide them with assistance and resources so that within a period of five years they could become economically self-sufficient. This, if successful, would not only permanently take care of the refugee population, but it would also help India's food needs by bringing unused land under cultivation. However, considering the immense difficulty governments and agencies normally encounter in resettling populations even intraculturally, this goal for Tibetans in India was certainly one of Herculean proportions.

Although the GOI would not bring all Tibetans together into one area, it also did not want to scatter them in small family units (as, for example, the Canadian government is doing with their Tibetans). The proposed settlements were a kind of compromise, because their envisioned size of three to four thousand was large enough to sustain Tibetan language and other institutions easily.

The GOI further facilitated this cultural preservation by allowing Tibetans considerable internal autonomy and, in particular, by permitting the DLG to exercise administrative control over the settlements. This does not mean that the GOI abdicated its authority over the Tibetans, for it did not. Rather it means that the GOI (and the State Government) had no objection to giving the DLG *de facto* internal administrative control of the camps and to working with the DLG instead of with the individual refugees, so long as the latter did not object. From the beginning, then, two critical aspects of the GOI's policy toward the Tibetan refugees were (1) the liberal "non-assimilative" framework, and (2) the broad "delegated" authority of the Tibetan leadership headed by Tibet's former ruler, the Dalai Lama.

The first of the rehabilitation agricultural settlements was located in the state of Mysore on forest land which in the past had sustained agriculture. The land itself was donated on a ninety-nine year lease by the state government of Mysore under whose jurisdiction and authority the settlement fell. In the early summer of 1961, after the trees had been cut and removed, the first Tibetan settlers arrived in Mysore to start the work of building the agricultural community. This settlement, the first of its kind in India, is called Mundakuppe.[2]

The plan for Mundakuppe called for the development in stages, over a period of several years, of a settlement consisting of three thousand acres. This land was to be allocated on the basis of one acre per person so that, in the end, the settlement would hold around three thousand Tibetans. Internally, Mundakuppe was to be divided into six camps, each of which would hold five hundred acres. The refugees who came down to Mysore in 1961 formed Camps One and Two.

As mentioned earlier, Mundakuppe was expected to achieve economic self-sufficiency after five years. During the "learning-experimental" years, the settlers were assisted in a number of ways. The first and second year, when permanent houses were being constructed and the fields cleared for cultivation, the settlers were paid a daily salary in addition to a regular food ration. By the third year, when the fields were initially planted, they received half-wages and rations. For the fourth and fifth years they received only quarter-rations. In the sixth year, 1966, the settlers were on their own.

I arrived in Mundakuppe in January 1966, at precisely the point when the first two camps were entering the total self-sufficiency stage. There would be no subsidies for the crop they grew that year. Not surprisingly, that spring there was a great deal of anxiety among the villagers as the time for sowing drew near. These anxieties, however, turned out to be totally unwarranted. The harvest that year (as well as in subsequent years) was excellent, and the settlement has become a tremendous economic success. Let us turn, then, and examine the techno-materialistic basis of the economic adaptation at Mundakuppe.

Mundakuppe is located in Mysore State between the cities of Mysore and Arracrem. It lies on a flat plain at an elevation of about 2700 feet. It has a pleasant climate with relatively cool evenings and an average rainfall of about 35 inches, an amount sufficient to support only one crop a year.

The settlement is spread out on two sides of a paved motor highway (see Map 1) which has regular bus service. The four camps south of the highway (Camps I–IV) are separated from neighboring Indian villages by stretches of forest, but the land to the north of the road (Camps V and VI) is contiguous on the east with the fields of local Indians. There is a small town (Aganlashuk) of several thousand people about three miles

---

[2] This is a pseudonym.

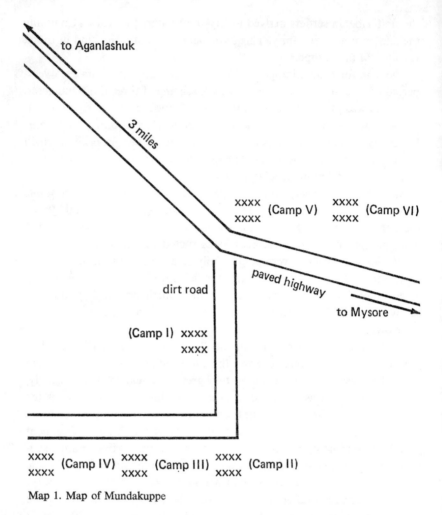

to Aganlashuk

3 miles

xxxx (Camp V)   xxxx (Camp VI)
xxxx   xxxx

dirt road   paved highway

to Mysore

(Camp I) xxxx
         xxxx

xxxx (Camp IV) xxxx (Camp III) xxxx (Camp II)
xxxx   xxxx   xxxx

Map 1. Map of Mundakuppe

northeast of the settlement on the main highway. At the point where the camp's dirt road intersects with the motor highway, a small trade/administrative complex has developed consisting of the offices and living quarters of the officials of the state government and a variety of Indian shops and restaurants.

The settlement itself is divided into six camps, each consisting of five hundred acres of farm land and roughly the same number of Tibetans. Each camp has a nucleated residential complex of one hundred tile-roofed houses around which the fields are arranged. Although the arable land was internally allocated on an individual basis to all Tibetans over the age of four, the basic jural unit in the settlement is a "household." Each household consists of five landholding persons who legally share one house. The household also possesses a number of agricultural tools as well as one draft animal for plowing. Because it is rare for a "real" family to coincide with the "legal" family, one house often contains two or more different and, not uncommonly, unrelated families. Neither the land nor the implements a person/household has can be sold. Furthermore, the land cannot be transmitted to one's heirs. Upon death, the land reverts back to the settlement.

The settlers of Mundakuppe were recruited and selected by the DLG from transit and road gang camps in north India. Almost all the main regional/sub-cultural groupings and social strata in Tibet are represented in the settlement. There are former "taxpayer" serfs, *dujung* serfs, traders, servants, craftsmen, monks, and various types of "unclean" castes. Although many of the settlers in Camp One have had previous agricultural experience in Tibet, this is not generally the case, and taking the settlement as a whole, the majority of settlers have had no prior farming experience.

The local staple crop is a variety of millet called *ragi*. Although Tibetans much prefer barley or wheat as food, because these cannot grow in Mysore, they have grudgingly adopted *ragi* as their main food crop. The technology associated with *ragi* cultivation, including the somewhat difficult transplanting process, was readily learned.

Aside from its taste, the main shortcoming of *ragi* is its relatively low yield potential. On the average, *ragi* yields only about 600 kilograms per acre and rarely exceeds 1000 kilograms per acre. Since *ragi* sold (in 1966/ 1967) for about 70 cents (*naya paise*) per kilogram, the gross monetary return per acre (using the 600 kilogram yield figure) comes to about 420 rupees.

Because of this low potential, various "experts" advised the cultivation of a more lucrative cash crop. Cotton and tobacco were tried but problems in procurement of seed and marketing led to their discontinuance. In 1966, a technical advisor recommended hybrid maize as an ideal crop. Although this idea met with considerable opposition from the settlers who remembered their previous experiences with cotton and tobacco and who were apprehensive about the large cash outlay maize requires for fertilizer, some were finally persuaded to plant maize and these were rewarded with a bumper crop. Since then maize accounts for about half of the acreage under cultivation.

Maize yields are much higher than those of *ragi*. Two thousand kilograms per acre is not unusual and the yields can run up to 3000 kilograms per acre. If we take 1600 kilograms per acre and 60 cents (*naya paise*) as the average yield and selling price, the gross monetary value of one acre of maize is about 960 rupees. After deducting the approximately 250 rupees paid per acre for fertilizer, seed, etc., the net yield of 700 rupees is still higher than even the gross figure for *ragi*. Maize is clearly a more lucrative crop.

We can get an idea of the relationship between this agricultural base and consumption requirements by looking at what the situation would be for a hypothetical family of three (with three acres). If they planted half maize and half *ragi*, their yield (taking the averages cited above) would be 2400 kilograms of maize and 900 kilograms of *ragi*. If they ate grain three times a day they would consume about 750 kilograms in a year (about 2 kilograms per day). Since Tibetans do not normally use maize flour, this would leave from the *ragi* yield about 150 kilograms. In addition to their grain needs, such a family would spend about 50 rupees a month (600 a year) on other foodstuffs such as oil, butter, milk, cigarettes, etc. Subtracting this from the 1050 rupees the maize yield converts to, the net cash remainder is 450 rupees. When the remaining 150 kilograms of *ragi* is similarly converted to a cash figure, the total profit for the three acres would be around 550 rupees.

Evidence from consumption patterns and standard of living bears out the contention that the settlement has been economically successful. In the period 1965–1967, there was a marked increase in consumption of what, in the settlement context, can be considered luxury items. Many of the Tibetan families who shared houses with other families moved out to their fields where they built new residences from their own funds. Those who had already moved to the fields made improvements such as replacing thatched roofs with tile roofs. There was considerable investment in new furniture and household possessions. Bicycles, and even some horses, became more and more common among the villagers. Gambling (ma jong and Tibetan dice) re-emerged although it had been initially banned. Furthermore, there was a tremendous increase in the use of Indian manual labor for field work. In spring and fall literally scores of Indians came daily to the camp seeking day-wage farm employment from Tibetans. A number of more affluent Tibetans were beginning to develop permanent employer/employee relations with particular Indians. Similarly, in 1967 it was becoming more common for impoverished young Indian boys to be taken in by Tibetan families. In return for room and board these Indian youths would do a variety of household tasks such as hauling drinking water from the wells. Another index of relative affluence can be seen in the way Mundakuppe has become a regular route for numerous Indian beggars, some of whom have gone so far as to learn to chant Tibetan prayers in Tibetan.

Mundakuppe's economic success has involved a delicate blending of traditional technology and customs with the increasingly effective utilization of modern agro-business technology. For example, on the traditional side, one type of plowing is done much as it was in Tibet with two-animal draft teams pulling a traditional type plow. Similarly, Tibetan methods of winnowing and threshing have been retained as have agricultural customs such as work songs. On certain days an observer would be hard pressed to know he was really in India and not in Tibet or some Himalayan kingdom.

On the other hand, Tibetans have been very open to change and have adopted a variety of both local Indian techniques and modern agricultural technology. The settlement has a cooperative society which has fourteen tractors and four trucks (run and maintained by Tibetans) and uses sophisticated hybrid maize seeds, different types of chemical fertilizers, and insecticides. The land has been contour bunded and there has been considerable development of tractor plowing by contours rather than by household holdings. There are several rat-proof grain warehouses which are used to maximize marketing profit. For example, one year the cooperative society took a 300,000 rupee loan from a bank to buy grain from the settlers at harvest time to be held until later in the year when the price would rise. Part of the profit difference was then redistributed among the farmers.

Economic self-sufficiency, however, is not the only criterion of successful resettlement and rehabilitation. Equally important are the cultural and psychological dimensions. In Mundakuppe, the continuity and vitality of Tibetan culture has been very successfully maintained. The Tibetan language is universally used in the settlement and all children learn not only Tibetan history and religion but also how to read and write the Tibetan language at a high level of proficiency. Similarly, Tibetan religion flourishes. Monks, lamas, and shamans function and there are several temples and monasteries. Religious rites and ceremonies are regularly performed, and the values and world view underlying the system are firmly accepted. Tibetan "national" identity is in many ways stronger and more explicit than it ever was in Tibet and there is tremendous pride in Tibetan culture and religion, as well as in the achievements of Mundakuppe. Tibetans feel no sense of inferiority vis à vis the Indians around them.

There is also very little manifestation of the dysfunctional behavior commonly associated with the "refugee" syndrome. There is little incidence of mental and emotional disorders and no incidence of alcoholism.

Crimes of property are few and occur within normal distribution parameters. Even though most of the Tibetans now realize it is not likely they will return to Tibet in their lives, the overall attitude of the people is positive.

This cultural adaptation has taken place along three lines. One of the most important of these has been the development of standards for intracultural interaction between Tibetans from the many diverse subcultural areas present in the settlement. Mundakuppe is a classic example of ethnic boundaries existing within ethnic boundaries. A kind of segmentary ethnicity has emerged. Within the Tibetan community, the major subcultural ethnic groups such as Khampas are clearly maintaining their identity vis à vis the other Tibetan groups although standards for intracultural (Tibetan) interaction have developed. For example, Lhasa Tibetan has come to be used as a *lingua franca* in the camp.

The second and equally important line of change has been the accommodation of traditional Tibetan political and social patterns to the democratic laws and institutions operative in India. For example, the DLG has written a constitution which, among other things, incorporates intraethnic (Tibetan) elections.

The third factor concerns Indo-Tibetan interaction. It is the least important of the three because Tibetan interaction with Indians has been restricted to fleeting encounters in the market place and sporadic contact in employer/employee situations where the Tibetans are in the dominant positions. There has been no interethnic development of personal or intimate relations, and marriage has been characterized by endogamy.

Space again precludes further discussion of these adaptations. In summary, however, the initial adaptation process in Mysore can be characterized as pervasive pluralism. Tibetan culture and identity have been conspicuously maintained and interethnic contact is almost completely limited to economic spheres. There has been virtually no assimilation to Indian cultural and social institutions. Concomitantly, there has been the impressive economic adaptation which combines traditional and modern agrobusiness techniques to exploit successfully the energy potential of a traditional niche. The economic success of the Tibetans is one of the most striking accomplishments of the program.

But what of the local Indian attitude to all this? Aliens are brought to their area and equipped with modern mechanized technology not available to them. These aliens not only become economically well off, but vigorously maintain their strange and alien cultural traditions. On the surface, this seems a fertile matrix for interethnic resentment, hostility, and conflict.

Whether or not there are strong feelings of resentment among local Indians is difficult to determine but, if so, it has not assumed behavioral significance. There have been few overt manifestations of hostility and conflict. Tibetans have generally had distant but cordial relations with local Indians and certainly do not feel unwelcomed or mistreated in the local area. The Tibetans, whose settlement has four stores run by their own cooperative society, regularly attend the weekly Indian market and go to the local Indian town. On any given day they can be seen shopping and going about their business in town. Because most of the older Tibetans know no Kannada, several of the Indian shopkeepers have actually learned a few words of Tibetan to facilitate business. Relations with the state government of Mysore have been very close and the Mysore government has shown an amazing capacity to understand and support the Tibetan population in Mundakuppe (and the other locations where Tibetans have been placed in Mysore). Local Tibetans genuinely have positive attitudes toward the Mysore government and India in general, and a number indicated that they would prefer to remain in Mysore rather than return to Tibet as it was under the old system (serfdom). All, however, would return under the new system.

How, then, do we account, on the one hand, for the economic, cultural, and psychological achievements of Tibetans in Mundakuppe and, on the other hand, for the absence of hostility and conflict between the Tibetans and the local Indians? Although a variety of factors, such as the policy of the GOI and the availability of resources, are relevant for this question, one factor — the internal political organization of the refugees — stands out as basic. In the new social and physical environment of India, the preservation of certain traditional Tibetan cultural patterns immediately offered the refugees competitive advantages. I contend that, in particular, traditional Tibetan political structure possesses a high "adaptive capacity" and is the single most important variable underlying the successful initial adaptation of the Tibetans. Let us, therefore, examine briefly aspects of both the traditional and the new (emergent) political structures.

The most important politico-economic institution in Tibet was serfdom. Except for a few hundred families of lords and religious corporate institutions, the remainder of the lay Tibetan population were serfs (*mi-ser*) of one sort or another, and these serf statuses were basically ascribed, that is, recruitment occurred automatically at birth through parallel descent lines. Serfs owed substantial service obligations to their lords who, in turn, were obligated to protect and provide subsistence for the serfs, this subsistence generally taking the form of arable land.

As in feudal Europe, the most important politico-economic resource was the manorial estate. Such estates were based on serf labor and were divided into a demesne section which the serfs worked as a corvée obligation and a testamentary section which consisted of the land the lord allocated to the serfs for their subsistence. Under this system the serfs were tied to the estate (i.e. they could not unilaterally and legally leave the estate) and they provided all the labor for the cultivation of the lord's demesne fields.

Estates were administered by stewards appointed for varying terms by the lord. These stewards were not local serfs but rather were selected from the household-administrative serf staff of the lord. Their main function was the overall administration of the lord's land to maintain a continual flow of products from the estate to the lord (in Lhasa). Under this general mandate the steward organized agricultural activities on the lord's demesne land, collected taxes, and intervened in any affairs (e.g. disputes) he felt might directly or indirectly affect the flow of goods. He was also the channel through which communication between the lord and the serfs took place and in some ways represented their individual and collective needs to the lord.

Among the serfs, however, we find an egalitarian structure. Within any given stratum of serfs each serf was the jural equal of all others, and competitive individualism pervaded the serf interactional system within a status. Although cooperative work and planning occurred under the authority of the steward, voluntary cooperation between the serfs was unusual.

Tibet, however, was characterized not only by a degree of feudal-like decentralization but also by centralization. The Tibetan political system can be described as a type of centralized feudal state. There was a central government headed by the Dalai Lama and administered by a bureaucracy consisting of an aristocratic and monastic official elite who ruled through a provincial administrative system comprising over one hundred district units. In each district, the central government posted one or two of its officials for terms usually of three years. Like the estate stewards, these district officials were primarily interested in maintaining the flow of goods and services that were owed the government from tax obligations. These officials, however, also adjudicated disputes, punished criminals, and represented the interests of the district to the central government. This government was the final source for adjudication and claimed ultimate rights over all land in Tibet. It alone could initiate national policy and it alone maintained an army. Suffice it to say that, although the exact parameters of any particular lord's authority varied, the central government was clearly paramount.

The central government was clearly dominated by religious orientations and personnel. The ruler, the Dalai Lama, was a bodhisattva (Avaloketisvara) who Tibetans believe has renounced his own nirvana to help all sentient creatures in general, and Tibetans in particular, to achieve final enlightenment. Furthermore, the regents who ruled in the Dalai Lama's infancy were also high incarnate lamas, and half of the governmental bureaucracy were monk officials recruited from the great Gelugpa monasteries around Lhasa. The overall orientation of the state, if there was one, was to promote the development of religion in Tibet. It was to provide a matrix conducive to the practice of religion. The entire governmental structure was thus intertwined with religion and its very legitimacy depended to a large extent on it.[2]

It was from this type of social system that Tibetans entered India by the thousands in 1959. From the beginning, as was indicated earlier, the old Tibetan government interceded with the GOI on behalf of Tibetans and succeeded in obtaining its consent to organize the refugees. Mundakuppe stands as one of the positive consequences of this détente between the Dalai Lama and the GOI.

In contrast to the traditional Tibetan social system, the new system in Mundakuppe emphasizes equality. All traditional ascribed differences have been legally eliminated. All the settlers have one acre of nonhereditary land whether they were beggars or wealthy traders in Tibet. Although former status differences continue to be recognized by some, and although notions of pollution persist, the jural and economic forces that supported these have been completely eliminated. These changes have been actively supported by the Dalai Lama and his government.

This democratic equality is, however, overlaid with political patterns of authority and hierarchy characteristic of the traditional Tibetan political system. There are no longer serfs and lords, and there are elections in the camp, but there is also paternalistic hierarchical rule.

As was described earlier, the settlement is divided into six camps each consisting of five hundred acres and five hundred persons (one hundred houses with five land-holding persons per house). The administrative hierarchy in the settlement consists of four levels of officials. The lowest level is the *cugpon (bcu dpon)*[3] or 'head of ten'. As his name implies, he represents ten households (fifty persons) and is concerned mainly with organizing labor "tax" obligations. These officials are elected annually and there are ten in each camp.

[2] For a more detailed discussion of the traditional Tibetan social system see the author's articles listed in the references.
[3] The transliteration system used here follows that described by T.V. Wylie (1959).

A more important official is the *chi-mi* (*spyi mi*) or camp leader. Each camp has two such officials who are elected on an annual basis. They receive a salary of 60 rupees a month which was initially collected from the residents of the camp but was later paid by the Cooperative Society.

Finally, there are the three *gardu* (*sgar 'thus*). These officials represent the three major ethnic subcultural areas: central Tibet (*dbus gtsang*), eastern Tibet (*khams* or *mdo smad*) and northeastern Tibet (*amdo* or *mdo stod*). They are elected for three-year terms and receive a monthly salary of 100 rupees from the DLG.

Above these positions are the appointees of the DLG. Chief among these is the camp leader. Unlike the lower camp officials, he is not a settler (has no land) and is not elected. He is, rather, an official of the DLG who was appointed by it to head the settlement. The camp leader during the time I was there was, in fact, a former monk official in the traditional Tibetan government. The camp leader heads an office called *döncö leygung* (*don gcod las khungs*) which contains a number of subordinate employees such as an English interpreter and a Tibetan secretary, and is considered a part of the DLG[4] which pays the salary of the officials. These officials are also not settlers but rather members of the DLG. Parallel but subordinate to the bureau office is the Cooperative Society. It also is headed by an official of the DLG who is under the camp leader and works hand-in-hand with him.

The camp leader is in charge of the overall administration of the settlement. Appointed by the DLG, he represents the needs of the settlers as a corporate collectivity to both the DLG and the Indian and foreign sectors. He and his staff plan and implement policy for the settlement with respect not only to technical-agricultural-marketing matters but also to social-cultural matters. For example, the use of beef and the playing of gambling games (dice and "big ma jong") have been forbidden in the settlement. Internally, the camp leader attempts to integrate and articulate the various diverse subcultural units and to present to them the policies and views of the DLG. He also plays an important role in maintaining the peace by using the prestige of his office to mediate disputes and altercations. Moreover he often acts on behalf of individuals in their dealings with Indian legal and political officials. In many ways, then, although the differences are as important as the similarities, the camp leader plays a role analogous to that of the district commissioner or estate steward in Tibet, and Mundakuppe resembles in some ways the type of estate in Tibet where the serfs (*dujung*) held only small plots of land for their lifetime. This resem-

---

[4]   It is formally titled: The Office of the Representative of His Holiness the Dalai Lama.

have a wonderful day

3202 ST JOE CTR RD
FORT WAYNE, IN 46835

THANK YOU

ST JOE   TEL# (260)485-8625

36 KS#13   S#1   Dec.12'05(Mon)20:22
STORE# 3107

1 10 MCNUGGETS MEAL	3.20
1 CKN CLUB-CPY MEAL	4.10
1 MED ROOT BEER	1.30
1 MED SPRITE	1.30
2 BBQ SAUCE	0.00

SUB TOTAL   9.90
TAKE OUT TAX   0.69

                                 10.59

CASH TENDERED   11.00

CHANGE   0.41

blance has not been lost on the settlers who jokingly refer to the rare settlement labor obligations (e.g. mending fences) by the name used for corvée taxes (*ula*) in Tibet. Similarly, the kinship patterns that have emerged in Mundakuppe follow those manifested by this type of serf in Tibet.

Mundakuppe is certainly not a feudal estate and the Tibetan settlers living there are not serfs, but the continuity in the type of hierarchical, appointive administrative leadership is striking. Although there has been a genuine democratization of many traditional Tibetan institutions, particularly with respect to land tenure, the camp leader's position represents a clear continuity with traditional Tibetan superordinate authority statuses.

As many anthropologists have pointed out in recent years, the retention of traditional sociocultural patterns in new environments is a function of the advantages they yield. Traditional sociocultural systems have different adaptive capacities in their new contexts and the manner and degree in which they are maintained depend on the competitive advantages they provide their holders. With respect to Tibetan refugees in the initial phases of contact, the Dalai Lama and his officials offered indisputable competitive advantages.

The Dalai Lama was an internationally known religio-political leader whose flight to India had drawn world-wide attention to the Tibetan situation. His exalted stature permitted him to negotiate with the GOI from a position of relative strength and facilitated the development of widespread lines of communication with numerous private and governmental personages and agencies both in India and abroad. Moreover, the ready availability of a core of highly experienced and competent governmental administrators provided the Tibetans a ready-made organization through which resources could be effectively aggregated and policy decided on and implemented. The DLG was able to monitor and coordinate activities and needs of Tibetan refugees all over India, as well as in Sikkim, Bhutan, and Nepal. The DLG offered the scattered Tibetan refugees a centralized and efficient organization that could integrate and represent their needs. This it has certainly done.

The very existence of a settlement in Mysore is an excellent example of this. The DLG, in conjunction with the GOI and various foreign aid agencies, developed the idea of resettling Tibetans permanently throughout India and worked out the specific details with respect to size, area, economic resources, etc. The DLG, furthermore, was responsible for implementing this policy within the Tibetan community. It convinced Tibetans to go to Mysore, an area which from North India seemed the end of the world. It also sent its officials to Mundakuppe in advance of the settlers and from the beginning organized activities internally and coordinated interaction with the Mysore and national governments. As needs and problems emerged, it was the representatives of the DLG who intervened and negotiated at length on whatever level was necessary. Given the traditional intrastratum individualism of Tibetan peasants, it is inconceivable that they could have so rapidly and effectively developed a leadership structure like that of the DLG. For example, even the DLG failed abysmally when they attempted in 1964 to institute communal (cooperative) labor in Mundakuppe. No one wanted to work for "the others."

However, unlike the old system, in Mundakuppe the settlers do not hold their land on the basis of tax and corvée obligations to a lord or the Tibetan government. Rather, each settler holds his acre from the GOI (and the Mysore State government) for the duration of his life regardless of whether he complies with the commands or decisions of the camp leader (or the DLG). This is the paradox of Mundakuppe. While on the surface there is political continuity in the form of a centralized hierarchical authority, in reality the hierarchical authority is extremely precarious.

The DLG found, and finds itself today, in the unenviable position of having no legal or constitutional status with respect to Indian law, and consequently it is not able to use coercive force to compel acquiescence with their policies. Its continued operation as a government depends completely on the voluntary compliance of the refugees, which, in turn, depends on the refugees' perceived self-interests and on their belief in the legitimacy of the DLG. But, even in the initial stages of the refugee situation, the latter was not completely unproblematic because significant numbers of refugees either had not been traditionally under the political authority of the DLG or had only recently come under it. It comes as no surprise, then, to find that the DLG has consistently and energetically attempted to reinforce these two general factors. The attempts of the DLG, however, are in large part responsible for the pluralistic character of the Tibetan's adaptation. It is my contention that the needs of the DLG in its new setting have produced policies that have been a powerful force for maintaining the initial ethnic differences and generating new ones. Let us first examine the self-interest variable.

The DLG actively attempted to aggregate relief funds for the refugees. It maintains offices not only in New Delhi but also in Geneva (where many of the relief agencies have headquarters) and New York City. It also publishes and distributes an English language newsletter throughout the world. Through its amazing intra-Indian and international organizational network, it has access to those in control of funds, and it has been very

successful in convincing them to recognize and deal with it as the legitimate leadership structure of the Tibetans. With two minor exceptions,
dissident groups of Tibetans have had little success in obtaining funds.

The DLG is also an important source of employment. It hires (for itself
and foreign sponsored projects) numerous Tibetans in various roles. It
has maintained the traditional prestigious titles and honorifics of government service but has opened service up to all strata. Thus, one of the
present council ministers was formerly a serf of one of the former council
ministers. The DLG also, to a large extent, monopolizes access to educational scholarships both in India and abroad.

In Mundakuppe this same pattern exists. In addition to the existence of
the camp itself, the office of the Dalai Lama (the camp leader) has managed
in a few short years to procure for the settlers tractors, trucks, scarce
hybrid seeds, chemical fertilizers, a medical clinic, electricity (in 1968–
1969), grinding mills, and so forth. The DLG has literally delivered the
goods to its constituency.

But while efforts to sustain old and discover new sources of aid continue, it is the ideological dimension that lies at the heart of the dynamics of
the adaptation of Tibetans to India. The strategy of the DLG in this
respect has taken several directions, all of which are oriented to maintaining cultural and social-relational boundaries. The DLG has actively
sought to maintain Tibetan social and cultural patterns and has fostered
a rigidly bounded plural adaptation for Tibetans.

The ideological policies of the DLG can be analytically separated into
three main dimensions:

1.   The development of an intense feeling of Tibetan cultural and political nationalism among Tibetans;

2.   The maintenance and expansion of the charisma and stature of the
Dalai Lama; and

3.   The fostering of social, political, and economic boundaries.

Nationalism is a rather new phenomenon for Tibetans. For centuries in
Tibet the relevant variable was not that of Tibet versus other national
entities but rather that of subcultural segments in conflict and opposition.
A good example of this is the term used for Tibet itself: *bod pa*. Actually,
this term, even in 1959, was used by eastern Tibetans to refer only to
central Tibetans. They considered themselves *khams pa* (eastern Tibetans) rather than *bod pa*, and many of them actively sought to remain, or
become, independent of the Tibetan (Dalai Lama's) government. Among
the Tibetans who arrived in India in 1959, the idea of a Tibetan national
identity was very poorly developed.

One factor immediately altering this state of affairs was the vivid realization of the fundamental similarities shared by all Tibetans that came as the result of their sudden immersion into the midst of a sea of Indians. The vast sociocultural distances initially felt to exist between the various Tibetan subcultural groups were significantly diminished, and this new awareness became an important foundation for the DLG's vigorous advocation of a Tibetan "national" (ethnic and political) identity.

Through its publications, such as the daily newspaper and the monthly newsmagazine, and through its control of the teaching staff and educational materials used in the Tibetan section of the school system, the DLG has effectively promoted the idea of a Tibetan nation and people, particularly among the young. Day in and day out this idea is expressed in the media and schools. Pride in one's language, customs, religious institutions, one's "modernized" government, and of course, in His Holiness, the Dalai Lama, are constant themes.

A new national anthem has been created which is sung daily in the schools and at public meetings. A new national holiday (March 10) commemorating the uprising of the Tibetan people against the Chinese in 1959 has also played an important part in mobilizing national sentiments. This March 10 holiday has been observed through various kinds of political demonstrations, some confined to the Tibetan settlements but many involving local Indian communities. Competition has developed between the various Tibetan communities as to which can produce the best celebration program, and this has been encouraged by the DLG which publishes detailed reports from each settlement on their activities. The scope of some of these celebrations is surprising. For example, in 1967 in Mundakuppe, the camp leader organized a massive truck demonstration for Mysore City. Fourteen open-topped trucks were rented and decorated with political slogans and statements. Handbills explaining in English the significance of the holiday were printed, and tapes reading the explanation were made in English, Kannada, Urdu, and Tibetan. Hundreds of Tibetans were loaded into the trucks and given the handbills to distribute while the tapes blared out the message through a portable public address system attached to the camp leader's car (which led the procession). For several hours these trucks drove throughout the city of Mysore, even stopping in front of the local Communist Party office. It was a great success and the Tibetans were received sympathetically by the local Indians. Although it was turning dark when the trucks returned to the settlement, the Tibetans who had to stay behind lined the settlement road and gave the participants a hero's welcome. It was a moving and uniting experience for the settlers.

A related theme is that of "returning to the homeland." Although the

DLG has advocated making the best of life in India, it has also vigorously maintained the position that there is hope of returning. The office of the DLG in New York has acted as a liaison with the United Nations and there have been repeated attempts to bring up the Tibetan question before that body. The various resolutions on human self-determination have been proclaimed by the Tibetan media as steps on the road of return to their country. The Tibetan media has given detailed, if not always accurate, coverage to the United Nations activities related to the Tibetan question.

Similarly, there has been a constant effort in the media to retain the idea of an overriding Tibetan nation by keeping before the people the plight of the Tibetan "brethren" left behind. There has been a steady diet of "eyewitness" accounts of the situation in Tibet by recent refugees; all having the theme of how lucky the refugees are in India and how the downtrodden brothers left in Tibet still believe in the Dalai Lama and earnestly desire a free Tibet headed by the Dalai Lama. Concomitantly, the Tibetan media continually expound on how the Chinese communists are trying to eradicate the Tibetan race in Tibet. It is, therefore, the duty of the refugees, led by the Dalai Lama and his government, to maintain the greatness and vitality of the Tibetan race and culture-nation.[5]

Underlying these perspectives is the theme of *rgyal zhen* or patriotism to the Tibetan cause. Support and compliance with the DLG is considered patriotic, whereas opposition and disagreement is considered traitorous because it allegedly harms the "Tibetan cause." The refugees have been continually exhorted in the media to exhibit true patriotism for Tibet (i.e. the DLG).

Another dimension of the development of a dynamic national consciousness has been the fostering of pride in selected Tibetan cultural traditions and a concerted attempt to maintain these in the alien socio-cultural matrix. Obviously, however, not all traditional cultural paraphernalia are compatible with the new "system" within whose parameters the DLG must act. For example, serfdom has no place in the "classless and casteless" ideology of the GOI. This feature of Tibetan society has been treated as a disgrace and is discussed with outsiders only with reticence. The attitude of Tibetan leaders and even peasants is that it is best forgotten.

This reticence instantly vanishes, however, when the conversation turns to Tibetan religion for it is this that all Tibetans hold up as the epitome

---

[5] For example, the following is a typical statement found in a recent Tibetan newspaper: *nga tsho ni gzhis lus bod mi'i re yul gcig po yin*/[We are the only hope of the Tibetans left behind in Tibet.].

of Tibetan cultural brilliance. Tibetans generally feel that their religion is superior to all others. The many foreigners who subscribe to Tibetan religion are the living proof for them of the inherent superiority of the "Tibetan way." Consequently, the DLG has actively and financially supported Tibetan religious and monastic institutions in India and has subtly encouraged the elimination of "little tradition" animistic elements such as oracles, shamans, etc. It has striven to keep monks together and to maintain monastic knowledge and learning and has financed a great deal of scholarship and publication in the religious sphere.

This elevation of religion to a place of intellectual and emotional superordination among the refugees leads us to the second dimension mentioned earlier, namely, the sustenance of the status of the Dalai Lama. For Tibetans who were adults when they came to India, the stature of the Dalai Lama was given. He was a great charismatic leader, the emanation of the bodhisattva diety, Avaloketiśvara, incarnated into human form to help Tibetans in particular and mankind in general to advance along the path to salvation. His presence, of course, was one of the main legitimizing factors underpinning the traditional government. In India, however, with the reconstitution of the DLG as a political entity devoid of either legal foundation or control of force, the legitimizing role of the Dalai Lama has become even more important than in Tibet, particularly among the new generation of refugees. Belief in the sanctity and extraordinariness (charisma) of the Dalai Lama and his rightful role of ruler had to be enculturated into the refugee youths and maintained among the adults if the DLG were to sustain itself in its new context.

This has been very successfully accomplished. Although many factors are relevant here, one of the most important has been the virtual monopolization by the DLG of informational input to the settlers. Through the school system and various publications, the reputation and accomplishments of the Dalai Lama have been consistently exalted. The Dalai Lama has been portrayed not only as the symbol or quintessence of Tibetan national identity but also as the patron of the Tibetan people who is directly responsible for their successful adaptation in India and their future expectations. There has been in-depth coverage of the activities of the Dalai Lama, and in many cases his speeches have been reprinted as separate pamphlets. Similarly, all Tibetan school children start their school day by singing, along with the national anthem, a prayer song composed by the Dalai Lama. Whatever the religious merit of the song, it is unquestionably associated in the minds of Tibetans with the Dalai Lama himself.

Deep belief and unfaltering reverence for the Dalai Lama are manifested continually by the people. In Mundakuppe, for example, the stereotyped phrase "by the kindness of the Dalai Lama" precedes almost all comments on the state of the refugees in India. All successes are attributed to the grace of the Dalai Lama. I have seen even very highly westernized Tibetans spontaneously prostrate themselves before the Dalai Lama. This continued belief in the Dalai Lama (which in some senses borders on cult fervor) as both the spiritual and the political leader has played a critical role in providing the DLG the legitimacy it needs to obtain compliance from the people for its policies. Perhaps the best indication of the overall success of this policy is the fact that starting from about 1968–1969, a voluntary program of taxation (literally: *zhal 'debs* or 'donations') was introduced by the DLG. This program has met with acceptance both throughout the refugee settlements in India and among Tibetans abroad. As usual, the Tibetan language media play an important role in sustaining this by publicizing donors and encouraging "friendly" competition between the different communities.

The development of strong feelings of national identity and the enhancement of the stature of the Dalai Lama have gone hand in hand with an attempt to maintain cultural and politicoeconomic boundaries. The DLG certainly does not encourage or support policies that facilitate intimate contact and interaction with aliens, either Indians or Europeans. Endogamy is vigorously encouraged and is intertwined with generalized notions of nationalism, in that it is portrayed as absolutely fundamental to the preservation of the Tibetan race, a race endangered by the actions of the communists in Tibet.

One of the most important policies of the DLG relevant to boundary maintenance concerns language. The DLG has energetically supported the use and teaching of Tibetan within the refugee community. The school system does a truly excellent job of teaching literary Tibetan to the refugee youth on a high level of proficiency, and the literacy rates among the young are extremely high. For the older refugees there are night schools that teach enough so that a person can read the newspapers (whose importance to the DLG has been indicated above). Spoken Tibetan is used throughout the Tibetan communities and in Mundakuppe the language is used not only in intimate, family contexts but everywhere in the camp in all situations. The settlers do not need to know any other language and most of the older ones do not. The camp leader's office (i.e. the DLG) provides the linguistic expertise and channels through which Tibetans can deal with Indians and Europeans.

Another aspect of boundary maintenance concerns the DLG's attitude toward Indian citizenship. Here we find, not surprisingly, that the DLG has taken a strong stand against Tibetans taking Indian citizenship even though this would seem to afford Tibetans competitive advantages. The current stateless status of the Tibetans places them under a variety of disadvantages with respect to such things as land ownership, business licenses, and freedom of movement within India. The DLG, however, has maintained the position that Tibetans taking Indian citizenship would diminish the strength of the refugees' claims to Tibet. Taking Indian citizenship, therefore, is considered as a renunciation of Tibetan cultural and national aspirations and is actively opposed. It is obvious, however, that a consequence of this policy (whether intentional or not) is the greater dependence of the refugees on the DLG. Because as individuals Tibetans are stateless "guests" of the GOI, their strength lies in their collectivity, and it is precisely the role of the Dalai Lama and the DLG to organize and represent that collectivity.

On the local (Mundakuppe) scene, an important policy concerns economic alternatives. In the initial phases of the settlement the camp leader and the GOI felt that it was critical for the refugees to focus all their attention on learning the necessary agricultural skills. To facilitate this, a policy was instituted whereby Tibetans were not permitted to engage in other private jobs or businesses either in the camp or in the neighboring areas. This, it was felt, would preclude the many refugees who had been traders in Tibet from seeking to earn their living in this way rather than from the land. Since the Mysore government refrained from issuing licences for shops, etc., without the recommendation of the camp leader (DLG), the settlers in fact were forced to devote all their attention to their land.

By 1966, however, this rule had outlived its utility. The settlement was an agricultural success but, as we shall see, needed supplementary sources of financial input which independent businesses could have offered. Yet the rule was not rescinded. It is difficult to avoid the conclusion that by 1966–1967, the initially nonpolitical policy had taken on manifest political dimensions. This policy obviously greatly increased the dependence of the settlers on the DLG since it eliminated one type of independent economic alternative. By making the settlers completely dependent on their land, the power of the DLG was enhanced because it, through the camp leader and the Cooperative Society, controlled the tractors, seeds, fertilizers, and the technical knowledge that supported the complex agrobusiness approach used in the camp. There were, in fact, several instances during my stay in the settlement when political opposition groups were refused permission to open small businesses in the nearby Indian town. This raises the question of negative sanctions. So far, we have examined only the DLG's use of positive or persuasive strategies. As one would expect, the DLG also employed negative sanctions. Basically, it used its control of resources to apply pressure on individuals to comply with its policies. For example, political opponents of the DLG find that their children do not receive scholarships for higher education or jobs in government related activities. An example from Mundakuppe will illustrate how such sanctions were employed in the settlements.

In 1963, the Cooperative Society was incorporated under the control of the camp leader and the DLG. Its membership was to consist of all the land-holding settlers, each of whom was supposed to purchase at least one 10-rupee share. While most of the Tibetans did this, a number did not. Not surprisingly, almost all of those who did not buy shares were from a subcultural area traditionally hostile to the DLG and a religious sect different from that of the Dalai Lama. In addition to these people, a number of others from that region had come to the settlement subsequent to the initial membership drive.

In 1966, the camp leader and the head of the Cooperative Society decided to try to increase the membership of the cooperative, particularly among that dissident segment. They used as leverage their control over rationed goods. The state government administered the ration quotas through agents who could pay for the goods in a lump sum and see to their collection and distribution. The Cooperative Society took on this job for the settlement. The items involved were important ones in the diet of the Tibetans, including such things as wheat and sugar. The camp leader, then, in 1966 informed the people that it would not issue rations to persons who were not members of the society as this was not fair to those who had paid for their shares. Because the nonmembers wanted these foodstuffs, they were effectively forced to join to obtain them.

These, then, comprise the main ways the DLG has attempted to maintain its authority. While changes have occurred in the traditional political system, political continuity in terms of hierarchical elitist authority is the single most important factor underlying the Tibetans successful adaptation. The pluralistic nature of the adaptation can be seen to result partly from the policies of the GOI but mainly from the policies and strategies of the DLG. The general pluralistic accommodation of Tibetans in Mundakuppe is as much a byproduct of political prerequisities as a valued end in itself.

But what of Indo-Tibetan contact within this adaptation? The relations between the two ethnic groups have been cordial. There has been no significant hostility or conflict even though the Tibetans share the same niche with Indians and are competing for resources with the Indians.

Part of the answer to this has already been discussed. The "farming only" policy of the DLG not only strengthened the office but also ARTI- FICIALLY delimited a sub-niche for the Tibetans. By voluntarily relin- quishing one major economic arena to the local population, the seemingly inevitable interethnic competition for resources has been decreased, if not eliminated. Consequently, the tremendous economic development of the surrounding area, particularly the town of Aganlashuk, has been con- trolled by Indians. By limiting themselves to the roles of primary pro- ducer and consumer, the Tibetans have provided the indigenous Indians a whole new source of wealth and income. This has aided the merchant class as well as others since the development of new and the expansion of old service industries has created many new jobs.

The coming of Tibetans has transformed the sleepy town of Aganlashuk into a bustling trade and business center. Moreover, during the two-year period I was in Mundakuppe, a new business area was developing at the intersection of the motor highway and the camp dirt road. What was initially a small administrative complex of the government of the state of Mysore had grown considerably; by the time I left it comprised several restaurants, grocery stores, and a bicycle repair and sales shop.

The presence of Tibetans has also benefited the poor landless Indians by affording them a new source of employment: working for Tibetans. Hundreds of Indians (men, women, and children) work in the fields for Tibetans on a day-wage basis. Furthermore, some Indian youths, as mentioned above, have begun to initiate relationships with Tibetan fam- ilies wherein they live with the Tibetans, receiving room and board in return for which they do odd jobs around the house. For the beggars, Mundakuppe has become a gold mine and is regularly plied by many of them.

In addition to the merchants and the poor, the wealthy landowners have also benefited financially from the settlement. The DLG has con- sciously attempted to alleviate the natural jealousy resulting from the Tibetans' possession of tractors and trucks by making the tractors avail- able on a rental basis to the Indian landowners. Many Indians have avail- ed themselves of this by hiring the tractors and drivers directly. Others have leased sections of unused land to the Tibetan cooperative, a practice very advantageous because there is no danger of the tenant not relin- quishing the land.

There is no question, then, but that the general area around Munda- kuppe has prospered as a result of the Tibetan settlement. It is not sur- prising, therefore, to find that in 1970–1971 a new settlement of four thousand Tibetans was started contiguous to Mundakuppe. Even more recently, several thousand monks have been resettled from Assam to an area also adjacent to Mundakuppe. In all, there are about ten thousand Tibetans living in that area. In Mysore as a whole, there are about seventeen thousand Tibetans.

The lack of ethnic hostility and conflict between Tibetans and Indians must be seen as a consequence of both the artificial restriction of resource competition and the general economic benefits, which the presence and success of the refugees has yielded for local Indians.

CONCLUSION

I have illustrated some of the main aspects of the initial process of adaptation of Tibetans in Mundakuppe, in particular, and India, in general. In the initial decade of residence in India the Tibetans, with the help of the GOI, the state governments, and the foreign sectors, have made tremendous adjustments to the new social and physical environment they encountered. Underlying the success of this adjustment has been the continuity of many traditional Tibetan sociocultural institutions, in particular, the governmental structure headed by the Dalai Lama. Although there have been many changes in the DLG in India with respect to recruitment, authority, and power, its fundamental traditional "legitimate political authority" has been continued. The DLG offered the disparate Tibetan refugees tremendous competitive advantages, particularly in the early years of settlement. What has been surprising, however, is the DLG's ability to maintain its superordinate position. I have tried to indicate some of the basic strategies the DLG has employed to accomplish this. I have also tried to show how basic political requirements have led the DLG to direct the process of adjustment in a direction emphasizing ethnic identity and integrity and how this has resulted in the pluralistic, cultural-separatist nature of the Tibetan adaptation in India.

It is difficult, however, to speak of the adaptation of Tibetans in India, for the concept of adaptation implies a dynamic process. As John Bennett (1969: 18) has written: "Adaptation is conceived as a process of potential adjustment to existing and changing conditions." With respect to the Tibetans, a number of changing circumstances ("inputs") have already (or will) set into motion important new responses. Although these will be better dealt with in a separate paper, it would be misleading to conclude without giving some indication of the nature of these new factors.

The new inputs are basically threefold. First, there is the question of the long-term economic stability of the settlement. Second, there is a pattern of the DLG being decreasingly able to aggregate resources and thus directly benefit the settlers economically. And third, the settlers themselves are becoming increasingly confident of their ability to exist alone in the Indian context, and therefore they are increasingly less apprehensive of undertaking independent courses of action.

One important dimension of the economic circumstances of Mundakuppe is the beginning of a disparity between output and population. Because of good medical care, the death rate has been dramatically reduced over what it would have been in Tibet. Since birth control is not used in the settlement (the DLG vigorously opposes it), there has been a steady population increase. However, the amount of land available is fixed. Thus, as the population increases, the surplus margin produced by the land will decrease, given the same level of productive output. Moreover, there is no likelihood that production will increase. Chemical fertilizers and insecticides are already in use and, as the land may be overworked, the output may even decrease. Given the nature of land tenure described above, it is also certain that settlers will not invest private capital to improve their land and generate higher output. Consequently, unless there is some form of out-migration of excess population or unless other, nonagricultural economic sources of income are developed, the long term future of Mundakuppe faces serious difficulties.

As to economic alternatives, although the "farming only" policy limits one obvious type of alternative, a number of settlers have taken to peddling woolen sweaters throughout India in the agricultural off-season. Tibetans, in fact, have become famous for this type of trading. How long the "farming only" policy can be maintained is another matter, and, even more seriously, what will happen to Indo-Tibetan relations when it ends, is at present imponderable.

Out-migration, on the other hand, is not a very likely alternative. Employment opportunities for Tibetans are very limited. However, more recently a new factor has emerged which may have an important impact. The creation, contiguous to Mundakuppe, of a large settlement of 3000 monks, all from Drepung monastery, has opened a potential population-absorbing channel. The monks will be able to work their land communally and thus will make maximally efficient use of the mechanization available to them. Their yield per capita will be considerably higher than that of individual families with their few acres. Consequently, they will be able to support numbers well in excess of the one person per acre ratio of the lay settlers. Moreover, it is not unreasonable to expect that the monastic units will also obtain income by taking up their traditional money-lending activities. They also will undoubtedly receive extensive gifts from the lay settlers. The significance of this for population distribution lies in the traditional Tibetan custom of giving children as monks to the monasteries and the monastery taking care of their sustenance. I expect that this traditional pattern will reemerge and become an important channel for population redistribution.

If these are some poignant future problems, the present also has produced important changes. Prime among these is the decreasing ability of the DLG to obtain foreign funds. Increasingly, the DLG is becoming dependent upon the voluntary "taxes" that the refugees (in India and abroad) have been paying. It has had to cut back much of the fat from the elaborate bureaucratic network it had developed in the earlier years. Thus, there are a growing number of young educated Tibetans who would have become DLG officials five years ago but who today have to find their own livelihood or otherwise to farm land in the settlements. This growing inability of the DLG to provide high status employment for the youth they have carefully reared and molded is beginning to weaken its position.

The best indication of this is the growing emergence (or better, reemergence) of political opposition groups. In recent years, associations and clubs from traditionally hostile regional and subcultural segments have begun to take a more active and open part in intra-Tibetan political competition. In some instances these groups have pursued actions independent of the Tibetan "national" framework. Among the young, there also has been an increase in independent thought and speech, including open criticism of governmental actions. In Mundakuppe, for example, there are those who would like to see the DLG appointed camp leader replaced by an ELECTED settler. While, on the whole, the DLG's vigorous policy of developing a national identity and spirit have been successful, it obviously has not eradicated traditional particularistic affiliations.

In conclusion, the situation among Tibetan refugees in India is far from settled. In the next decade, these populations will be confronted by very serious economic and political problems. Whether their initial emphasis on a cultural-pluralistic or ethnic strategy will prove workable in the long run is problematic. For the present, such a strategy has greatly facilitated the resettlement and rehabilitation of large numbers of Tibetans in an alien cultural milieu. However, its success thus far has depended upon a very delicate balance of institutional processes that have served to regulate intra- and interethnic relationships in respect to the competition for limited environmental resources.

REFERENCES

BENNETT, JOHN W.

1969   *Northern plainsmen.* Chicago: Aldine.

GOLDSTEIN, MELVYN C.

1971a Taxation and the structure of a Tibetan village. *Central Asiatic Journal* 15(1):1–27.

1971b Serfdom and mobility: an examination of the institution of "human lease" in traditional Tibetan society. *Journal of Asian Studies* 30(3): 521–534.

1971c Stratification, polyandry and family structure in Tibet. *Southwestern Journal of Anthropology* 27(1):64–74.

1971d The balance between centralization and decentralization in the traditional Tibetan political system: an essay on the nature of Tibetan political macro-structure. *Central Asiatic Journal* 15(3):170–182.

1973   The circulation of estates in Tibet: reincarnation, land, and politics. *Journal of Asian Studies* (May).

GOODENOUGH, W.

1970   *Description and comparison in cultural anthropology.* Chicago: Aldine.

WYLIE, T. V.

1959   A standard system of Tibetan transcription. *Harvard Journal of Asiatic Studies* 22:261–276.

CONCLUSION

Toward a Theory of
Ethnic Phenomena

LEO A. DESPRES

It may be recalled from the introduction that the papers included in this volume were prepared with a view toward focusing comparative attention on the relationship that might exist between the genesis and persistence of ethnic boundaries, the political incorporation of ethnic populations, the organization of inter-ethnic relations, and competition for environmental resources. It is transparently evident from the work of several contributors that such an inquiry could not proceed without interrogating at least some of the conceptual apparatus attending the study of ethnic and racial phenomena. That this was necessary should not come as a surprise to those who are familiar with the literature: in the absence of an established and generally acceptable theoretical framework, it needs to be considered how observations will be ordered and interpreted. And so, quite apart from their respective substantive foci, these papers are not devoid of important theoretical discussions. Thus, in assessing the results of this exercise, it is only logical to consider first the nature of these theoretical discussions in reference to the more general context from which they seem to have arisen.

In 1973, at least two events served to mark the research interests that are most current among anthropologists. At the Spring meetings of the American Ethnological Society (AES), the entire program of symposia was structured with a specific focus on problems relating to the investigation and comparative analysis of ethnicity and ethnic group relations. Later in the year, and on a much grander scale, many of the substantive, conceptual, and theoretical issues that attended the AES discussions were revisited at the IXth International Congress of Anthropological and Ethnological Sciences, where approximately 200 of the more than 1200 contributed papers were organized in seven different sessions devoted to the discussion of comparative ethnic studies.

From the perspective of intellectual history, there is a curious dimension to this current preoccupation with ethnic phenomena among anthropologists. Most scholars who are concerned with ethnic studies are quite familiar with anthropology's contributions to the biology of race. Also well known is anthropology's long tradition of ethnographic and ethnological research. However, with some notable exceptions (e.g. Kuper 1947; Wagley 1952; Wagley and Harris 1958; Harris 1964; Smith 1965), the literature of anthropology suggests that relatively few social and cultural anthropologists have been theoretically stimulated to inquire into the role of racial and ethnic phenomena in relationship to the organization of groups or, for that matter, the organization of total societies. Introductory texts generally tell us what the field is all about and they serve to illustrate the point. Beginning with the index to Tylor's (1916) introduction to the study of man and civilization, and including texts by Lowie (1920, 1940), Linton (1936, 1955), Nadel (1951), Keesing (1959), Goldschmidt (1960), Bohannan (1963), Beattie (1964), Mair (1965), Hoebel (1966), and Keesing and Keesing (1971), ethnic, ethnic group, ethnic relationships, or the like are accorded no special listing. Ethnology and ethnography are described; ethnocentricism is often defined; but, if employed in any context, the word "ethnic" appears without definition or analytical significance. It may well be that in these works ethnic phenomena are subsumed under other labels. However, even were that the case, unless we adopt the cognitive structure of Trobrianders, we have to assume that the introduction of new labels marks some sort of shift in our thinking.

A more general review of the social science literature suggests that studies of racial and ethnic phenomena have fallen largely within the province of sociology.[1] In conceptualizing ethnicity, sociologists have drawn heavily upon anthropological studies of culture. However, the substantive and theoretical significance of most sociological investigations

---

[1] Among the sociological classics, one should mention Thomas and Znaniecki's (1918–1920) five-volume work on Polish peasants, Wirth's (1928) study of a Jewish community, Drake and Cayton's (1945) study of urban adjustment among Negroes, and Frazier's (1949) overview of Negro life in America. There has been a relatively continuous flow of sociology texts treating race and ethnic relations; some of the better known of these are: Park (1950), Hughes and Hughes (1952), Lind (1955), Berry (1958), Simpson and Yinger (1958), Shibutani and Kwan (1965), Banton (1967), Blalock (1967), van den Berghe (1967), and Schermerhorn (1970).

derive their intellectual force from the concern that sociologists have shown in a broad range of social problems related to the incorporation of racial and cultural minorities in urban and industrial societies. In this vein, it is interesting to note that the index to Beals and Hoijer's (1971) most recent anthropology text contains a reference to "ethnic" populations in urban ghettos. Similarly, the index to Harris' (1971) text also provides a listing under "ethnic" by way of reference to cultural and racial "minorities."[2]

Reflecting more specifically upon the literature of anthropology, one is tempted to consider ethnic studies B.B. and A.B. (i.e. Before and After Barth, editor, 1969). Before Barth, excluding a few important studies of racial and cultural minorities (e.g. Wagley 1952, Wagley and Harris 1958), ethnic phenomena receive their most explicit theoretical attention in the work of those anthropologists who are concerned with the organization of plural societies. The single most important contributor to this area of research (Smith 1969: 104) has emphasized that ethnic combinations are clearly strategic in the study of social and cultural pluralism.[3]

However, quite apart from the strategic significance of ethnic populations in the study of social and cultural pluralism, it has not followed that the concept of ethnicity has received a great deal of analytical refinement in the literature relating to plural societies.[4] That this is the case is most evident in some of the writings of M. G. Smith. For example, in a recent article treating pluralism in pre-colonial Africa, M. G. Smith (1969: 104–105) defines ethnicity to denote "... common provenience and distinctness as a unit of social and biological reproduction; it accordingly connotes internal uniformities and external distinctness of biological stock, perhaps of language, kinship, culture, cult, and other institutions."[5] The theoretical and methodological difficulties attending this conception are simply too obvious to warrant discussion. Suffice it to say that neither M. G. Smith nor any other anthropologist concerned with the study of plural societies has applied this biocultural conception of ethnicity to the collection and analysis of data. More generally, plural theorists have given emphasis to the cultural differentiation of population units within an

---

[2] One cannot help but wonder if it is necessary to conceptualize ethnicity differently for populations in the "bush" and in the city; or, is it perhaps that anthropologists who come to town view populations differently?

[3] See also Smith (1957, 1960, 1965), Rubin (1960), Benedict (1961, 1962), and Despres (1964, 1967, 1969).

[4] This statement is not to include sociologists who have been concerned with the study of plural societies. For example, see van den Berghe (1970: 3–16).

[5] This conception of ethnicity is reminiscent of Seligman's (1930) description of the races of Africa.

overall system of such units. Apart from this general emphasis, the concept of ethnicity has not assumed strategic significance within the system of concepts that characteristically form the framework of plural theory.

All of this is to suggest that ethnic phenomena did not receive a great deal of theoretical attention among anthropologists until the publication of Barth's investigations of the populations inhabiting the Northwest province of Pakistan and the adjoining frontier areas of Afghanistan (Barth 1956, 1959, 1964). Regarding these investigations, it would appear that Barth's interest in ethnic boundaries followed upon his collection of data and was perhaps as much determined by the ethnographic complexity of the area in which he worked as by any pre-established theoretical interest in ethnic problems as such.

To state the matter more concretely, the populations of Northwest Pakistan presented difficulties of description and analysis not unlike the difficulties which Evans-Pritchard (1940) and Fortes (1945) had encountered in reference to the Nuer and the Tallensi. For example, as in the case of the Nuer and the Dinka (Evans-Pritchard 1940), the Pathans and such neighboring groups as the Baluchi revealed no precise or determinate relationships among their linguistic, cultural, social, and political boundaries. Apart from the social heterogeneity of many Pathan communities, among themselves, Pathan populations disclosed a variety of economic adaptations and styles of life. In the North, where Baluch tribes encroached upon these populations, large parts of some Baluch tribes acknowledged Pathan origins (Barth 1969b: 117–134). With reference to Nuer-Dinka relationships, Evans-Pritchard (1940: 192–248) had emphasized that structurally significant boundaries were drawn primarily on the basis of categorical ascriptions. This also appeared to be the case in Northwest Pakistan. However, whereas Evans-Pritchard, and also Fortes (1945), had elected to largely ignore the theoretical import of such observations, much to his credit, Barth did not.

As Barth viewed the situation in Northwest Pakistan, the Pathan and Baluch populations disclosed a more inclusive system of ecologic, political, social, and cultural relationships, and the structure and organization of their respective communities could not be explained apart from the analysis of this system. Because this more general system of relationships enjoined ascribed statuses that were presumptively determined in reference to social origin and cultural background, Barth elected to conceptualize it as one of a poly-ethnic type. Accordingly, he further conceptualized ethnicity as a largely subjective process of status identification. It followed from all of this (Barth 1969a: 13–16) that ethnic groups are formed to the extent that actors use ethnic identities to categorize themselves and others for purposes of interaction. It also followed that a stable system of inter-ethnic relations presupposes a structuring of inter-action along the boundaries of ethnic groups; that is to say, it presupposes a set of rules governing situations of inter-ethnic contact.

Without detracting from the merit of these more recent works, it is apparent that a theoretical framework capable of informing comparative ethnic studies has not yet emerged. Various contributions to the present volume serve to illustrate the point. Skinner (cf. 152), for example, emphasizes that the plural society model tends to obfuscate the political factors that determine how complex societies function. On the other hand, van den Berghe, who is often identified as a pluralist, underscores (cf. 75) the extreme subjectivism associated with Barth's conception of ethnicity. Still another view is presented by Hoetink (cf. 18) who, after noting that ethnicity may ambiguously subsume a variety of exclusive or overlapping ascriptive loyalties, prefers to discard altogether the concept of ethnic group in favor of analyzing these loyalties in terms of their ascriptive content and their greater or lesser correlation.

Notwithstanding these and other elements of disagreement, the papers that form this volume do reveal, even if in nascent form, a convergent line of theoretical development. On one level this is expressed by the similar preoccupation of different contributors with a relatively focused range of conceptual and theoretical issues. To note but one example, all of these papers are inclined to take issue with the subjectivist conception of ethnicity which is thought to derive from the work of Barth. At the same time, however, they seem to agree that an exclusively objectivist, or cultural, conception of ethnicity is equally unserviceable. This makes theoretically problematic not only the relationship between cultural distributions and categorical ethnic ascriptions but also the role and overall significance of the subjective element in respect to such ascriptions.

On another level, a convergent line of development is evidenced by a glossary of concepts which includes, *inter alia*, ethnic and/or racial diacritica, identity, and status; ethnic boundaries, populations, groups, and stratifications; and boundary maintenance and incorporation processes such as accommodation, assimilation, and conflict. These conceptions repeatedly insinuate themselves in related discussions, suggesting perhaps that they are key elements and form an essential starting point for any critical examination of ethnic phenomena. Except for brief excursions, the central focus of this volume has not stimulated individual contributors to give a great deal of formal attention to the definition or clarification of these conceptual elements. Notwithstanding this fact, we ought to inquire into the problems attending the use of these concepts and determine how they might provide a more serviceable framework for future research.

Several of the contributors to this volume seem to agree that ethnicity is both an objective and a subjective phenomenon. This view is most clearly expressed by van den Berghe (cf. 72) who states: "Ethnic groups are defined BOTH by the objective cultural modalities of their behavior (including most importantly their linguistic behavior), and by their subjective views of themselves and each other."

At first blush, this conception of ethnicity seems clear enough. However, certain ambiguities attend its construction so as to seriously impair its heuristic value. For example, in any complex situation there is the problem of ascertaining the distribution of cultural modalities, including modalities of language and dialect variation. Judging from the literature of anthropology, there is every reason to suppose that such distributions in most instances will not disclose unambiguous and definitive boundaries, particularly in respect to populations that have been relatively contiguous over long periods of time. Accordingly, the definition and significance of such boundaries will be drawn in reference to criteria which are theoretically meaningful to the observer. It follows from this realization that the question must be posed as to whether or not boundaries so drawn will correspond to cognitive orientations which the populations in question might evince in respect to themselves and others. To ascertain this, the observer will need to impose other criteria according to which the significance of still another set of distributions may be determined. The relationship that exists among these various distributions poses still another order of problems.

A more concrete feeling for some of these difficulties can be gleaned from Whitten's penetrating analysis of ethnicity among the Jungle Quechua. Based upon data relating to the distribution of cultural and linguistic modalities among the populations of the Oriente, Whitten (cf. 47) concludes that the Canelos Quechua are not homogeneous in their ethnic make-up. However, with reference to the contrastive identities which the Canelos Quechua apply to themselves and to others, Whitten also concludes that "... they are nonetheless a self-identifying, if highly individualistic, indigenous aggregate with clear cultural markers ..." Thus, for purposes of defining the Canelos Quechua as an ethnic population, Whitten gives predominate emphasis to the stereotypic and contrastive identities which the Canelos Quechua ascribe to themselves and to others.

While taking issue with the subjectivist view of ethnicity, none of the contributors to this volume would disregard altogether the significance of subjective elements attaching to ethnic identities. Nevertheless, important conceptual and theoretical problems remain obscured for lack of formal consideration. The papers by Despres, Goldstein, Holloman, van den Berghe, and Whitten provide discursive data in support of the conclusion that categorical identities are highly relativistic. They vary according to language and dialect and according to the referent populations for which contrasts are being drawn. They vary according to whether they are achieved or ascribed. If ascribed, they also vary according to whether they are self-ascribed, ascribed by others, or both.

Ethnic identities which are self-ascribed need not correspond to the identities which others impose. This implicates the problem of relative power. For example, if individuals are accorded ethnic identities by others, and if these identities enjoin imperative statuses in the sense that such individuals are denied rights and privileges which others enjoy in the public domain, then it would seem to be a rather moot methodological point as to whether or not these individuals assert, or otherwise subjectively acquiesce in, the status identities which are imposed upon them. However, the contrary is the case. As Holloman shows for the Cuna, Whitten for the Canelos Quechua, Goldstein for Tibetan refugees, and Despres for Afro- and Indo-Guyanese, the assertion of ethnic status identities may provide an ideological basis for the corporate or political organization of ethnic populations.

It also emerges from these papers that not all categorical identities are ethnic; and related to this is the fact that ethnic identities are rarely inclusive of the full range of social identities structured into poly-ethnic societies. Thus, from a social organizational point of view, ethnic identities may vary according to the variety of social situations in which they may be appropriately expressed. It follows from this that individuals need not play ethnic roles all of the time in order that poly-ethnic systems persist; that the ethnic identities ascribed to population aggregates do not make of those aggregates corporately or politically organized groups; and that corporately organized ethnic groups need not be the only politically important groups to which individuals might belong in a poly-ethnic society. And it follows from all of this that the behavioral significance of ethnicity, for individuals as well as for the groups they form, cannot be ascertained apart from a rather comprehensive analysis of the overall social system.

Thus, whether one wishes to pursue the notion of plural societies, as employed by van den Berghe and others, or substitute for it the notion of ethnic or poly-ethnic systems, as proposed by Skinner, it is necessary to keep clear the various levels at which ethnic phenomena are socially engaged and analytically interrogated. Except for Holloman, who makes reference to the distinction between macro- and micro-structure, and

Despres, who relates ethnic phenomena to differentiated levels of analysis, this structure remains somewhat oblique in most of the papers under consideration.

To summarize, the papers which comprise this volume suggest that prevailing conceptions of ethnicity are perhaps too ambiguous in their overall construction to significantly advance the comparative study of ethnic phenomena beyond the work of Barth. Clearly, such phenomena are multidimensional. They simultaneously engage elements that tend to be conceptualized differently in reference to the analysis of cultural systems, organized groups, and individual transactions. Unless these elements are ordered within some more systematic and inclusive theoretical framework, it will be difficult to derive and comparatively establish generalizations in respect to poly-ethnic societies.

In the direction of such theoretical development, there appears to be some agreement among various contributors to this volume that ethnicity is but one of several possible forms of status ascription which may be contrasted to all forms of status achievement. These dissimilar forms of social differentiation give issue to correspondingly dissimilar stratification structures. Accordingly, ethnic phenomena might best be understood from the point of view of stratification theory or perhaps even more general theories of power.

Whether ethnic statuses are self-ascribed or ascribed by others, they characteristically differ from other possible forms of status ascription in that their social definition incorporates presumptive evidence of differential cultural origins. The diacritica by which such ascriptions are cognitively and symbolically expressed are quite variable. They may range from socially recognized cultural differentiae of language, tradition, dress, and demeanor to include the aggregate use of culturally defined phenotypical features. It would follow that systems which enjoin cultural definitions of race are best thought of as a special type of polyethnic system. Because ethnic markers in these systems do involve diacritica that individuals cannot easily discard or change, perhaps these systems are inclined to disclose an extreme rigidity of boundaries with reference to ethnic populations.

Although this definition of ethnic statuses tends to underscore the cultural origins which they impute, it does not follow that these status ascriptions are entirely putative or devoid of historical validity. Clearly, in one way or another, all the papers of this volume reveal that ethnic populations disclose historical experiences relevant to the circumstances affecting their identity, organization, and system of relationships. However, the significance of ethnic statuses does not devolve ultimately upon

the historical veracity of imputed cultural origins: rather, their significance derives primarily from the imperative relationships which they
enjoin. The theoretical and methodological implications of this point are
such as to justify their brief discussion.

All social statuses enjoin imperative relationships in reference to persons and groups as well as material resources. However, these relationships can be viewed as imperative in two very different ways. On the one
hand, they can be considered imperative in terms of the rights and obligations which they prescribe. On the other hand, they can be considered
imperative because they establish a determinate relationship to material
resources. Rights and obligations are not of the same epistemological
order as material resources. The former admit of individual interpretation
and, therefore, their empirical determination inevitably discloses a range
of subjective variation. Whatever this range of subjective variation might
be, unless it has been socially contested in one way or another, it is only
presumptive to consider it normative. By way of contrast, imperative relationships in respect to material resources do not impose such methodological restrictions in regard to their empirical determination. The distribution of material resources can be empirically established quite independent
of the rights and obligations that may be thought to regulate their access
and control. It would seem logical, therefore, to independently consider
these different status imperatives — i.e. rights and obligations on the one
hand and resource distributions on the other — and to leave their
relationship open to empirical inquiry.

If ethnicity is viewed as one form of social stratification, it needs to be
emphasized that social class is quite another. Ethnic stratifications derive
their structural features from categorical status ascriptions. By way of
contrast, class stratifications are more evidently based upon status identities which are achieved. In theory, these two forms of stratification exist
in contradiction. In fact, they may co-exist in complex ways according to
the historical, techno-environmental, economic, and political parameters
of the particular societies in which they are found. While this point
receives some attention in the papers by Otite and Whitten, it is given
more extensive treatment in the papers by van den Berghe, Hoetink,
Skinner, and Despres.

As previously noted, ethnic phenomena simultaneously engage elements that may be operative in reference to population aggregates, corporately organized groups, and individuals. It is consistent with most
stratification theories or theories of power that these units not be con-
fused. Population aggregates, even when ascribed a categorical identity,
are not corporately organized groups. By definition, corporately orga-

nized groups disclose determinate boundaries and membership, an analytic feature they share in common with categorically identified population aggregates. Beyond this, however, corporate groups differ from population aggregates in that they generally have a common estate, a unitary set of external relations, a relatively exclusive body of common affairs, and procedures which are more or less adequate to the administration of these affairs. In other words, corporate groups are politically organized units. Internally, they reveal governmental processes; externally, they generally reveal a determinate set of political relationships. It follows from this that ethnic populations are one type of structural phenomenon and ethnic groups are quite another, and each type may differently influence the system of inter-ethnic relations that might obtain among individuals.

Figure 1 diagramatically shows how these various dimensions of ethnic phenomena can be ordered so as to examine the relationships that might exist among them.

Having related what these papers seem to suggest by way of promising conceptual and theoretical developments, it is appropriate to consider matters of a more substantive nature. Specifically, what relationships do these papers tend to reveal between the genesis and persistence of ethnic boundaries, the political incorporation of ethnic populations, the organization of inter-ethnic relations, and the competition for environmental resources? In addressing this question, it is not necessary to burden the reader with summaries of individual papers which, in every instance, have been summarized by their respective authors. Instead, attention will be focused primarily on those findings that are thought to be of general significance.

Perhaps because of the limitations imposed, historical data relating to the genesis of ethnic boundaries do not receive detailed treatment in any of the papers of this volume. However, none of the contributors is inclined to ignore such data. It is evident from Whitten's paper that ethnic boundaries of one type or another existed in the Oriente long before the intrusion of Europeans. The same can be inferred from Skinner's overview of Africa. In any case, it is apparent from these and other studies that ethnogenesis involves processes by which populations become more or less culturally differentiated as a consequence of their economic and social adaptation to different techno-environments. It is apparent also that such processes engage varying degrees of competition in different types of resource domains. While Skinner asserts this to be the case almost by definition, it may be equally asserted as a conclusion which receives somewhat detailed support from the papers offered, respectively, by Despres, Goldstein, Holloman, Otite, and Whitten.

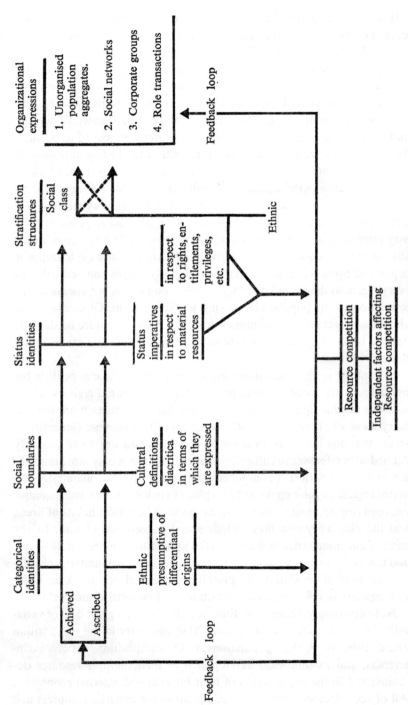

Figure 1. Framework for the comparative study of ethnic phenomena

It is equally apparent from these papers that the character and persistence of ethnic boundaries assume somewhat different dimensions according to the circumstances affecting the competition for resources. For example, there are those circumstances in which indigenous but low-energy populations seem to have competed with one another in various resource domains over long periods of time. Some of the preliminary data which Whitten relates on Lowland Ecuadorian populations would suggest that under these circumstances ethnic boundaries are inclined to be quite flexibly drawn in reference to cultural diacritica, the historical origins of which are remote and which also reveal a great deal of mythological, ritual, and genealogical content. It would seem that the contrastive identities based on these diacritica are easily altered in response to the cooperative or competitive relationships that develop as small population units may intrude upon one another's resource domains. The resources available in these domains are primary in their nature. Their exploitation is dependent upon technologies that are relatively simple and accessible to everyone. And the overall quantity of these resources is not always scarce in relation to the populations seeking to exploit them. Of course, these are largely speculations and more research of a precise nature needs to be done in order to specifically establish the role of ethnic ascriptions under these circumstances.

In contrast to these situations are those in which the competition for resources exists under colonial, post-colonial, or imperial regimes. These societies commonly reveal complex poly-ethnic systems that are the primary focus of attention in all of the papers of this volume. Generally, it seems that the ethnic boundaries of these systems are more precisely defined with reference to cultural diacritica that are not only more immediate in their historical development but which also are manifestly less mythological in their content. Examples of such diacritica are language, national origins, modalities of institutionalized behavior, habits of dress, and the like. They also may include social conceptions of race. In any case, ethnic boundaries in these societies appear to be more rigidly drawn and the ascription of status identities in respect to such boundaries characteristically involves claims and disabilities which clearly mark an order of inequality in reference to the distribution of material resources.

Not surprisingly, these poly-ethnic societies reveal a great deal of variability in their historical development. They also vary in the composition and distribution of their populations; in the composition, variety, exclusiveness, and technological development of their multiple resource domains; and in the organization of their internal and external economies. All of these factors relate to the competition for material resources and they need to be researched much more precisely in order to establish the nature of their co-variation and to ascertain further the extent to which they are determinative of the equally variable ethnic stratifications that obtain in these societies. Nevertheless, it may be concluded that the case studies presented here do provide considerable data which are suggestive of at least some of the relationships we might expect to find between the conditions affecting the competition for resources, the persistence of ethnic boundaries, and the organization of ethnic populations.

By definition, ethnic boundaries express some organization of status identities to which status claims of one type or another are attached. With respect to material resources, to the extent that these status claims confer competitive advantage upon the populations who assert them, social boundaries supportive of categorical ethnic identities will persist. Conversely, when such claims confer no particular advantage in this regard, ethnic boundaries weaken and the assertion of ethnic identities appears to diminish. The first of these propositions receives considerable support from data presented, respectively, in the papers by Holloman, Whitten, Despres, Otite, Skinner, and Goldstein. Data presented in support of the second of these propositions are given more specific treatment in the papers by van den Berghe, Despres, and Skinner.

In regard to the competition for resources, it should be noted here that Hoetink develops views that are not only interesting but which demand further consideration. According to Hoetink (cf. 9), the concept of competition implies that within some social context there are groups for whom membership and internal cohesion are ideally determined by noneconomic factors. It would follow that perhaps resource competition is more determined by, than determinative of, ethnic ascriptions. This particular thesis is more fully developed by Hoetink in an earlier work (Hoetink 1964), and it has been recently discussed in a review article by Mintz (1971: 437–450). This thesis does not receive a great deal of support from the case studies under consideration, but then it proceeds from theoretical conceptions that are somewhat different from those which these studies are inclined to reflect.

This particular disagreement aside, Hoetink builds upon the work of Nieboer (1900) and proceeds to suggest that in any social context the competition between groups presupposes an equilibrium of power and a correspondence of values. In other words, a competitive relationship can exist between groups only if they share a subjective assessment of the resources for which they are competing and, in addition, if they enjoy relatively equal access to those domains in which such resources are lodged. Nevertheless, Hoetink also emphasizes that resource domains vary objectively, according to whether they are open or closed and, also, according to the technologies available for their exploitation.

That a competitive relationship among groups necessarily presupposes a correspondence of values and an equilibrium of power is certainly debatable. However, it seems indisputable that ethnic boundaries give issue to social strategies which are designed to monopolize particular resources or, in some instances, entire resource domains. Whitten describes how the Canelos Quechua have recently assumed a "*nativo*" or "*Indio*" identity in order to exercise status claims to lands that have come under competitive pressure from blanco-mestizos. Otite describes how Ikale populations monopolize the ownership of agricultural lands by exercising ethnic status claims. And, in reference to the same land, Urhobo populations similarly secure tenancy rights and thereby monopolize the local oil palm industry. Holloman likewise relates how the San Blas Cuna have contrived to reinforce ethnic boundaries in order to monopolize land for the cash cropping of coconuts. Thus, to the extent that ethnic strategies succeed in monopolizing particular resources, they also have the effect of reducing the competition that might otherwise exist for these resources. It follows from these data that ethnic strategies may serve either to institute or maintain an order of inequality in respect to material resources.

Judging from the data of several papers, ethnic stratifications may have either a positive or a negative valence in respect to the overall integration of the societies in which they are found. This condition may follow upon a multiplicity of factors. To speculate on various data reported by Despres, Goldstein, Holloman, and Otite, it seems that stable ethnic stratifications generally depend upon the availability of resource domains that are relatively adequate to the population pressures exerted upon them. In addition, these domains must be heterogeneous in their resource composition, relatively open, and relatively stable in their technological and manpower requirements. These conditions are approximated in Guyana between 1840 and 1940; in India in respect to Tibetan refugees and neighboring Indian settlements; in the San Blas Islands since 1925; and in the Okitipupa Division of Western Nigeria. Accordingly, the ethnic stratifications that existed in these areas reveal a series of resource monopolies in reference to which ethnic populations are symbiotically or noncompetitively aligned, and there is little evidence to suggest that relationships among these populations are disruptive of the larger societies in which they are found.

However, it needs to be emphasized also that ethnic stratifications derive a positive valence from circumstances which are rather unusual in their combination. Population aggregates are not typically stable in their demographic composition. Similarly, resource domains can change rather rapidly in their number, heterogeneity, and relationship; in their exploitive technologies and manpower requirements; in their accessibility; and in their capacity to support populations of varying density. Changes in the magnitude of these factors are particularly evident under colonial and post-colonial economic regimes. Accordingly, ethnic stratifications more commonly reveal a negative valence in respect to the overall integration of the societies in which they are found. That is to say, such stratifications seem to relate significantly to the instability of these societies. Most of the papers under discussion are supportive of this conclusion, but the papers by van den Berghe, Despres, Skinner, and Whitten are particularly relevant for the attention they give to the relationship between poly-ethnic systems and various patterns of colonial and post-colonial domination.

Without exception, these case studies reveal that poly-ethnic or plural societies most generally combine ethnic and social class stratifications in their overall social systems. The problems relating to the co-existence of these dissimilar stratifications are numerous and complex. Only a few of these problems are disclosed, mainly in the papers by van den Berghe, Despres, Hoetink, Skinner, and Otite. From their discussions, it is apparent that each of these stratifications can be supportive of status identities that give issue to claims which directly relate to the organization of groups, social networks, and interpersonal role transactions. It also seems that these stratifications are rarely coterminous and, thus, they give issue to social discontinuities which may constitute an independent source of conflict in respect to groups as well as individuals. However, from the limited data presented, it is not entirely clear how the intercalation of these stratifications is related to specific factors affecting the competition for material resources. Comparative research of a more extensive and focused nature is needed in regard to this and related problems.

The corporate or political organization of ethnic populations presents an important area of problems which is given little formal attention by most of the contributors to this volume. Despres describes in some detail how segments of the Afro- and Indo-Guyanese populations have been stimulated to organize various political and economic associations in response to developments affecting the competition for material resources. Goldstein similarly describes the political efforts which Tibetan refugees have made to develop and secure resource domains that are needed for their cultural survival. And Holloman relates how the San Blas Cuna have attempted to establish themselves as a political community in response to pressures which others have exerted on resource domains that the Cuna consider to be theirs. These analyses are sufficiently suggestive as to invite speculation and further research.

As previously noted, the ascription of ethnic identities to population aggregates does not make of these aggregates corporately organized groups. In general, it would appear that the corporate organization of ethnic population segments seems to derive its motivational force more or less directly from the negative status claims which attach to most ethnic stratifications. These claims seem to be politically excited when they enjoin resource monopolies that are disturbed or in some manner re-opened for competition. This state of affairs may follow upon changes relating to a multiplicity of techno-environmental factors.

To mention but a few of the techno-envoronmental factors of which these papers are suggestive: there are first of all those that seem directly related to the size, composition, and distribution of ethnic populations. For example, in Guyana, malaria control, the organization of a rural health delivery system, and improved sugar estate housing all contributed to a relatively recent explosion in the East Indian population and this, in turn, served to increase the competition between Indians and Africans for agricultural land. Also important are technological factors that contribute to the deterioration of old resource domains or the development of new ones, or factors that might otherwise affect the quantity, quality, and overall accessibility of particular resources. Still another important set of factors affecting the competition for resources are those relating to the organization and development of local and international resource markets and the exploitive effects these markets may have on particular population segments. Also related to the competition for resources are changes resulting from developments in systems of transportation, communication, and education; these too may stimulate the corporate organization of ethnic populations.

In the same regard, perhaps international developments are deserving of special mention. Van den Berghe, Despres, Skinner, and Whitten give particular emphasis to the relationship between ethnic and social class stratifications and the international competition for local resources. One effect of this competition, certainly evident in Guyana and in Ecuador, is that local populations are left usually to compete among themselves for unexpropriated resources. More often than not, it seems that these unexpropriated resources are of a primary nature and are found in domains that are both marginal and labor-intensive in their technologies. These conditions may be particularly selective for the competitive organization of groups on the basis of ascribed status identities to which particularistic loyalties are attached.

To speculate further upon limited data, except perhaps for low-energy societies which are either marginal to or outside of colonial or post-colonial economic and political regimes, it seems that corporately organized ethnic groups are not generally co-extensive with the population aggregates from which their memberships are drawn. For example, in Guyana where political parties have catered extensively to the exclusive interests of ethnic populations, the memberships of these parties are not inclusive of the populations in question. Similarly, the memberships of those corporate groups which are ethnically exclusive are also but small segments of the populations from which they are drawn. This would suggest perhaps that corporately organized ethnic groups are in some sense selective of their memberships in reference to factors that may not relate to ethnic identities. Or, alternatively, ethnic populations may be quite heterogeneous in characteristics that do not derive from their ethnic statuses, and these variable characteristics may be as significant for the corporate organization of these populations as ethnicity itself.

In theory, the inequalities which attach to ethnic stratifications are not necessarily corporate inequalities. That is to say, it does not follow from such stratifications that these populations are accorded differential corporate rights and entitlements in the all-inclusive public domain. Moreover, it is at least apparent that the political constitution of some poly-ethnic societies does not give ethnic populations special consideration or make of them objects of political discrimination or oppression. Whether or not this is in fact the case remains to be demonstrated. Nevertheless, it is more than apparent that in a great many plural societies ethnic populations are differentially incorporated and some of these societies disclose the most inhumane and repressive political orders known to man.

Among the contributors to this volume, three touch more or less directly upon problems relating to the differential incorporation of ethnic population. In reference to Guyana, Despres suggests that ethnic populations tend to become the object of de facto political discrimination whenever a corporately organized ethnic group succeeds in monopolizing control of all or most of the resource domains within any relatively closed environment. In practical terms this means that such a group has seized control of the instruments of state. This generalization may be construed as a general description of certain colonial, post-colonial, and imperial regimes to which other contributors make reference. Certainly the African colonial regimes to which Skinner refers, and perhaps also some of the post-colonial regimes that he mentions, reveal processes of incorporation not unlike those that Despres describes for Guyana. And, as Whitten relates, these processes are also in evidence in the Ecuadorian Oriente where Indian disenfranchisement and ethnic annihilation rushes on in a manner that is all too reminiscent of developments in North America. Still, these discussions are brief and they are only suggestive of the determinate relationships that might be involved.

In conclusion, the papers that comprise this volume reveal a convergent line of development toward a comparative theory of ethnic phenomena. The conceptual framework that emerges suggests that these phenomena might best be understood from the point of view of stratification theory or perhaps more general theories of power. Admittedly, this conceptual framework is in need of further discussion and refinement. However, notwithstanding such discussion, it has been shown that this approach is particularly productive of hypotheses relating various dimensions of ethnic phenomena to a wide range of objective, and presumably independent, factors affecting the competition for material resources. The comparative validity of these hypotheses remains to be established.

Perhaps all that one can safely conclude from the case materials presented in these papers is that significant relationships are more than apparent between factors affecting the competition for resources and the persistence, corporate organization, and differential incorporation of ethnic populations. This conclusion does not have the ring of something new or astounding: indeed, the literature would suggest that many social scientists have suspected as much for a very long time. However, the focus of most of the research available on ethnic phenomena belies these suspicions. The precise nature of these relationships and the extent to which they are determined by material factors, which presumably admit of political alteration, remain to be closely investigated.

REFERENCES

BANTON, MICHAEL
    1967   *Race relations*. New York: Basic Books.
BARTH, FREDRIK
    1956   Ecologic relationships of ethnic groups in Swat, North Pakistan. *American Anthropologist* 58:1079–1089.
    1959   *Political leadership among the Swat Pathans*. London School of Economics Monographs on Social Anthropology 19. London.
    1964   "Ethnic processes on the Pathan-Baluch boundary," in *Indo-Iranica*. Edited by G. Redard.
    1969a "Introduction," in *Ethnic groups and boundaries*. Edited by Fredrik Barth, 9–38. Boston: Little, Brown.
    1969b "Pathan identity and its maintenance," in *Ethnic groups and boundaries*. Edited by Fredrik Barth, 117–34. Boston: Little, Brown.

BARTH, FREDRIK, *editor*
1969 *Ethnic groups and boundaries.* Boston: Little, Brown.
BEALS, RALPH L., HARRY HOIJER
1971 *An introduction to anthropology.* New York: Macmillan.
BEATTIE, JOHN
1964 *Other cultures.* New York: Free Press of Glencoe.
BENEDICT, B.
1961 *Indians in a plural society: a report on Mauritius.* London: Her Majesty's Stationary Office.
1962 Stratification in plural societies. *American Anthropologist* 64:1235–1246.
BERRY, BREWTON
1958 *Race and ethnic relations.* Boston: Houghton Mifflin.
BLALOCK, HUBERT M., JR.
1967 *Toward a theory of minority-group relations.* New York: John Wiley and Sons.
BOHANNAN, PAUL
1963 *Social anthropology.* New York: Holt, Rinehart and Winston.
DESPRES, LEO A.
1964 The implications of nationalist politics in British Guiana for the development of cultural theory. *American Anthropologist* 66:1051–1077.
1967 *Cultural pluralism and nationalist politics in British Guiana.* Chicago: Rand McNally.
1969 Differential adaptations and micro-cultural evolution in Guyana. *Southwestern Journal of Anthropology* 25:14–44.
DRAKE, ST. CLAIR, HORACE CAYTON
1945 *Black metropolis.* New York: Harcourt, Brace.
EVANS-PRITCHARD, E. E.
1940 *The Nuer.* London: Clarendon Press of Oxford.
FORTES, MEYER
1945 *The dynamics of clanship among the Tallensi.* London: Oxford University Press.
FRAZIER, E. FRANKLIN
1949 *The Negro in the United States.* New York: Macmillan.
GOLDSCHMIDT, WALTER
1960 *Exploring the ways of mankind.* New York: Holt, Rinehart and Winston.
HARRIS, MARVIN
1964 *Patterns of race in the Americas.* New York: Walker.
1971 *Culture, man and nature.* New York: Thomas Y. Crowell.
HOEBEL, E. ADAMSON
1966 *Anthropology: the study of man.* New York: McGraw-Hill.
HOETINK, H.
1964 *The two variants in Caribbean race relations.* London: Oxford University Press.
HUGHES, E. C., HELEN MCGILL HUGHES
1952 *Where peoples meet: racial and ethnic frontiers.* Glencoe: Free Press.

KEESING, FELIX M.
1959   *Cultural anthropology.* New York: Rinehart.

KEESING, ROGER M., FELIX M. KEESING
1971   *New perspectives in cultural anthropology.* New York: Holt, Rinehart and Winston.

KUPER, HILDA
1947   *The uniform of colour.* Johannesburg: South African Institute of Race Relations.

LIND, ANDREW W., *editor*
1955   *Race relations in world perspective.* Honolulu: University of Hawaii Press.

LINTON, RALPH
1936   *The study of man.* New York: Appleton-Century-Crofts.
1955   *The tree of culture.* New York: Alfred A. Knopf.

LOWIE, ROBERT H.
1920   *Primitive society.* New York: Liveright.
1940   *An introduction to cultural anthropology.* New York: Rinehart.

MAIR, LUCY
1955   *An introduction to social anthropology.* London: Clarendon Press of Oxford.

MINTZ, SIDNEY
1971   Groups, group boundaries and the perception of race. *Comparative Studies in Society and History* 13:437–450.

NADEL, S. F.
1951   *The foundations of social anthropology.* New York: Free Press of Glencoe.

NIEBOER, H. J.
1900   *Slavery as an industrial system: ethnological researches.* The Hague: Martinus Nijhoff.

PARK, ROBERT EZRA
1950   *Race and culture.* New York: Free Press of Glencoe

RUBIN, VERA, *editor*
1960   *Social and cultural pluralism in the Caribbean.* Annals of the New York Academy of Sciences 83.

SCHERMERHORN, RICHARD A.
1970   *Comparative ethnic relations: a framework for theory and research.* New York: Random House.

SELIGMAN, C. G.
1930   *Races of Africa.* London: Home University Library.

SHIBUTANI, TAMOTSU, KIAN M. KWAN
1965   *Ethnic stratification: a comparative approach.* New York: Macmillan.

SIMPSON, GEORGE, J. MILTON YINGER
1958   *Racial and cultural minorities.* New York: Harper.

SMITH, M. G.
1957   "Ethnic and cultural pluralism in the British Caribbean," in *Ethnic and cultural pluralism in inter-tropical countries,* 439–447, Brussels: INCIDI.
1960   "Social and cultural pluralism," in *Social and cultural pluralism in the*

      Caribbean. Edited by Vera Rubin, 763–777. Annals of the New York
      Academy of Sciences 83.
1965   *The plural society in the British West Indies.* Los Angeles and Berkley:
      University of California Press.
1969   "Pluralism in precolonial African Societies," in *Pluralism in Africa.*
      Edited by Leo Kuper and M. G. Smith, 91–151. Berkeley and Los
      Angeles: University of California Press.
THOMAS, W. I., FLORIAN ZNANIECKI
1918–1920   *The Polish peasant in Europe and America,* five volumes. Boston:
      R. G. Badger.
TYLOR, EDWARD B.
1916   *Anthropology.* New York: D. Appleton.
VAN DEN BERGHE, PIERRE L.
1967   *Race and racism.* New York: John Wiley and Sons.
1970   *Race and ethnicity.* New York: Basic Books.
WAGLEY, CHARLES, *editor*
1952   *Race and class in rural Brazil.* Paris: UNESCO.
WAGLEY, CHARLES, MARVIN HARRIS, *editors*
1958   *Minorities in the New World.* New York: Columbia University Press.
WIRTH, LOUIS
1928   *The ghetto.* Chicago: University of Chicago Press.

Biographical Notes

LEO A. DESPRES (1932) was born in Lebanon, New Hampshire. He received his B.A. and M.A. from The University of Notre Dame, and Ph.D. from Ohio State University (1960). Formerly he was Professor and Chairman of Anthropology, Case Western Reserve University; presently he is Professor and Chairman of Sociology and Anthropology, The University of Notre Dame. His field work and publications focus on ethnic relations in Guyana and the West Indies; he is author of *Cultural pluralism and nationalist politics in British Guiana* (Rand McNally, 1967) and numerous articles.

MELVYN GOLDSTEIN (1938) received his B.A. (1959) and M.A. (1960) from The University of Michigan and his Ph.D. (1968) from the University of Washington. At present he is Associate Professor at Case Western Reserve University. His publications on Tibet include: *Modern spoken Tibetan: (Lhasa dialect)*, University of Washington Press, 1970; *Modern literary Tibetan: a grammar and reader*, volume five of the papers of the Wolfenden Society on Tibeto-Burman Linguistics, 1973.

HARMANNUS HOETINK (1931) studied at the University of Amsterdam and received his doctorate in sociology at the University of Leiden. He was the first director of the Latin American Research Center at Amsterdam and taught at the University of Rotterdam (1964–1968), he has also directed the Institute of Caribbean Studies, University of Puerto Rico. Presently he is Professor of Sociology, University of Puerto Rico. He has been visiting professor at Yale University and The University of Texas at Austin, and has lived in different Caribbean countries for nearly twenty years. His four books and many articles are on comparative race relations and in the field of historical sociology. In 1970 he received the Annual Award from the Conference on Latin American History, American Historical Association.

REGINA E. HOLLOMAN (1931) did her undergraduate work at Ohio State University and holds three degrees from Northwestern University, an M.A. in sociology (1956) and both M.A. (1967) and Ph.D. (1969) in anthropology. She did fieldwork among the San Blas Cuna of Panama in 1966 and 1967 and among Latins and Appalachins in Chicago (1974). She has also done postdoctoral work in computer simulation. She has been associate professor of anthropology at Roosevelt University since 1970. Her areas of emphasis are cognitive anthropology, urban anthropology, and Latin American studies.

ONIGU OTITE (1939) was born in Okpara, Nigeria. He was educated at University of Nigeria, Nsukka, B. A. Hons. Sociology 1963, and at University of London, Ph.D. Social Anthropology 1969. From 1963 to 1965, he was Government Administrative Officer for Western and Midwestern Nigeria and from 1969 he has been Lecturer at the University of Ibadan, Nigeria. He is the author of *Autonomy and dependence: the Urhobo Kingdom of Okpe in modern Nigeria* 1972; *Rural migrants and economic development* (forthcoming); and numerous articles on the Nigerian Society, the Urhobo, encapsulated systems, and on family and social organization in Nigeria.

ELLIOTT PERCIVAL SKINNER (1924) was born in Trinidad-Tobago, West Indies. He received his B.A. from University College, New York University in 1951 and his M.A. and Ph.D. from Columbia University in 1952 and 1955, respectively. From 1954, he has taught primarily at Columbia University, where today he is Chairman of the Department of Anthropology. His many articles and books specialize in African ethnology, with interests in political organization, religion, and urbanization. They include: *The Mossi of Upper Volta* (Stanford University Press, 1964), *A glorious age in Africa* (Doubleday, 1965), *African urban life: the transformation of Ougadougou* (Princeton University Press), *Peoples and cultures of Africa: an anthropological reader* (The Natural History Press), and *African traditional life* (with Margo Jefferson; Doubleday, 1973).

PIERRE L. VAN DEN BERGHE (1933) was born in Lumbumbashi, Zaire. He has received his B.A. and M.A. from Stanford University and Ph.D. from

Harvard University. Currently, he is Professor of Sociology at the University of Washington, Seattle. His fieldwork and publications are on ethnic relations in South Africa, Kenya, Nigeria, Mexico, Guatemala, Brazil, and Peru.

NORMAN E. WHITTEN, JR. is Professor of Anthropology at the University of Illinois, Urbana. He took his Ph.D. in 1964 at the University of North Carolina, Chapel Hill. Besides field work with the Lowland Quechua of Ecuador, Whitten has worked extensively with black cultures in Nova Scotia, Canada, the southern United States, Colombia, and Ecuador. He is author of two books: *Class, kinship, and power in an Ecuadorian town: the Negroes of San Lorenzo* (1965, Stanford: Stanford University Press), and *Black frontiersmen: a South American case* (1973, Cambridge, Massachusetts: Schenkman Publishing) and senior editor of *Afro-American anthropology* (1970, New York: Free Press). He is currently writing a book on Lowland Quechua social structure and cultural adaptation in the face of massive changes in the Amazonian Lowlands.

Index of Names

Adams, Richard N., 63
Aguirre Beltrán, Gonzalo, 27
Alland, Alexander, Jr., 113
Azikiwe, Nnandi, 143

Banton, Michael, 1, 87, 128, 188
Barth, Frederik, 2–3, 19–21, 29–30, 75, 87–88, 90, 112–113, 120, 189–191, 194
Barton, W. D., 33–34
Baudouin I (King of Belgium), 145
Beals, Ralph L., 189
Beattie, John, 188
Bell, Wendell, 87
Benedict, Burton, 87, 189
Bennett, John W., 113, 183
Berry, Brewton, 188
Blalock, Hubert M., Jr., 188
Blundell, Michael, 142
Bohannan, Paul, 188
Braithwaite, Lloyd, 89
Burnham, L. F. S., 90, 101, 104, 106

Capriata, Jorge, 72
Casagrande, Joseph B., 58–59
Cayton, Horace, 188
Cohen, A., 126–127
Cohen, Ronald, 88
Colson, Elizabeth, 137
Conombo, Joseph, 143
Cotler, Julio, 72
Crespo Toral, Hernán, 41
Cross, Malcolm, 89

Dalai Lama, 159–185
Despres, Leo A., 1–7, 87–117, 187–207
Drake, St. Clair, 188

Es Sadi, 135
Evans-Pritchard, E. E., 190

Flores Ochoa, Jorge, 72
Fortes, Meyer, 190
Frazier, E. Franklin, 188
Fuenzalida, Fernando, 72, 73
Furnivall, J. S., 112, 119

Geertz, Clifford, 113
Ghai, Y. P., 141–142, 147
Gillette, Cynthia, 41, 58–59
Gluckman, Max, 128
Goldschmidt, Walter, 188
Goldstein, Melvyn C., 5, 87, 159–186, 193, 196, 199, 200, 201
Goodenough, Ward, 160
Gowon, General, 151

Hanna, Marwan, 149
Harris, Marvin, 15, 113, 189
Hegen, Edmund E., 61
Hoebel, E. Adamson, 188
Hoetink, Harmannus, 3, 9–25, 87, 191, 195, 199–200, 201
Hoijer, Harry, 189
Holloman, Regina E., 3, 27–40, 193–194, 196, 199, 200, 201–202
Houphouet-Boigny, Felix, 146
Hughes, E. C., 188
Hughes, Helen McGill, 188

Jácome, Nacanor, 41

Kantule, Nele, 33, 35–36

Keesing, Felix M., 188
Keesing, Roger M., 188
Kenyatta, Jomo, 145
Kuper, Leo, 87, 88
Kwan, Kian M., 1, 87, 188
Kwayana, Eusi, 103, 104

Lewis, Gordon K., 89
Lind, Andrew W., 188
Linton, Ralph, 188
Lowie, Robert H., 188
Lumumba, Patrice, 145

Mabogunje, A. L., 126
Macdonald, Theodore, 41
Mair, Lucy, 188
Maquet, Jacques, 128
Marsh, Richard O., 33
Marshall, A. H., 92
Marshall, Lorna, 88
Marx, Karl, 38, 119
Mason, Philip, 1, 79–80
Matos Mar, José, 72
Mboya, Tom, 145
Middleton, John, 88
Mintz, Sidney, 199
Mobuto, General, 151

Nadel, S. F., 188
Naranjo, Marcelo, 41
Nash, M., 87
Nath, Dwarka, 104
Nieboer, H. J., 199; *Slavery as an Industrial System*, 10–12
Nkrumah, Kwame, 144, 150–151
Nuñez del Prado, Oscar, 72
Nyerere, Julus, 103

Okonjo, C., 126
Otite, Onigu, 4, 119–130, 195, 196, 199, 200, 201

Pareja Diezcanseco, Alfredo, 58
Park, Robert Ezra, 188

Radcliffe-Brown, A. R., 87
Rappaport, Roy A., 113

Rouch, J., 128
Rubin, Vera, 189

Schermerhorn, Richard A., 1, 87, 188
Seligman, C. G., 189
Senghor, Léopold S., 144
Shibutani, Tamotsu, 1, 87, 188
Simmel, Georg, 132–133
Simpson, George, 188
Sjoberg, Gideon, 87
Skinner, Elliott P., 4–5, 131–157, 191, 193, 195, 196, 199, 201, 202, 203
Smith, M. G., 18, 30, 87, 88, 90, 112–113, 133, 189
Smith, Raymond T., 89
Speckman, J. D., 87

Thomas, W. I., 188
Thompson, Stephen I., 58–59
Todd, Garfield, 142
Toynbee, Arnold, 30
Tschombe, Moise, 145
Tsundru, Chandra, 159
Tylor, Edward B., 188

Van den Berghe, Pierre L., 1, 3, 4, 71–85, 87, 188, 189, 191, 192, 193, 195, 199, 201, 202
Van Liere, R. A. J., 87
Vayda, Andrew P., 113
Velasco Ibarra, José María, 53

Waag, Michael, 41
Whitten, Dorothea S., 41
Whitten, Norman E., Jr., 3–4, 41–69, 192, 193, 195, 196, 198, 199, 201, 202, 203–204
Wirth, Louis, 188
Wurfl, Margarita, 41
Wylie, T. V., 171

Yameogo, Maurice, 151
Yinger, J. Milton, 188
Young, Philip D., 58–59

Znaniecki, Florian, 188
Zubaida, Sami, 1

Index of Subjects

Acculturation, 132

Achuara Jívaro, 52

Adaptive strategies, among Canelos-Quechua, 64–65

ADM. *See* Anti-Discrimination Movement

Afghanistan, 190

Africa, 119, 133, 196; colonial regimes in, 78, 203; conquest states in, 134–135

African independence, ethnic strangers and, 143–145

African nationalism, colonial-type ethnic systems of, 142–145

African societies: European conquest of, 135–138

African Society for Cultural Relations with Independent Africa (ASCRIA), in Guyana, 102–104, 108, 110

African states, 131

Afrikaaners, 136–137, 138

Afro-America, socioracial stratifications in, 13–16

Afro-Guyanese: as bauxite workers, 98; corporate entitlements of, 91; and ethnic associations, 100–105, 201, 202; and government, 99; and internal markets, 95–96; and sugar plantations, 92; in urban population, 93–94

Agency for International Development, 97

Agrarian reform, in Peru, 76–77

Agricultural lands, distribution of, in Guyana, 91–92, 94

Agricultural settlements, among Tibe-tan refugees, 164–166

Alama (Quechua term of reference), 44–45

Ambomu, 134

American Ethnological Society, 187

Amerindians, in Guyana, 102

Andean agriculture, 76

Andean Indians, isolation of, 77

Andean Quechua, compared to Jungle Quechua, 45

Angola, 143

Anthropologists, and ethnic studies, 188–189

Anti-Discrimination Movement (ADM), in Guyana, 104, 111

ASCRIA. *See* African Society for Cultural Relations with Independent Africa

Ascriptive identities, bases for, 23–25

Ascriptive loyalties, and culture, 16–17

Ashanti, 137, 145

Asia, 119

Asians, in Africa, 138, 141–142, 147–148

Auca, as identified by Quechua, 45–46

Awishiri, compared to Quechua, 42

Ayllu (kinship groups among Canelos Quechua), 50–51, 52

Aymara, in Peru, 74

Baganda, 139, 144

Bakongo, 144

Baluba, 144

Baluchi, 190

Bangala, 144

Belgian Congo. *See* Zaire
Belgium, 78
Beni, 144
Berbice (Guyana), 92
Bhutan, 173
Biafran secession, 151
Bilingualism, in Peru, 73–74, 79
Black communities, in Ecuador, 59
Blanco-mestizos, and Canelos-Quechua, 42, 45, 57–60, 64–65
Blancos, in Peru, 79
Bobonaza River (Ecuador), 42, 45
Boers. *See* Afrikaaners
Boundary crossing, in Peru, 77
Boundary maintenance: by Canelos-Quechua, 64–65; by San Blas Cuna, 35–39
British Guiana. *See* Guyana
Brokerage agencies, in Ecuador, 62
Burundi, 134
Bushmen, 133

Canelos Quechua: clans of, 52; cultural identity of, 42–46; ethnic composition of, 47–48; fish poisons, use of, by, 49; kinship among, 50–51; resource competition among, 64–65, 192, 200
Caseríos, in Comuna de San Jacinto, 56
Categorical ascriptions, 190
Categorical identities, relativity of, 193
Categorical social relationships, defined, 60
Cattle trade, in Ibadan, 126–127
Census categories, as categorical identities, 89
Central African Federation, 142–143
Chicha, use of, by Canelos Quechua, 49
Chiga, 137
Chinese, in Guyana, 92, 95–96, 102, 176, 177
Cholo, concept of, 79; in Peru, 74; in San Jerónimo, 80–81
Class stratification: and ethnic stratification, 195; in Latin America, 83
Cofán, compared to Quechua, 42
Collective farms, in Nigeria, 124
Colombia, and San Blas Cuna, 28
Colonialism, 132
Colonial-type ethnic systems, 135–142
Colonists, 54, 56, 60–61
Colonizations, 59, 62, 119
Color-class continuum, 107–108

Competition: conception of, 9–10, 199; and slavery, 11–12
Competitive equilibrium, in Guyana and Surinam, 9
Competitive strategies, among San Blas Cuna, 34–38
Comuna, 53–57, 64–65
Comunidades, in San Jerónimo, 81
Confederation of Tribal Associations of Katanga, 144
Conflict theory, 119
Conquest states, and ethnic systems, 134–135
Contrastive identities, among Quechua, 44–45
Convention Peoples Party (Gold Coast), 144–145
Cooperatives: in Peru, 76–77; among Tibetan refugees, 172, 180–181
Copper Belt, 140
Corporate groups, defined, 196
Corporate inequalities, in Guyana, 90–91
Cultural adaptation, among Tibetan refugees, 167–168
Cultural pluralism, 119, 189. *See also* Pluralism; Plural society
Culture: conceptions of, 16–17; and stratification, 21–22
Curaray River (Ecuador), 42
Cuzco, 80; ethnicity in Department of, 82

Dagomba, 134
Dahomeans, 139–140, 146
Dali Lama government: and ethnic boundary maintenance, 179–180; future of, 183–185; negative sanctions of, 181; and Tibetan nationalism, 161, 172–176; and Tibetan religion, 177–179
Demerara (Guyana), 92
Democratic centralism, in Peru, 77
Demographic shifts, in Ecuador, 59
Descent, concept of, among Canelos Quechua, 52
Differential adaptation, 113
Differential incorporation: and ethnic populations, 109, 203–204; and resource monopolies, 114
Dinka, 190
Dioula. *See* Yarse
Direct rule, in Africa, 136
Dutch Huguenots. *See* Afrikaaners

East Indians: corporate entitlements of, 91; ethnic associations of, 100–105, indentured workers among, 91–92; internal markets of, 95–96; sugar workers among, 98; urban population of, 93–94

Ecological anthropology, and ethnic studies, 113–114

Ecuador: blanco-mestizo culture of, 66; Instituto Ecuatoriano de Reforma Agraria y Colonización of, 60; Ministerio de Previsión Social of, 41, 45, 56, 58, 60, 65, 202

Egba, 125

Elites, as agents of change, 29–30

Essequibo (Guyana), 92

Estates, manorial, 170

Ethnic annihilation, 65–67, 204

Ethnic areas, in Tibet, 172

Ethnic ascriptions, 194

Ethnic associations, in Guyana, 100

Ethnic boundaries: and boundary crossing, 77–78; and elite strategies, 29–30; among Lowland Quechua, 3; persistence of, 30–31, 198–199; in Peru, 4, 73; and resource competition, 132; among Tibetan refugees, 5, 168, 179–180; as type of Suzerainty, 28; in Western Nigeria, 4

Ethnic categories: in colonial-type systems, 137–138, 140; and imperative statuses, 90; among Quechua, 45, 52

Ethnic claims, and identities, 108–109

Ethnic competition: in Guyana and Surinam, 10, 14; and internal markets, 95–96

Ethnic conflict: in Africa, 143–145; and Nigerian elites, 128; and resource competition, 72, 124

Ethnic diacritica: in Guyana, 110; in Peru, 73–74, 79; phenotypical, 136–137

Ethnic disenfranchisement, in Ecuador, 63–67

Ethnic groups: and colonialism, 132; as corporate units, 110–111; defined, 18–19, 72, 131, 190–191; inequality among, 77; study of, 71

Ethnic identities: ascriptive bases of, 24–25; among Canelos Quechua, 64–65; in Guyana, 89; in Ibadan, 127; among Ikale and Urhobo, 123; and resource competition, 114; and status claims, 108–109, 199; among Tibetan

refugees, 176; variable features of, 193

Ethnic inequalities, in Africa, 149–150

Ethnicity: and agrarian reform, 76; and ascriptive loyalties, 191; and cholificacion, 79; conceptions of, 60, 72, 87–88, 112, 189, 191–192, 194; and cultural origins, 194–195; and economic orientations, 120; in Guyana, 89, 111; and kinship, 58; and language, 75; and military regimes in Africa, 151; phenotypical images of, 107–108; plural theory of, 190; in post-colonial Africa, 145–149; and resource competition, 88; in San Jerónimo 80–81; in small-scale societies, 133; and social class, 71–75, 77–79, 83, 195

Ethnic monopolies, among Hausa, 126

Ethnic occupations, in Nigeria, 121

Ethnic passing, 77–78, 83

Ethnic phenomena: levels of analysis of, 193–194; study of, 1–3; universality of, 88

Ethnic politics, 143–145

Ethnic populations: adaptation of, 91–94; corporate organization of, 110–111, 114, 195–196, 201–203; differential incorporation of, 203–204

Ethnic relations: in Guyana, 105–109; in Nigeria, 123–126; in Peru, 72–74; study of, 71–72

Ethnic strangers: in colonial-type systems, 139–145; in post-colonial Africa, 145–149

Ethnic strategies: and associations, 100–105; in Ecuador, 63–67; and resource domains, 139, 200

Ethnic stratification: in Africa, 128; and corporate inequalities, 203; in Guyana, 4, 96–100, 110; positive and negative valence of, 200–201; techno-environmental determinants of, 202; types of, 77–78

Ethnic systems: and conquest states, 134–138; model of, 152–153; origins of, 131–132

Ethnogenesis, 196

Etiquette codes, and ethnicity, 108–109

Europeans, 97–98, 135–139, 196

Families, in Comuna de San Jacinto, 56

Feudalism, in Tibet, 169–171

Fingos, 139

Free-Town. *See* Sierra Leone
French Africa, 137, 144
Fulani, 134, 139

Georgetown (Guyana), 92
Ghana, 128, 134, 150
Gold Coast, 143, 144, 146
Greeks, in Africa, 138
Guatemala, 79
Guyana: ethnic associations in, 100–
   105; ethnic composition of, 89; ethnic
   relations in, 105–109, 200, 202–203;
   ethnic stratification in, 96–100; gov-
   erment of, as resource domain, 99;
   internal markets in, 95–96; public
   service in, 90; resource domains in,
   97–99; urban populations in, 93–94
Guyana Mine Workers Union, 103
Guyana Rice Corporation, 101
Guyanese, national identity of, 106–107
Guyanese populations: distribution of,
   92; origins of, 91
Guyanese society: perceptions of, by
   Guyanese, 90–91; plural character of,
   96

Haciendas: in Ecuador, 63; in Peru, 76–
   77, 81
Haiti, socioracial groups in, 14
Hausa, 125–127, 134–135, 140, 144–145
Hausa immigrants, in Ghana, 128
Highland Indians, in Ecuador, 59
Hima, 134
Hispanization, 83
Horticulture, among Canelos Quechua,
   47–48, 54
Huarani, compared to Quechua, 42
Huasi (Canelos Quechua household
   units), 51
Hutu, 128

Ibadan, 120, 125–127
Ibos, 125–126, 140, 143–144, 151
Ife, 125
Ijebu, 125
Ijo, 121
Ikale, 120–124, 200
Immigrants, Urhobo as, 120
Inca communalism, 76
Incorporation processes, 29–30, 88–89,
   90
Indentured workers, in Guyana, 92
India, 161, 200; government of, and
   Tibetan refugees, 161–162, 180–181,
   183

Indian-blanco relationships, in Ecuador,
   63–64
Indian disenfranchisement, in Oriente,
   57, 65
Indian protest, in Ecuador, 61
Indians, Peruvian, 73–76, 79
Indirect rule, in Africa, 136
Indo-Guyanese, 201–202. *See also* East
   Indians
Indo-Tibetan relations, 168–169, 181–
   183
Infrastructure, in Ecuador, 61–63
Instituto Ecuatoriana de Reforma
   Agraria y Colonización, 57
Inter-ethnic encounters, in Guyana,
   106–109
Internal colonialism, in Ecuador, 58–61
International Commission of Jurists, 90
Intra-ethnic elections, among Tibetan
   refugees, 168
Isoko, 121
Itsekiri, 121
Ivory Coast, 145–146

Jívaro, in Ecuador, 41–43, 49, 64
Jungle Quechua. *See* Canelos Quechua

Kafir War, 138
Kamba, 139, 144–145
Kantanga. *See* Zaire
Kanuri, 140
Kenya, 139, 142, 144–145, 147–149
Kenya African Democratic Union, 145
Kenya African National Union, 145
Khampas (Tibetan ethnic group), 168
Kikuyu, 139, 149
Kikuyu-Luo alliance, 144, 145
Kilwa, 135
Kola trade, among Hausa, 127
Kwale, 120, 124–125

Landowners, Ikale, 120
Land tenure, among Tibetan refugees,
   174
Language, and ethnicity, 74, 78–79, 81–
   83
League of Coloured Peoples, in Guy-
   ana, 102
Lebanese, in West Africa, 138, 141
Liberia, 143
Limean ologarchy, 74
Llacta (Canelos Quechua territorial
   groups), 50–51
Lowland Quechua, and resource com-
   petition, 62, 64

Lulua, 144
Lumpenproletariat, in Lima, 83
Lunda, 144

Maha Sabha, 101–102
Malaria eradication, in Guyana, 93
Malawi, 140, 143
Mali Federation, 144
Masai, 139
Masufa, 135
Mau Mau, 142, 147
Mendes, 149
Mestizos: in Ecuador, 58–60; in Peru, 73–76, 79–82
Mexico, 79
Mid-Western States (Nigeria), 120, 122, 124
Military bases, in Ecuador, 63
Military conquest, and ethnic groups, 75
Military coups, in Africa, 150–151
Minifundias, in Peru, 76
Minorities, cultural and racial, 189
Miscegenation, in Guyana, 91
Missions, in Ecuador, 43, 62–63
Monks, among Tibetan refugees, 184–185
Mossi, 134–135, 137, 140, 143–144
Mouvement National Congolais, 145
Movement against Oppression, in Guyana, 107
Mozambique, 143
Multiracial stratifications, 11–20
Mundakuppe. *See* Tibetan refugees
Mysore, 162–163, 169
Mythology, among Canelos Quechua, 51–52

National Council of Nigeria and the Cameroons, 143
Nationalism, in Ecuador, 65
Nepal, 173
Network relationships, 60
Ngoni, 140
Nigeria, 120–121, 124, 128, 137, 139, 143–144, 146, 148, 151, 200
Ninisi, 134
North America, 204
Northern Rhodesia. *See* Zambia
Nuer, 190
Nupe, 125
Nyasa, 140
Nyasaland. *See* Malawi

Occupations, among rural people, 120
Oil exploitation, in Oriente, 53, 61
Oil palm industry, in Nigeria, 121–122
Okitipupa Division (Nigeria), 120–123
Opposition groups, among Tibetan refugees, 185
Oriente. *See* Canelos Quechua; Comuna; Ecuador
Orogun (Nigeria), 120, 124–125
Ouagadougou, 134–135
Oyo, in Ibadan, 125

Pakistan, 190
Pathans, 190
Patterns of incorporation, among San Blas Cuna, 27–28
Peace Corps volunteers, in Ecuador, 63, 65
Peoples National Congress, in Guyana, 100–102, 104
Peoples Progressive Party, in Guyana, 100–101, 104
Peru, 76, 78–80
Peruvian social structure, characteristics of, 72–74
Petroleum companies, in Ecuador, 63
Phenotypical diacritica, and ethnicity, 107–108, 114
Pioneering, in Upper Amazon, 61–62
Plantations: in Guyana, 92; in Oriente, 48, 54
Plateau Tonga, 137
Pluralism, 58, 74, 112–114, 168, 174
Plural society, 82–83, 87, 119, 193, 201; corporate inequalities in, 203; model of, 152–153, 191
Political culture, 65
Political economy, in Ecuador, 61–63
Political organization: of ethnic populations, 201–203; in Tibet, 169–171; among Tibetan refugees, 171–173
Political parties, in Nigeria, 127
Poly-ethnic systems, 4, 193; stratification structures of, 201; variability of, 198–199
Population aggregates, categorical identification of, 105–106
Portuguese: in Congo, 138; in Guyana, 95–96, 102–103
Power brokers, in Peru, 77
Power domains, in Ecuador, 56–57, 61, 63
Pre-Columbian civilizations, in Peru, 74–75

Purina treks, of Canelos Quechua, 64
Puyo Runa, Canelos Quechua, 52–53, 57, 63
Pygmy populations, in Africa, 133

Quechua: of Bobonaza drainage, 44–52; of Comuna de San Jacinto del Pindo, 53–58; cultural and linguistic divisions of, 42–43; ethnic strategies of, 58–65; in Highland Peru, 74–75; speakers in San Jerónimo, 80, 82
Quichua. *See* Quechua
Quijos. *See* Quechua

Race, and ethnicity, 194, 198
Racial imbalances, in Guyana's public service, 94–95
Racist ingredient, in allocation of resources, 11–13
Racist societies, 78
Radicalism, among Peruvian intellectuals, 77
Refuge areas, in Oriente, 43, 64
Refugee relief funds, and Tibetans, 174–175
Refugees, problems of, 160
Religion, among Tibetan refugees, 177–179
Resource allocation, and ascriptive stratifications, 20
Resource competition: in Africa, 123–128, 131–133; in colonial-type ethnic systems, 138–143; and ethnic associations, 100–105; and ethnic boundaries, 3–5, 198; and ethnic conflicts, 72; and ethnic relations, 129; in Guyana, 9, 91–100; international dimensions of, 202; in Oriente, 54–67; in San Blas Islands, 31, 34–35
Resource distributions, and ethnic identities, 107–108
Resource domains: open and closed, 10–12; and stratification systems, 114
Resource monopolies: and differential incorporation, 114; ethnic stratifications in, 200–201
Revitalization movements, in Guyana, 102–103
Rhodesia, 78
Rice Marketing Board, in Guyana, 100–101
Ruanda, 128, 134
Runa: defined, 44; divisions of, 46

Sabo (Hausa settlement), 126–128
Salon radicalism, in Peru, 76
San Blas Cuna: competition of, for resources, 34–35; cultural adaptation of, 36–38, 200–201; internal colonialism among, 3; relation of, to Panamanians, 31–33
San Jacinto del Pindo, Comuna de. *See* Comuna
San Jerónimo (Peru), 80–81
San Lorenzo (Ecuador), 59
Secoya, compared to Quechua, 42
Senegal, 144
Shell Oil Company, in Oriente, 53
Sierra Leone, 128, 149
Sikkim, 173
Siona, compared to Quechua, 42
Slavery, 10–13
Social boundaries, attributes of presentation of, 22–25
Social circumscription, among Canelos Quechua, 32
Social class: and ethnicity, 72–74, 82; in Guyana, 107–108
Social differentiation, and ethnicity, 194
Social status, in Peru, 81–83
Social structure, Peruvian, 72–74
Societies, small-scale, 133
Society for Racial Equality, in Guyana, 102
Socioeconomic mobility, among Canelos Quechua, 50
Socioeconomic stratification, and ascriptive stratification, 13
Sociologists, and ethnic studies, 188–189
Sociology of dependence, 73–75
Socioracial groups, in Western Hemisphere, 10–25
Sofala, 135
South Africa, 78, 136–138, 143
Southern Rhodesia, 143
Spanish, in Highland Peru, 75, 82
Spanish America, ethnic patterns in, 78
Spatial mobility, among Canelos Quechua, 50
Status imperatives, defined, 195
Stranger groups, in Africa, 132–133, 135, 137–138
Stratification systems, and culture, 20–21
Structure of domination, in Peru, 75
Sudan, ethnic systems in, 135

Sugar plantations, in Guyana, 92
Suzerainty relationships, defined, 28
Swazi, 134
Switzerland, ethnicity in, 78
Syrio-Lebanese, 148–149

Tallensi, 190
Tanganyika. *See* Tanzania
Tanzania, 140
Technology, and resource domains, 11
Temmes, 149
Territorial encapsulation, in Oriente, 57
Tibet, 160, 169–170. *See also Dalai Lama* government
Tibetan cultural traditional, 177
Tibetan nationalism, 175–177
Tibetan race, 177
Tibetan refugees: characteristics of, 160–161; economic rehabilitation of, 165–168; future prospects of, 183–185, 200–201; and Indian citizenship, 179–180; political organization of, 169–173; recruitment of, 165; religion of, 177–179; settlement of, in Mysore, 162–164
Tibetans, in India, 159–160
Timbuktu, 135
Togo, 150
Togolese, 139, 146
Trade, among Canelos Quechua, 49–50, 54
Tutsi, 127

Uganda, 137, 139–140, 144, 148
United Nations, and Tibetan question, 177
United Party, in Gold Coast, 145
United States: ghetto culture in, 18; socioracial groups in, 18
Universal incorporation, as ideology, 109
University of Cuzco, 80
University Guyana, 97, 104–105
Untssri Shuara. *See* Jívaro
Upper Volta, 144–145, 151
Urhobo, 120–125, 200
Urhobo-Isoko Federal Native Authority, 125

Visionary experiences, among Canelos Quechua, 49, 51

Western States (Nigeria), 120–121

Xhosa, 138

Yarse, 134–135, 145
Yoruba, 125–126, 137, 140, 144

Zaire, 137–138, 144, 146–147
Zambia, 137, 140, 143, 148
Zande. *See* Azande
Zanguete. *See* Hausa
Zanzibar, 148
Záparo, among Canelos Quechua, 42, 44, 47

M